Praise for

TANTRA
FOR EROTIC EMPOWERME(

D0886445

"*Tantra for Erotic Empowerment* offers a refreshing perspective on the connection between Tantric teachings and sexual power . . . Although it's a serious work based on a great deal of study and rooted in ancient traditions, Mark and Patricia have made it accessible to the everyday person. In fact, it's simultaneously traditional and completely new and radical."

—From the foreword by Tristan Taormino,
Village Voice and nationally syndicated columnist

"*Tantra for Erotic Empowerment* combines traditional wisdom and insight with true sensitivity and compassion, to become a valuable guide for the modern Tantric seeker. Mark and Patricia weave classic teachings with the reality of living in the modern Western world in a thorough and grounded way, accessible to students of all orientations."

—Christopher Penczak,
author of *The Mystic Foundation* and *Gay Witchcraft*

"Mark and Patricia have written a book on Tantra that deals with my favorite kind of sex—with oneself. Without having to wade through Eastern traditions, even a professional masturbator like me learned a few new tricks that furthered my own Erotic Empowerment."

—Betty Dodson, Ph.D.,
author of *Sex for One*

"Informative, challenging, inspiring and readily accessible to the serious student of tantric practice, *Tantra for Erotic Empowerment* is unquestionably one of the best books on tantric sexuality to be recently published in English. The exercises and specific instructions it offers are powerful, enjoyable and enlightening. Although it is provocative and even controversial in certain respects, this is an outstanding source of teaching and required reading for anyone open to tantric ways of growing and becoming more empowered in our lived bodily experiences."

—Barnaby B. Barratt, Ph.D., DHS,
Director of the Center for Tantric Spirituality
and author of *What Is Tantric Practice?*

"*Tantra for Erotic Empowerment* is a very authentic Tantra book, but perhaps more importantly, it's commonsensical and easy to understand. Mark Michaels and Patricia Johnson present Tantric principles and philosophy in clear, accessible ways. So even those with no background or interest in Eastern traditions can benefit from the great treasures Michaels and Johnson have to offer. Read it and be erotically empowered, because you're worth it."

—Annie Sprinkle, Ph.D.,
author of *Dr. Sprinkle's Spectacular Sex: Make Over Your Love Life*

"If you are embodied enough to seek authentic teaching about your erotic potential, try out the wisdom, exercises, reflections, and meditations that make up this book. Mark Michaels and Patricia Johnson are teachers whose intention is to guide and inspire you on your own exuberant journey. Their approach is astonishingly creative."

—Joseph Kramer, Ph.D.,
The New School of Erotic Touch

"With *Tantra for Erotic Empowerment*, Mark Michaels (Swami Umeshanand) and Patricia Johnson (Devi Veenanand) have risen to the challenge of writing a practical guide to Tantra. They have taken a tricky subject that could easily have been mishandled, and created a useful tool that could easily become a classic preparatory text in this genre."

—Raven Kaldera,
author of *Pagan Polyamory* and
Hermaphrodeities: The Transgender Spirituality Workbook

"This is a fearless and brilliant work, at once scholarly, technically accurate, challenging, and immensely readable. The writing is economical and lucid. The exercises are absorbing and profoundly therapeutic in the 'human' sense. It is a genuine original, and I enjoyed it immensely."

—Paul Skye (Swami Ajnananda Saraswati),
author of *The Mastery of Stress*, award-winning poet and short story writer

TANTRA
FOR EROTIC EMPOWERMENT

About the Authors

Mark A. Michaels (Swami Umeshanand Saraswati) and **Patricia Johnson** (Devi Veenanand) are a devoted married couple and have been teaching Tantra and Kriya Yoga together since 1999. Their first book, *The Essence of Tantric Sexuality,* won the National Best Books 2007 award in the Health/Sexuality category and was a finalist in the Religion/Eastern Religions category. They have written and appeared in two instructional DVDs: *Tantric Sexual Massage for Lovers* and *Advanced Tantric Sex Techniques* (Alexander Institute, 2007), and have contributed articles to various online and print publications, including *Chronogram* and *Debonair.*

Michaels and Johnson have taught throughout the United States, as well as in Canada, Europe, and Australia. They have been featured on television and radio and in numerous publications, including the *Village Voice, Metro, Latina, Jane, RockStar, Breathe, Redbook, The Complete Idiot's Guide to Tantric Sex,* and *The Complete Idiot's Guide to Enhancing Sexual Desire.* Their teaching combines a traditional lineage-based Tantric approach with the best contemporary methods so that students can bring heightened awareness and an expanded capacity for pleasure into all aspects of everyday life.

The authors are senior students of Dr. Jonn Mumford (Swami Anandakapila Saraswati) and have been named lineage holders of the OM Kara Kriya system for the Americas and Europe. Sunyata, coauthor of *The Jewel in the Lotus,* named Michaels his lineage holder in 2001. They have also studied Bhakti Yoga with Bhagavan Das and Tantra with Dr. Rudolph Ballentine.

Michaels is a graduate of New York University School of Law, is a member of the Bar in New York State, and holds master's degrees in American Studies from NYU and Yale. A playwright and translator, he translated and adapted Goldoni's *The Mistress of the Inn* for New York's Roundabout Theatre Company and cowrote *The Thrill of Victory, The Agony of Debate,* which premiered at New York's Primary Stages. Patricia Johnson is a professional operatic soprano who tours extensively throughout the United States, Europe, and South America and has performed with the New York City Opera, the Houston Grand Opera, and the Berlin Komische Oper. They make their home near New York City.

TANTRA
FOR EROTIC EMPOWERMENT
the key to enriching your sexual life
Mark A. Michaels & Patricia Johnson

Llewellyn Publications
Woodbury, Minnesota

First Edition
First Printing, 2008

Author photo by Adrian Buckmaster, www.adrianbuckmaster.com
Cover design by Gavin Dayton Duffy
Cover image © Beauty Photo Studio / age fotostock / Superstock
Interior book design by Joanna Willis

Llewellyn is a registered trademark of Llewellyn Worldwide, Ltd.

Illustrations:
Pages 12 (fig. 2), 45, 58, 90, 215, 219–220: Llewellyn art department. Pages 110 and 119: Mary Ann Zapalac. Page 105: Matthew Archambault. Page 12 (fig. 1): from Arthur Avalon, *The Serpent Power* (Madras: Ganesh & Co., 1931). Pages 16 and 218: from Thomas Inman, *Ancient Pagan and Modern Christian Symbolism* (New York: Bouton, 1880). Page 148: from Edward Moor, *The Hindu Pantheon* (Madras: J. Higginbotham, 1864). Page 199: from W.J. Wilkins, *Hindu Mythology: Vedic and Puranic* (Calcutta: Thacker and Spink and Co., 1882).

Quotation on page 194 from Song 31, *While There Is Still Passion,* in Bhaskar Bhattacharyya with Nik Douglas and Penny Slinger, *The Path of the Mystic Lover: Baul Songs of Passion and Ecstasy* (Rochester, VT: Destiny Books, 1993), www.InnerTraditions.com. Copyright 1993 by Bhaskar Bhattacharyya. Used with permission.

Library of Congress Cataloging-in-Publication Data
Michaels, Mark A., 1959–
 Tantra for erotic empowerment: the key to enriching your sexual life / by Mark A. Michaels and Patricia Johnson.—1st ed.
    p. cm.
 Includes bibliographical references and index.
 ISBN 978-0-7387-1197-3
 1. Sex—Religious aspects—Tantrism. 2. Tantrism. 3. Sex instruction. I. Johnson, Patricia, 1964– II. Title.
 HQ64.M538 2008
 306.77—dc22

                                                                            2007050297

Llewellyn Worldwide does not participate in, endorse, or have any authority or responsibility concerning private business transactions between our authors and the public.
 All mail addressed to the author is forwarded but the publisher cannot, unless specifically instructed by the author, give out an address or phone number.
 Any Internet references contained in this work are current at publication time, but the publisher cannot guarantee that a specific location will continue to be maintained. Please refer to the publisher's website for links to authors' websites and other sources.
 Cover model used for illustrative purposes only and may not endorse or represent the book's subject.

Llewellyn Publications
A Division of Llewellyn Worldwide, Ltd.
2143 Wooddale Drive, Dept. 978-0-7387-1197-3
Woodbury, MN 55125-2989, U.S.A.
www.llewellyn.com

Printed in the United States of America

To our students. Your dedication and bravery have inspired us. We hope *Tantra for Erotic Empowerment* inspires you.

Contents

Exercises

Illustrations

Foreword

by Tristan Taormino

I have written three books on sex, taught hundreds of workshops on various topics, spoken to thousands of people about their sex lives, and answered several thousand questions on every imaginable erotic topic. As a sex educator and columnist, it's my job to keep my eye on trends in the field of sexuality. Tantric sex is undoubtedly one of the hot topics that people want to know more about. In the last decade, nearly two dozen books have been published on the subject. Countless classes, events, and websites are dedicated to it. It has garnered high-profile mainstream media attention, from magazine articles such as *Cosmopolitan*'s "The Secret to Tantric Sex" to an episode of HBO's *Real Sex*.

So why all the interest? Some people are quick to zero in on the latest hip new thing in sex, regardless of what it actually is. Others have heard rumors that Tantric sex leads to multiple orgasms and relationship bliss (and who doesn't want that?). But people who are serious about learning more about Tantra are often looking for sexual experiences that go deeper than some sweaty fun between the sheets. They are searching for a language to describe those experiences, and they are searching for techniques to improve their skills for achieving them. They want greater awareness of their sexuality. They want to connect with their partners and, in some cases, with a higher power. They want sex to be meaningful, transformative, and profound.

Various people have tackled the topic of Tantra and Tantric sex with varying levels of knowledge and credibility. When I first began to investigate Tantra—for both professional knowledge and personal curiosity—it didn't exactly spark my interest right away. As described in the popular literature, Tantra seemed to be rigidly couples-centric, heterosexual, and decidedly un-kinky. In other words, I felt pretty alienated right off the bat.

The books all seemed to fall into two categories. Some were old information recycled as new; others were wildly abstract. In the first category, many of the writers seemed to cobble together various new-age concepts and catch phrases and call them Tantric. One passage I read described how Tantra "embraces and enhances all forms of creative expression, such as movement and dance, massage, martial arts, the fine arts, healing, and music. Through experiencing and glorying in the delights of the body, the body becomes a temple in which you experience the sacred. It becomes a doorway to spiritual evolution."[1] This concept and others I read about sounded vaguely familiar, but it wasn't clear how they related to this thing called Tantra.

At the other end of the spectrum were texts that were not easy for me to grasp. They were esoteric, inaccessible, and too "out there." In one book, the authors declared, "To help us understand the tantric philosophy, we need to make a distinction between a higher plane of reality, a state of cosmic consciousness, which we will refer to as Reality with a capital R, and our microcosmic or worldly reality, which we will call reality with a lowercase r."[2] Language like that made Tantra seem impenetrable to me. I couldn't see how any of the ideas related to real life in general, or my life in particular.

Even within circles of sexually savvy folks, people have a hard time explaining what Tantric sex is; they just know they should be doing it. It wasn't until I took Barbara Carrellas's Urban Tantra class in New York City that anything about Tantra made sense to me at all. Finally, I heard concepts explained in a way I could relate to. Some elements of Barbara's own brand of Tantra began to be clearer to me, and I was interested to learn more.

---

1 Jwala, *Sacred Sex* (San Rafael, CA: Mandala Publishing, 1994).

2 Charles and Caroline Muir, *Tantra: The Art of Conscious Loving* (San Francisco: Mercury House, 1989), 16.

Then I met Mark Michaels and Patricia Johnson. I was introduced to them at a sexuality event I co-produce, which features six days of workshops, demonstrations, rituals, and special events. It covers a broad range of human sexuality, so it attracts people of all genders and sexual orientations from all walks of life. What unites them is an interest in sexuality in all its forms. Presentations typically cover subjects such as BDSM, swinging, Tantra, Paganism, genderqueer identities, polyamorous relationships, fantasy role-playing, and the intersections of sex and spirituality.

Mark and Patricia weren't as flashy or gregarious as other sexuality teachers I knew. They were quiet, straightforward, and warm. The fact that they had shown up at all made me sit up and take notice, since other teachers in their field had snubbed the gathering as too sexual, too kinky, or not focused enough on "pure" Tantra. Mark and Patricia were clearly interested in bringing their wisdom to a diverse group of people. When they expressed an interest in presenting at a future event, I decided to give them a shot. They sent me descriptions of their classes, and I knew immediately theirs was a different kind of Tantra, not the one I felt excluded from. It wasn't just about straight, partnered, gentle lovemaking. No, theirs was a world of Tantra that was stimulating, exciting, and new.

At a later event, I attended their class on Aghora Tantra, described as covering "some of the more extreme Tantric practices, in which social and personal boundaries are consciously crossed for the purpose of spiritual evolution." It wasn't exactly Tantra 101—it sounded more like the "dark side" of Tantra—but I was intrigued. And their teaching style fit so well with the ethos of the event: they were open-minded and open-hearted, inclusive of all gender and sexual identities, and accessible to beginners, experts, and everyone in between. I could see clear connections between their philosophies and those behind such seemingly differing subjects as body modification and sadomasochism. They discussed practices that echoed the methods and goals of people who engage in other intense erotic practices to achieve a higher consciousness. After class, I shared this epiphany. They seemed perfectly at home in this unique melting pot of a community. Their presence cemented one point in my mind: that vastly different teachings on diverse topics can, in fact, overlap, intersect, and work together beautifully. They have taught me how much we can learn from one another, no matter how different our sexual and spiritual practices.

Tantra for Erotic Empowerment embodies that same spirit: it brings together wide-ranging knowledge and experience with a broad array of people and communities. It offers a refreshing perspective on the link between Tantric teachings and sexual power, and is a wonderful example of how to bridge the gap between Tantra and the current sex-positive movement. Although it's a serious work based on a great deal of study and rooted in ancient traditions, remarkably, Mark and Patricia have made it accessible to the everyday person. It is, in fact, simultaneously traditional and completely new and radical. For people like me who've found Tantra too abstract, this book approaches it in a practical, understandable way. Through guided journaling and exercises, the authors lead us on a personal journey of self-discovery and self-empowerment. In the process, they outline an entirely new way to think about one's body, desires, and fantasies.

As writers and teachers, Mark and Patricia are reassuring and encouraging. They take care not to push the reader too far or to make unreasonable demands on the beginner. But make no mistake: they are also demanding. What the authors ask of you can be rigorous and difficult. Be prepared to be challenged. If you commit to the challenge, be prepared to reap the rewards. And be prepared to change.

Introduction

Tantra for Erotic Empowerment is a book for those who want to get a taste of Tantric sexuality firsthand, for those who wish to understand their own sexuality more deeply, enhance the sexual component of their relationships, or explore some simple meditation techniques that embrace sexuality as a tool for spiritual growth. For the most part, we have avoided focusing on arcane material or emphasizing complicated energetic practices, which can often seem baffling to the first-time reader.

At the same time, *Tantra for Erotic Empowerment* is not solely for beginners, since it explores both the theoretical and practical aspects of Tantra in some depth and includes exercises that even readers who are familiar with contemporary Tantra and Neo-Tantra should find both challenging and original.[1] Today, Neo-Tantric workshops abound, but this book goes deeper, taking a longer-term, more searching approach to sexuality. We focus on consciousness, an experimental attitude, and, above all, pleasure. Experienced readers will likely find new dimensions in even the more familiar Neo-Tantric practices included here.

---

1 The term Neo-Tantra was coined in the early twentieth century by a group of Indian nationalists who were attempting to reclaim Tantra as a valid spiritual tradition. It was later used by Bhagwan Shree Rajneesh (Osho) to describe his system, which melded Tantric philosophy with a variety of other spiritual and psychological approaches. Osho has influenced almost all Western Tantra teachers, so most of what is available in the West can accurately be described as Neo-Tantra. The meaning of the term should become clearer as you work through this book.

The Genesis of This Book

This book grew out of our experience together as Tantra teachers and practitioners. In our early explorations, we were exposed only to Western Neo-Tantra, initially through reading and then in workshops. We first met in 1999, and on our first date, we discussed our shared interest in Tantra and discovered that we had very similar attitudes about the conscious exploration of sexuality. As a result, we decided to practice sexual Tantra together. We soon discovered that we wanted to delve into the Tantric tradition more deeply, so we began to study with Dr. Jonn Mumford (Swami Anandakapila Saraswati), one of the few Westerners with traditional Tantric training. Dr. Mumford later named us lineage holders of the OM Kara Kriya system and initiated us as Swami Umeshanand Saraswati and Devi Veenanand.

Gradually, under Dr. Mumford's influence, the substance of our teaching became somewhat more traditional as we sought to fuse the best elements of contemporary Neo-Tantra with the material we learned from him. We shared the sense that much of what passes for Tantra in the West places too much emphasis on technique, and not enough on consciousness, and many books on sexual Tantra struck us as difficult to grasp. We had already benefited by studying with Dr. Mumford online, so we decided to use that medium. We designed a course, "The Fundamentals of Tantric Sexuality," and began offering it over the Internet in 2001.

The response of our online students inspired us to write *Tantra for Erotic Empowerment,* and the title reflects feelings they expressed to us. As a result of their work during the course, many of our students have reported greater groundedness, an increased capacity for pleasure in life, and an improved ability to handle difficult situations, in sexual contexts and in life generally.

Tantra for Erotic Empowerment expands upon "The Fundamentals of Tantric Sexuality," incorporates a few key concepts from our first book, *The Essence of Tantric Sexuality*, and includes exercises that we have developed over the last eight years in our workshops and private teaching. Most of our students have been heterosexual couples, but we have taught workshops for singles, couples, polyamorous people, members of the gay, lesbian, bisexual and transgendered communities, and practitioners of BDSM. We have learned from everyone we have taught, and we are deeply committed to inclusiveness in both our teaching and our writing. Tantric practices are valid for anyone, regardless of gender, sexual orientation, degree of physical fitness, or lovestyle. We encourage you to adapt this book's exercises to suit your own circumstances.

This book also incorporates some historical background and social commentary. Few Westerners know much about the Tantric tradition, and most of us have been heavily influenced by cultural attitudes toward sexuality. In order to develop a form of Tantric practice that is at once suitable for contemporary life and true to the authentic tradition, it is important to have a sense of history and an understanding of how culture has shaped us. Thus, strictly speaking, this is not a book on traditional Tantra, although we do borrow from that profound body of knowledge, doing our best to present it with integrity and respect. Tantra is pragmatic and does not require a rigid adherence to abstract notions of authenticity. If you bring awareness and an open attitude to the exercises, your work will be in harmony with the spirit of classical Tantra.

Practical Considerations

Your journey through this book's fourteen *dalas,* or chapters, will be one of sexual self-discovery. Although you are welcome to pace yourself as you wish, we recommend spending at least one week on each dala. Your practice will include a brief daily meditation as well as a total of fifty-two exercises, several in each dala.

Tantra for Erotic Empowerment is designed for both individuals and partners. Many single people are reluctant to explore Tantra due to the misguided belief that it is for couples only. In fact, most Tantric practices are solo practices. Most people are so focused on relationships with others that they tend to lack awareness of their own internal worlds. It is very important to cultivate this relationship with the self, since it provides the strongest possible foundation for interacting with others in a positive way. Thus, some exercises are presented in two formats, solo and partnered, and couples will benefit from doing both forms. We invite polyamorous readers to use their imaginations and adapt the exercises accordingly.

This book should engage your intellect and inspire thoughtful self-exploration. At the same time, the exercises make the process highly experiential. Some of these exercises involve reflection and writing. Some involve using sexual energy without any explicitly sexual activity. Others call for sexual activity with an emphasis on awareness and a spiritual focus; many involve a highly conscious approach to self-pleasuring. Even if these approaches seem radical and challenging at first, if you progress through the exercises with an open mind and a sense of dedication, you will at the very least arrive at a much deeper understanding of your own sexuality. You may even experience dramatic positive changes in yourself.[2]

Keep your personal safety in mind as you explore this book and do the exercises. Of course, in the age of HIV-AIDS, safer sex practices and conscious decision-making about risks are essential. But safety has deeper and subtler implications, too. Be aware of your comfort level and boundaries, and choose deliberately when and how to explore their limits. While this book aims to demystify Tantra's sexual aspects, partly by encouraging you to examine and gently expand your sexual horizons, do not underestimate the depth and complexity of the sexual self. This is a delicate arena, even for the most experienced practitioners. We are not professional sex therapists or psychologists, and this is not a self-help book, at least not in the conventional sense. With this in mind, we suggest that you move at your own unhurried pace.

We also ask you to be kind to yourself and avoid any reiteration of feelings of shame or past hurt. Focusing on such feelings can not only be painful in the moment, it can also create a reflexive pattern that may become habitual—a repeated reopening of old wounds. Indeed, this emphasis on revisiting past hurts may be one of the most troubling aspects of the "sexual healing" movement that is often associated with modern Tantra. We have found that pleasure is the most valuable tool for inspiring growth and learning. Healing can happen in this context, but it is a by-product, not a goal. You need not suppress or deny any painful feelings, nor do you need to emphasize them or let them overwhelm you. If such feelings arise, we suggest that you simply notice and observe them, without dwelling on or trying to interpret them. You may find that doing so enables you to bypass the discomfort and move into a realm of pleasure, or that it lets pain move through you and dissipate. Another approach is to shift your focus to whatever pleasure you

---

2 If you wish to work through this book with our direct guidance and feedback, details are available at our website, www.tantrapm.com.

can find. Focusing on pleasure in the present moment is one of the most effective ways to loosen the grip of past negative experiences.

If you cannot find any pleasure at all in what you are doing, then we suggest you take a break and try it again in a few days. If the same negative feelings emerge, along with the same inability to discover a source of pleasure, then the exercise is probably not for you. Simply move on. You can always choose to work at a slower pace, take time to digest the information and your experience, or take a break from the practices altogether.

Ultimately, we hope that this book helps you integrate your sexuality more fully into all aspects of your life, that you discover enhanced comfort with yourself as a sexual being and new pathways to greater enjoyment. According to the *Kularnava Tantra*, *"Yogo bhogoyate," yoga* (union) can be attained through *bhoga* (enjoyment), so do keep pleasure in mind at all times. Embracing pleasure, and particularly sexual pleasure, with consciousness and intention is one of the keys to personal empowerment.

Sexuality and Self-Development

Although only a small percentage of traditional Tantric practices are physically sexual in nature, and little of the literature addresses sexual matters directly, a strong case can be made that sex is what most clearly distinguishes Tantra from most spiritual traditions. Thus, this book will begin with that small percentage, offering sexuality as the gateway to an embodied understanding of Tantric principles, and this is fitting. One of the great insights of the Tantric sages was that orgasm is a mystical experience. They also understood that, for many, it is the most readily accessible mystical experience of all.

If you are only interested in the sexual aspects of Tantra, that is fine, although we hope this book will encourage you to explore this rich tradition more deeply. The practice of Tantra can help you discover ecstasy and bliss in all aspects of life. If you want to experience the full power of Tantric sex, you must establish a strong foundation in non-sexual practices. Bringing awareness to sexuality can be challenging at times. Even bringing awareness to life's less complicated areas can take effort, because modern Western consumer culture tends to encourage unconscious behavior. For these reasons, when we work personally with students either privately or in groups, we generally move very slowly before addressing sexuality directly.

In this book, we take a more direct approach, so in a sense *Tantra for Erotic Empowerment* will give you the icing off the cake, which is not a bad thing. Life is short, and we Westerners have a very complex and uncomfortable relationship with pleasure. Sometimes it really is best to eat dessert—or even the sweetest part of it—first. At the same time, as we grow more sophisticated, we may discover that the flavor of the icing is richer and more complex when it is still on the cake.

Sex, Society, and Modern Tantra

Sex is a powerful and loaded subject. In the words of our teacher, sexual energy is rocket fuel. In mainstream American society, sex is everywhere; we are bombarded with titillating images and promises of erotic exhilaration. At the same time, American attitudes toward sexuality generally remain puritanical and profoundly negative. Similar attitudes are found in cultures around the world, although not in such a dramatically vexed and ambivalent form. Culture plays a central role in shaping our beliefs about sexuality, something we will discuss in detail in these pages.

Tantric practitioners—*Tantrikas*—seek freedom, including freedom from social constraints. The process of becoming free requires developing an understanding of what confines us. We offer our perspective on these constraints, which may seem somewhat harsh, with the hope that it will open you up to new possibilities. Tantric practice can point to a way of living differently. No one can completely escape culture's mixed messages, but exploring Tantric sexuality may help you become a freer person, sexually and in every aspect of your life.

A great deal of information about Tantra is readily available today. Some of it is very good, and some is not. At one end of the spectrum are the theoretical, historical, and academic tomes written by scholars who often have a profound knowledge of Sanskrit and of Tantric literature and, in some instances, direct practical experience and initiation. Miranda Shaw's *Passionate Enlightenment: Women in Tantric Buddhism* is an outstanding example of this genre. At the other extreme are teachers with no training of any kind, offering an amalgam of New Age therapies, mystifying mumbo-jumbo, and invented sex rituals under the commercially enticing rubric "Tantra." We are not academics, but we are initiates and committed practitioners, and we bring that perspective to both our writing and our teaching.

Many books purportedly on "Tantric sex" and "sacred sexuality" can be found on the market today. So can books that promise to enhance intimacy, improve sexual performance, and intensify pleasure using techniques borrowed from Tantra, Taoism, Reichian therapy, and the human potential movement. Some of these works have influenced us to some extent, even though our approach is more traditional than that of many other authors. We hope this book fills a niche by giving you practical, powerful tools to begin an authentic exploration of the Tantric path.

While Tantra is an all-encompassing approach to living, which may not be for everyone, anyone can benefit from incorporating certain Tantric practices into daily life. Some of these practices are simple and take little time. If doing the exercises in this book inspires you to explore Tantra more deeply, you will be richly rewarded. On the other hand, even if you do only a few of the exercises here, you will reap some benefits, possibly significant ones.

As a companion to this book, we highly recommend *Ecstasy Through Tantra,* by our teacher, Dr. Jonn Mumford—it was required reading for our on-line course. Dr. Mumford is an initiate trained in India and is one of the few Westerners to have written a popular, accessible book on the sexual aspects of Hindu Tantra from that perspective. It has been our privilege to learn from him.

The Tantric Approach

Some beginning students are drawn to Tantra by popular depictions that emphasize extended lovemaking, bigger, better, longer-lasting orgasms, and so on. This goal-oriented attitude—a *Guinness Book of World Records* approach—is antithetical to fundamental Tantric principles. In Tantra, presence, awareness, and nonattachment are central. While Tantric practice and techniques can enhance sexual pleasure, this happens only in the absence of goal orientation. This book offers tools not only to expand your capacity for pleasure, but also to approach sexuality as a goalless process to be experienced and enjoyed fully without regard to outcome. We wish you much pleasure in your exploration of Tantric sexuality.

How to Use This Book

Tantra is the magic of transforming your consciousness and thereby transforming your entire being.

—SWAMI UMESHANAND SARASWATI AND DEVI VEENANAND

This book has fourteen chapters called *dalas* (Sanskrit for petals), forming a flower, which will unfold for you as you read. The word dala is a reference to the classical Tantric *chakra* system in which each chakra is visualized as a lotus with a specific number of dalas.[1] In Tantra, as in many other Eastern traditions, the lotus is a metaphor for the human being. Like the lotus, we humans may have our feet in the mud, but our heads are reaching for the sky—truly a more generous and inclusive understanding than the nearest Western equivalent, Oscar Wilde's famous aphorism: "We are all in the gutter, but some of us are looking at the stars." This idea is expressed in more explicitly Tantric terms in a line from the *Kularnava Tantra*, "Success is obtained by those very things which lead to fall."[2] Another translation puts a slightly different gloss on it: "By that which people fall, by that may people rise." Your attitude toward these things is the key.

Ultimately, the Tantric view can lead to the conclusion that the distinction between falling and rising, between the mud and the stars, is illusory. Still, the lotus is an important symbol. In many parts of Asia, it also has a specific sexual meaning. It is a symbol for the female genitalia or *yoni,* a term you are likely to encounter whenever you read about Tantra. The well-known Tibetan Buddhist mantra *Om mani padme hum* translates as "Om, the jewel in

---

1 *Chakra* means wheel in Sanskrit. The term also refers to energetic centers within the body. An intimate knowledge of the chakra system is important in the advanced study of Yoga and Tantra but is beyond the scope of this book.

2 Arthur Avalon, *Kularnava Tantra*. M.P. Pandit, Sanskrit Text ed. Taranatha Vidyaratna (Delhi: Motilal Banarsidass Publishers, 1965, reprinted 1984, 1999), 8.

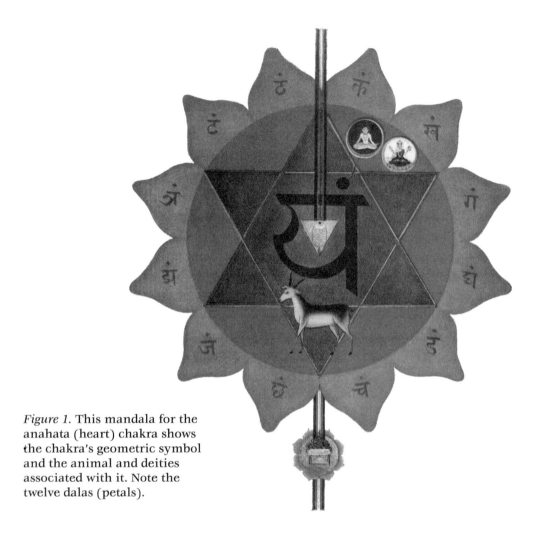

Figure 1. This mandala for the anahata (heart) chakra shows the chakra's geometric symbol and the animal and deities associated with it. Note the twelve dalas (petals).

Figure 2. The renowned mantra "Om mani padme hum" is shown here in Tibetan script.

the lotus, hum." (*Om* and *hum* are mantric syllables that do not translate.) This is a sexual reference from a living Tantric tradition.[3]

We suggest that you do the practices in this book slowly and methodically, spending at least one week on each dala. Take your time and let the exercises and information sink in before you move on. The exercises are incremental, and the dalas are designed to build on each other to facilitate your growth and understanding.

The first few dalas are informational and theoretical in focus, so that you can begin your exploration with some basic knowledge about Tantra and an understanding of what we mean when we write about Tantric sexuality. In the third and fourth dalas, we will ask you to begin to examine what sexuality and spirituality mean to you. Subsequent dalas will include more experiential learning but will also involve both intellectual engagement and a contemplative approach. In our view, one of the significant problems of the contemporary New Age movement and its embrace of alternative spiritual technologies has been a widespread tendency to elevate emotion and experience at the expense of intellect. This has produced a streak of anti-rationalism that, at its worst, borders on fundamentalism. Tantric practitioners strive to balance all the elements that make us human. Life is not a zero-sum game, and using your intellect to the best of your ability does not necessarily require you to deny your emotions or your body.

At the same time, your own experience is the heart of your Tantric journey. While you can learn much by reading, you will learn far more by doing—if you approach it consciously. Applying intellectual understanding to your experience will lead you to a more multifaceted form of knowledge. Therefore, it is best to approach the exercises systematically. First read each dala in full, unless instructed otherwise (for example, we may ask you to stop and write in your spiritual journal, as discussed in more detail below). Before beginning the exercises, make sure you understand the material presented in each dala.

As you progress through the book, you may find that we are asking you to examine your awareness, perceptions, and sexuality more deeply than you

3 For more on the lotus and its sexual symbolism, see our previous book, *The Essence of Tantric Sexuality*, page 166.

ever have before. Such self-exploration can have a profound impact because most of us are trained to avoid introspection, particularly in the sexual realm. Although the rewards are great, looking inward can sometimes pose challenges. For this reason, we advise you not to undertake the exercises in this book during times of stress or if you are having difficulties in your relationship. Wait until the stress has subsided before you begin.

In the classical Tantric and Yogic traditions, spiritual practice is generally seen as distinct from healing or therapy, and spiritual aspirants are expected to be fundamentally healthy. The study of Tantra is not a substitute for psychotherapy or couples therapy, although it may be useful, indeed highly rewarding, to begin your exploration in conjunction with either individual or couples therapy, provided your therapist is supportive and open-minded. While we are very wary of using Tantra as a healing modality, we do note some analogies between the Tantric and psychoanalytic approaches. For example, both emphasize becoming aware. Thus, while Tantra is not a substitute for therapy, you may find that practicing has therapeutic value. Still, it is best to view this value as a fringe benefit and not an objective.

These exercises have the potential to ignite a hidden reservoir of energy and draw you into a new, more passionate intimacy with your partner, but if your relationship is troubled, you may find that this work makes your problems more acute and deepens the divide between you. If you are in a relationship, we encourage you to practice together—but only if you are already reasonably satisfied with your bond, communicate well, and are committed to growing together. Under these conditions, practicing as a couple can be immensely enriching.

As a general rule, we discourage people in relationships from exploring Tantric sexuality unless all partners participate enthusiastically. When a partner's reluctance is an issue, we encourage the potential student to explore the many non-sexual practices that cultivate inner energy, increase awareness, and expand consciousness. Pressuring a partner can lead to disharmony and create more problems than it solves. Frequently, couples come to us because one person is dissatisfied and believes that exploring Tantra may be a way to fix the relationship (or "fix" the other partner). The partner, meanwhile, may be going along as a gesture of appeasement and unenthusiastically at best. This level of disharmony usually makes it difficult, if not impossible, to engage in meaningful partnered Tantric study and is generally best addressed in the context of couples therapy.

But that general rule for couples need not apply here because this book is designed to take you on a journey of sexual *self-discovery*, one that partners in a relationship can take either as individuals or as a couple. Some of the students who have completed our online course on Tantric sexuality without their partners' participation have found that the practices enriched both their inner lives and their relationships. So if your partner is not interested, you can still benefit from working independently; however, we encourage you to be open about your decision to do so.

While we are an opposite-sex, pair-bonded couple, and most of our students identify as heterosexual, the exercises in this book can be explored by anyone, regardless of sexual orientation or gender identity. And, as we noted earlier, we encourage people in polyamorous relationships to discover ways to work on this material in accordance with their own configurations. To the best of our knowledge, all the translated Tantric scriptures that discuss sexuality

Figure 3. **A group sex scene depicted in Indian temple art, circa 1600. Detail from a panel on the Kaladi Temple in the town of Sagar, Karnataka.** *(Photograph by K. L. Kamat, www.kamat.com)*

Figure 4. Ardhanarishwara, a hermaphroditic form of the God Shiva

describe heterosexual activity; however, we also note that many Tantric texts have been destroyed or remain untranslated, and classical Indian erotic temple art depicts the full spectrum of human sexuality.

Since it is a fundamental Tantric tenet that every human being contains both male and female aspects, external genitalia are of less consequence than the capacity to imagine and activate these inner qualities. The ability to visualize is more important than mere biology, and the mind is the only limit on the capacity of a same-sex couple—or any person, couple, or group—to practice Tantra. Thus, it is best to view the references to the masculine and feminine in

Tantric texts (and in this book) as metaphors, rather than take them literally, and to use the practices to explore the nuances of gender within yourself.

This book is based on our understanding of the Tantric tradition. We are not dogmatic and recognize that other interpretations may differ. Some strict traditionalists may take issue with the emphasis we place on sexuality, but we believe that sexuality is one of the richest arenas for Tantric exploration, and thus for personal empowerment, precisely because it can be so fraught, so emotionally charged, and yet so seldom examined with any seriousness. We hope that this book is valuable for all readers, including those who choose not to do the exercises, and that it inspires all of them to explore their sexuality more deeply.

In addition to informational text, each dala includes the five elements discussed below. (Together, the practices and exercises contained in each dala are called *sadhana*.)

- *Reflection:* Each dala begins with a quotation from a Tantric source.

- *Tratak:* In this brief meditation, you gaze for three minutes at a candle flame immediately after reading the reflection. The purpose is not to reflect on the meaning. Simply focus on the flame and observe what happens in your mind and body.

- *Exercises:* We have developed a range of exercises designed to engage your mind and body and thereby enrich your spirit. You can work through them at your own pace.

- *A Message from Swami Umeshanand and Devi Veenanand*: At the close of each dala we offer further insights, often based on our own experience.

- *Nyasa:* Answering these six to eight brief questions at the end of each dala will help you absorb your experience more fully and deepen your practice. We suggest that you record your answers in your spiritual journal.

We encourage you to use all the elements of this book, but some readers may choose to focus on the text itself without engaging in the sadhana (the active practices). Therefore we have done our best to present clear, reliable information on the Tantric tradition in a way that has value independent of the sadhana.

Many popular books on Tantra include wildly inaccurate descriptions of its history and philosophy, and we have heard some teachers make outlandish statements about its origins. (One couple claimed to have received channeled Tantric teachings from Babylon.) Unfortunately, this serves only to trivialize what is a rich but culturally specific tradition. By contrast, scholarly publications on Tantra may be fact-filled, insightful, even fascinating, but they can seem obscure to the general reader, particularly one with little prior knowledge. We hope that this book fills a need for accurate yet accessible background. Anyone engaging in a practice that might be labeled "Tantric" will benefit by understanding the actual tradition at the root of the practice.

As we have noted, this book also discusses current social and cultural attitudes and their evolution. Popular notions about the history of sexuality—from the way gender is constructed, to what Puritanism means, to how masturbation became such a taboo—are often at odds with the historical record. Becoming erotically empowered entails having a clear sense of what the culture expects from us and why and how sexual roles of all kinds have become entrenched. The more fully we understand these issues, the freer we can become. If you do nothing more than read the text itself, you should come away with a deeper understanding of Tantric theory and practice and of the history and structure of Western sexual mores, both of which are valuable in their own right.

This book includes a glossary of terms (see page 239). Our approach is not highly esoteric, but some of the concepts and terminology we use may be unfamiliar. Use the glossary to clarify or refresh your memory as needed. You will also find a bibliography listing the resources we have drawn on for this book, as well as other recommended reading.

Sadhana and Your Spiritual Journal

Daily *sadhana,* or spiritual practice, is central to Tantra. Some forms of traditional Tantric sadhana are complex and may last for hours, but here the daily practice is simple and not overly time-consuming. Sticking with it should be fairly easy. The key is to cultivate a commitment to some form of daily spiritual work, even if your time is limited. By building such a foundation, you will make sadhana a natural aspect of your daily life. In our own lives, for ex-

Figure 5. The practice of eye-gazing is a powerful technique for creating intimacy and sustaining harmony. *(Photograph by Teresa Ambrose)*

ample, we used to devote several minutes a day to eye-gazing together during the early stages of our relationship. Now eye-gazing has become second nature to us, and we no longer set aside a time for it. Instead, it happens spontaneously several times a day. (More on this practice in dala 7, "Energy.") In this book, sadhana refers to everything you do as you work through each dala: reading the reflection, practicing tratak, doing a variety of exercises, writing in your spiritual journal, and responding in writing to several questions at the end of each dala *(nyasa)*. The more fully you dedicate yourself to daily sadhana, the richer your experience will be.

Keeping a journal is an integral part of this process. Doing so can enhance your awareness on many levels and initiate a process of self-empowerment that may lead to profound and positive changes in all aspects of your life. Your spiritual journal need be nothing more than a simple notebook in which you record your observations and experiences.

Documentation is the key. Do not interpret or attempt to evaluate anything you describe in your spiritual journal. Simply make a record as a scientist would when collecting data. It is important to avoid interpretation for a number of reasons. Attempting to interpret will take you out of the intensity of the experience and disrupt the process, and it is likely to create expectations for the future. This may impede your ability to approach the practices with openness and curiosity. Evaluation leads to self-consciousness, and this may make it difficult to observe and record objectively. Analysis tends to inspire value judgments and hierarchical thinking, both of which can interfere with pure experience. You will have ample time to return to your results and analyze them in the future.

Keeping a journal is a traditional practice in Western Magic, one used by John Dee and Aleister Crowley among others. Swami Sivananda (our guru's guru's guru) also recommended it. Thus, journaling has been recognized as a tool in both Eastern and Western traditions.

In addition to creating a record, this form of journaling also helps you develop what is known as "witness consciousness." The capacity to witness is central to most meditative spiritual traditions (and to psychoanalysis, for that matter). In the simplest terms, the witness is the part of you that is aware you are reading this book right now. Refining your witness consciousness will enhance your ability to make conscious choices. You will be better able to stand aside from your immediate, reflexive, emotional reactions to events and thereby exercise a greater degree of choice when you do decide to act. We will explore witness consciousness more fully in dala 8, "Meditation."

Reflection

Each dala begins with a quotation offering a glimpse into authentic currents of Hindu Tantric thought. As you progress through the book, spending at least a week on each dala, read the opening reflection every day during that period. Do not try to analyze the passage or concern yourself with its literal meaning. Simply read it and practice tratak (described below). You will absorb its essence, regardless of whether you understand it intellectually.

Some of these reflections are from classical Hindu Tantric texts; others are from more modern Indian sources. Each quotation is briefly attributed, and the full citation can be found in the "Reflection Sources" section at the back of this book. Many Western books on Tantra tend to mix Hindu and Buddhist material indiscriminately—something we have avoided, since we are trained in Hindu Tantra. We have also avoided using passages from the *Kama Sutra*, *Ananga Ranga*, or other texts that are essentially sex or marriage manuals. These works, however interesting and valuable, are often mistakenly described as Tantric. While they emerged from the same cultural matrix that gave rise to Tantra, they serve a more secular purpose.

Tratak

After reading the reflection each day, you will practice tratak on a candle flame. It is best to practice tratak just before bed, but if that is difficult, find a time that works for you. The word tratak means, literally, to gaze without blinking. It is a classical Tantric technique and a powerful tool for transformation. In this form of tratak, you gaze directly at a candle flame. This practice hones concentration, opens up deeper levels of consciousness, and integrates the reflection indelibly into your entire being.

You will need a single candle, preferably red. Place it on a table or stool with the flame at eye level. As you sit and gaze, make sure your eyes are relaxed. You should try to inhibit the blinking reflex, but you need not suppress it altogether. The practice should not be strenuous. Many people find it helpful to relax the eyelids to the point where they are slightly lowered over the eye. You may notice a variety of interesting visual effects while gazing and immediately thereafter.

Figure 6. Practicing tratak with a flame as a couple *(Photograph by Teresa Ambrose)*

Figure 7. Individual tratak with a flame *(Photograph by Teresa Ambrose)*

If you are practicing with a partner, sit facing each other with the candle between you and gaze at the flame together. As you do so, an energetic circuit is activated between you, often with very beneficial results—strengthening your bond and enhancing your relationship in a delightfully effortless way.

We suggest you do the practice for three minutes at first. Once you are comfortable with the technique, you may benefit by extending it to five minutes or more. (Using a timer will free you from preoccupation with the time.) After completing the meditation, record any spontaneous thoughts, sensations, or other observations in your spiritual journal.

Exercises

Each dala includes several exercises designed to engage your mind and body, heighten your awareness, and expand your consciousness. Many of these are intellectual and involve writing in your spiritual journal. Some are physical. Others will require you to work with your awareness in various ways, both specific and general.

Some of these fifty-two exercises are truly traditional; some are influenced by more modern, Westernized forms of Tantra. We developed others in our own teaching, often with student input. They are designed to lead you to yourself: self-knowledge is the key to becoming an erotically empowered human being. This is an incremental process, so it is best to do the exercises in sequence. If you do them with a truly open mind, you are likely to notice significant benefits. Try to approach each one with a childlike sense of curiosity and wonder, as if it were some new landscape. If you avoid anticipating any outcome, you are likely to make some surprising and delightful discoveries about your sexuality and yourself.

Nyasa

Nyasa means, literally, "writing down." In each dala we will ask you several questions and have you record your reponses in your spiritual journal. The act of writing out the answers will help to implant the key concepts of this book into your consciousness.

Nyasa also refers to a traditional Tantric technique in which the practioner implants mantric syllables into various parts of the body, inscribing it with the power of the sounds. Traditional nyasa is truly an advanced practice that can only be transmitted from teacher to student, "mouth to ear." It is beyond the scope of this book to provide instructions in true nyasa, but we have borrowed

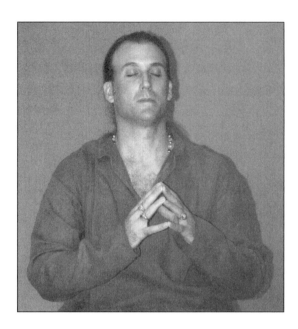

Figure 8. Nyasa
(Photograph by Teresa Ambrose)

the term to remind you that writing is powerful and because it evokes the traditional practice.

A Message from Swami Umeshanand and Devi Veenanand

We are delighted that you have chosen this book to help you explore Tantric sexuality.

Our interest in Tantra grew out of our interest in sex. Early in life, we both realized that sexuality could be a gateway to profound experiences. We also saw that the conventional Western way of having sex is very limiting—extraordinary things can happen, but usually at random and almost by accident. That was certainly our experience, but we had a sense of hidden possibility that led us to Tantra. We started by reading a few books, which made little sense to us. Some years later, we decided to study more formally. At first, we were merely seeking to improve our sex lives, but we soon discovered that for us, Tantra is a way of life. It need not become one for you, but we are confident that working through this book will make your sexual experiences both more enjoyable and more meaningful. You may also discover other benefits, perhaps some surprising ones.

Each dala will conclude with a message from us. We will tell some stories about our own experience with Tantra, discuss the ways that it has changed our lives, and share some of the knowledge we have gained in our years of study and practice.

And now the journey begins!

Hari Om.

DALA 2

Paradox

Mystical ecstasy isn't subject to dualistic thought. It is completely free from any notion of location, space, or time. This truth can only be touched by experience.

— *Vijnanabhairava Tantra*

Tantra is a highly contested and paradoxical subject. Even very knowledgeable people struggle to define and explain it. In this dala, we will consider several definitions of Tantra. Examining apparent contradictions can lead to a deeper understanding of the word and its nuances, one that goes beyond the intellectual. Developing the capacity to live with, indeed to embrace, ambiguity and paradox is an important skill—in Tantric practice and in life.

As you work through dala 2, read the reflection on the opposite page every day. Then practice tratak on a candle flame for three to five minutes (see page 22 to refresh your memory). Do not try to understand or interpret the text. Instead, let yourself absorb the passage on multiple levels and give your intellect a rest. Record your experiences and observations in your spiritual journal. Do this daily for a minimum of seven days.

Defining Tantra

People often ask us, "What is Tantra?" There is no simple answer. Scholars debate its origins, characteristics, and antiquity, and providing a clear, straightforward definition is a challenge. Let's begin by looking at four very different attempts to do so.

According to author N. N. Bhattacharyya, Tantra is a

> . . . general term for any system serving as the guiding principle of work. In the religious sense, Tantra first came to mean "the scripture by which knowledge is spread" . . . Tantra came to mean the essentials of every religious system and subsequently, special doctrines and rituals found only in certain forms of various religious systems.[1]

---

1 N. N. Bhattacharyya, *Tantrabidhana: A Tantric Lexicon* (Delhi: Manohar Publishers, 2002), 160.

André Van Lysbeth wrote:

> Depending on the context, *Tantra* means a shuttle (in weaving), the warp (of a fabric), continuity, succession, descendence, a continuous process, the carrying out of a ceremony, a system, a theory, a doctrine, a scientific opus, or a section of a book. *Tantra* is also a mystical or magical doctrine or any piece of work based on such a doctrine.[2]

Dr. Jonn Mumford (Swami Anandakapila Saraswati) has described it this way:

> Tantra is the way of the Hero (Vira) who neither rejects nor fears any aspect of life. The Tantrist seeks freedom (Moksha) through life (sensation, sentient, sensual) and not through escape (abstinence, abstaining, absence), using the body as an instrument of evolution. In the words of a Tantric proverb, "He who would rise must first thrust himself up with the aid of the earth."[3]

Popular Neo-Tantric teachers and authors Charles and Caroline Muir state that:

> The word Tantra refers specifically to a series of esoteric Hindu books that describe certain sexual rituals, disciplines and meditations. These ancient Indian books, over 2,000 years old, were written in the form of a dialogue between the Hindu god Shiva, who is "the penetrating power of focused energy," and his consort, Shakti, who represents the female creative force and is sometimes called "the Power of Tantra."[4]

These four descriptions make it clear that no single definition will suffice. Indeed, the word's meaning is so elusive that historian David Gordon White has argued, "The various waves of 'Tantric revival' have only further clouded the picture, everything becomes Tantra because nothing is Tantra. In the

---

2 André Van Lysbeth, *Tantra: The Cult of the Feminine* (York Beach, ME: Samuel Weiser, Inc., 1995), 3.

3 Jonn Mumford, *Ecstasy Through Tantra* (St. Paul, MN: Llewellyn, 1988), 33.

4 Charles and Caroline Muir, *Tantra: The Art of Conscious Loving* (San Francisco: Mercury House, 1989), ix.

late 20th century, New Age Tantra has rushed in to fill the vacuum."[5] The Muirs' definition, which is the most specific, is unfortunately the least accurate on a number of counts, and such inaccuracies are in part the source of White's disdain for "New Age Tantra."[6] The definitions provided by N. N. Bhattacharyya, André Van Lysbeth, and Dr. Mumford are more helpful but still may leave the novice befuddled.

The dominant popular myth that Tantra is little or nothing more than sexual Yoga originated in nineteenth-century accounts of what were then considered "licentious" Indian rituals. According to the Abbé DuBois, a French Jesuit chronicler of Indian customs during the early 1800s:

> Amongst the most abominable rites practised in India is one which is only too well known, it is called *sakti-puja*; *sakti* meaning strength or power. Sometimes it is the wife of *Siva* to whom this sacrifice is offered; sometimes they pretend that it is in honour of some invisible power. The ceremony takes place at night with more or less secrecy. The least disgusting of these orgies are those where they confine themselves to eating and drinking everything that the custom of the country forbids, and where men and women, huddled together in indiscriminate confusion openly and shamelessly violate the commonest laws of decency and modesty.

The shocked Abbé went on to claim that when the participants in these rituals, which often included opium and other drugs, were "completely intoxicated, men and women no longer keep apart, but pass the rest of the night together, giving themselves up to the grossest immorality without any risk of disagreeable consequences."[7] This emphasis on Tantra's sexual aspects has persisted into the modern era, albeit in celebratory rather than scandalized terms. It has been perpetuated by books such as Omar Garrison's *Tantra: The Yoga of Sex*, Margo Anand's *The Art of Sexual Ecstasy* and the Muirs' *Tantra: The Art of Conscious Loving*. Popular magazines have added to this myth,

---

5 David Gordon White, *Kiss of the Yogini: "Tantric Sex" in Its South Asian Contexts* (Chicago: University of Chicago Press, 2003), 257.

6 Swami Umeshanand's first teacher training with was Charles Muir, and while our approach to Tantra has taken us in a different direction, the Muirs have given many couples powerful tools for enhancing their relationships.

7 Abbé J. A. Dubois, *Hindu Manners, Customs and Ceremonies*, trans. Henry K. Beauchamp (Oxford: Clarendon Press, 3rd ed. 1906), 286, 287.

Figure 9. Temple art from Khajuraho, India, circa 1000. Such depictions of sexual behavior on temple walls must have shocked early European visitors. *(Photograph by K. L. Kamat, www.kamat.com)*

suggesting that Tantra "promises longer sexual staying power for men and more sustained and frequent orgasms for women."[8]

When we ask people to define Tantra, many of them give voice to the popular stereotypes, and answer that it is something celebrities do, that it is about better sex and marathon lovemaking sessions. Others suggest that it is a way of bringing spirituality into sex, although from our perspective, the spiritual element is always present in consensual sex. The challenge lies in becoming aware of this fact. Some think Tantra is merely an extended hand-job conducted in a candlelit room with New Age music in the background, as a good friend of ours once joked, or that it is something flaky and grotesque, as depicted in *Sex and the City's* notorious "Tantra" episode.

As Westerners and products of our culture, we cannot avoid the influence of this popular mythology, but in our practice and study we strive for a deeper and, we hope, more authentic understanding. Let us consider, then, what the word Tantra means and what it does not mean, beginning with a brief historical overview. Remember, however, that the history of Indian civilization and the history of Tantra are still the subjects of scholarly debate, so this basic introduction is by no means definitive.

8 White, *Kiss of the Yogini*, xiv.

The Muirs' reference to a body of religious literature originating in India is accurate, although the first such texts that can be dated with any confidence were written in the sixth century CE, and some were written as recently as the sixteenth and seventeenth centuries, notably two of the most influential Tantric scriptures, the *Gheranda Samhita* and the *Shatchakra Nirupana* (translated as *The Serpent Power*). The latter is perhaps the most authoritative and widely used treatise on the chakras.[9]

Like much religious literature, the written Tantras probably represent—to a significant extent—formalized compendia of material drawn from a more ancient oral tradition. The Tantric scriptures contain instructions for a vast array of spiritual and magical practices, and information about esoteric anatomy, alchemy, and other arcane subjects. Some also describe sexual rituals, and some are indeed dialogues between Shiva and Shakti in one of her manifestations.

Tantra thrived on the Indian subcontinent (in Hindu, Buddhist, and Jain forms) until the Islamic conquests that began in the late twelfth century. It reached what was perhaps its greatest level of refinement in tenth- and eleventh-century Kashmir, particularly in the writings of Abhinavagupta, a renowned Tantric guru and author of several significant Tantric texts. David Gordon White, however, has suggested that Abhinavagupta's classic writings were an attempt to bring occult and extreme practices, specifically the use and consumption of sexual fluids as offerings to ravenous feminine deities, into the Hindu mainstream by redefining them in more "spiritual" terms.

As White sees it, the texts generally deemed to be classics of traditional Tantra actually represent a medieval "Neo-Tantric" reinterpretation of a tradition that had been outside the religious mainstream. White correctly emphasizes the magical, almost shamanic, dimension of Tantra, an element that many scholars have downplayed in an effort to make the tradition more "respectable." In any event, the Islamic invasions had a devastating impact on Indian Tantra, and much Tantric literature was lost as a result. The Himalayan region, including Nepal and Tibet, along with Tamil Nadu in South India,

---

9 It could be argued that these texts, the *Gheranda Samhita* in particular, are Yogic rather than Tantric, but there is no bright line that separates Yoga from Tantra. Both texts were, at the very least, heavily influenced by the Tantric tradition.

escaped most of the impact of the Islamic conquests and preserved a strong Tantric tradition into the modern era. Tantra also survived in Bengal. In other parts of India, Tantra persisted, sometimes underground.

Indian Tantra had a revival of sorts in the late nineteenth and early twentieth centuries in the context of the Indian nationalist response to British colonialism. Ironically, a leading figure in this renaissance was Sir John Woodroffe (1865–1936), also known as Arthur Avalon, an Indian-born British judge who sat on the High Court of Calcutta. To some degree, the Tantric revival as promoted by Avalon and others imbued Tantra with the Anglo-Saxon culture's ambivalence toward sexuality, since Indian adherents and their British supporters wished to advance the idea that Indian civilization deserved respect. Indeed, one of Woodroffe's most important books was titled *Is India Civilized? Essays on Indian Culture.* For this reason, and perhaps because of his own reticence, Woodroffe's writings and translations of Tantric texts downplayed the sexual elements of Tantric ritual.[10]

We discuss the recent history of Tantra and its evolution in the United States in *The Essence of Tantric Sexuality.* For the purposes of this book, suffice it to say that Tantra emerged as a popular Western phenomenon in the 1970s, along with many other Eastern spiritual traditions, and other alternative religious approaches that can be loosely labeled "New Age."

If Avalon and other early twentieth-century advocates deemphasized sex, most "New Age" Tantrists have taken the opposite approach. We have even heard Tantra defined as "sacred sexuality," a woefully incomplete definition. In many instances, New Age practitioners blend aspects of Hindu Tantra, Tibetan Buddhist Tantra, Taoism, and Western psychotherapy—among other things—inventing something with virtually no relationship to the original tradition. It is not surprising, then, that we see many prospective students who think that Tantra and Tantric sex are synonymous, that Tantric sex is synonymous with male multiple orgasms and female ejaculation, with some "emotional clearing work" thrown in for good measure, and that intercourse must last for hours.

---

10 Even so, Woodroffe may have participated in sexual rituals. See Kathleen Taylor, *Sir John Woodroffe, Tantra and Bengal: 'An Indian Soul in a European Body?'* (Richmond, Surrey, UK: Curzon Press, 2001), 109–111.

How unfortunate that this rich and complex tradition has been reduced to such a banal stereotype! Nevertheless, many people, including us, were drawn to Tantra because of its sexual aspects, and we believe that consciously exploring sexuality is a rich and meaningful path, leading to a way of being in the world that may be more truly described as Tantric. Thus, we hope to strike a balance between the rigorous view of scholars such as White, who dismiss "New Age" Tantrism with scorn, and the superficial approach of the popularizers who preach the gospel of Tantric sex yet know little or nothing of Tantra's history and, moreover, have not been initiated into a traditional lineage.

By now you probably realize that Tantra is a confusing and even paradoxical subject. With that in mind, we offer the following thoughts in the hope that they will both confuse you further and offer some new ways of thinking about the meaning of the word. Swami Anandakapila has often told us that "confusion precedes fusion." In other words, you gain understanding only through a process of shedding certainty and preconceived ideas. It is in this state of doubt or confusion where the greatest potential for insight lies.

Tantra is—

- Tantra is an ancient tradition that recognizes sexual energy as a source of personal and spiritual empowerment. This sets it apart from most Western traditions and helps explain why most Westerners have reduced it to its sexual elements alone.

- Tantra is the magic of transforming your consciousness and thereby transforming your entire being. Your body is the most powerful tool for bringing about this transformation.

- Tantra is a spiritual science. Tantric techniques have been tested and have proven effective for many centuries. If you practice diligently, you will experience results.

- Tantra can be quite simple. Everyone has had Tantric experiences, but it is not always so easy to notice them.

- Tantra can be embraced in whole or in part. A few simple practices can often produce profound and lasting results.

- Tantra is goalless, unless exploring and expanding consciousness can be called a goal. Goal orientation is one of the biggest obstacles faced by the aspiring Tantrika. Abandoning specific goals and focusing on what you are doing in the moment, with as much awareness as you can muster, are the keys to effective practice.

- Tantra is a way of life. The Tantric approach to exploring your own consciousness is an ever-evolving process of discovery that emerges from daily practice.

- Tantra can provide you with the means to deepen your sense of connection to self, to your partner, to all that is.

- Tantra is a technology of mind and body that will lead you to know yourself deeply.

- Tantra is for people of "heroic" temperament who are already mentally healthy. Ideally, an aspiring Tantrika has done extensive work on the self. Traditionally, this might mean years of Yogic study and practice. For Westerners, psychotherapy may be the best preparation, since it provides tools for the self-exploration that is central to Tantra.[11]

- Tantra is a practical way to loosen the bonds of unconscious, habitual behavior and thereby start to live more freely and fully.

- Tantra is the discipline of becoming yourself completely. In the end, there is nothing at all to do.

- Tantra is pragmatic and non-moralistic. You can utilize whatever tools are at hand for the purpose of expanding consciousness.

One way to define Tantra is to say it is the science of self-exploration.

---

11 "In the West, we have a particular type of Yoga . . . called psychotherapy; it is one of the most valuable heritages that Western civilization has produced," wrote Dr. Jonn Mumford, noting that psychotherapy is essential for those seriously interested in Yoga. The same applies for Tantra, but the Tantric and psychotherapeutic approaches are radically different, and actually blending them is probably unwise. Dr. Jonn Mumford, *A Chakra & Kundalini Workbook: Psycho-Spiritual Techniques for Health, Rejuvenation, Psychic Powers and Spiritual Realization.* (St. Paul, MN: Llewellyn, 1997), 154.

Tantra is not—

- Tantra is not sacred sexuality, although it may include sexual practices among many uses of the body as a tool for spiritual development.

- Tantra is not a set of techniques for better sex. Increased pleasure, deeper intimacy, and new lovemaking skills are often the by-products of the practices, and many people are drawn to Tantra out of an interest in developing these abilities. Such goals are valid, but it is unlikely that they will be attained until they are discarded.

- Tantra is not psychotherapy, although many practices may have psychological benefits. Some modern teachers use 1960s-era emotional release techniques, which are of questionable efficacy and are potentially dangerous. They have nothing to do with traditional Tantra.

- Tantra is not an easy fix for personal or relationship problems. Partnered practice can deepen intimacy, but it can also magnify existing tensions. Similarly, solo practice—particularly meditation—may ease some personal problems, but not always. If the psychological or interpersonal issues are serious, they should be addressed with a trained therapist.

- Tantra is not for the faint-hearted, the ungrounded, or the emotionally fragile. We all have these qualities in some respects at some times, but if you feel you are not fearless enough to practice Tantra, there are many other approaches that may serve you better. Whatever path you choose, it is best to make the choice with as much self-awareness as possible.

- Tantra is not a healing modality, although practicing can significantly benefit both physical and emotional health.

- Tantra is not a religion in the conventional Western sense; however, it has helped shape both Tibetan Buddhism and many branches of Hinduism. Tantric ideas can be found in most of the world's religions.

- Tantra is not magic in the popular sense—mere trickery or spellcasting —but many Tantric texts include recipes and instructions for creating amulets, casting spells, and obtaining magical powers. In addition, the effects of practicing can be quite magical in an entirely different way.

- Tantra is not easy. You can't learn it by reading a book or attending a week-end workshop. It requires sustained experience. (In French, the word *ex-périence* means experiment, and that definition applies as well.)

- Tantra is not a set of physical practices, Yogic exercises, or sexual gym-nastics. Physical practices are merely tools for conditioning the body and changing the consciousness. In Tantra, everything one does in daily life can function as a tool.

- Tantra is not a form of sexual Olympics, even though Tantric sexual practices can transform sexuality into a divine—Olympian—experience.

- Tantra is not a massage technique, genital or otherwise. Unfortunately, "Tantric massage" has become a euphemism for erotic massage in many circles. Any form of massage can be given and received Tantrically—with awareness, a sense of sacredness, and as a means to cultivate and direct energy—but calling something Tantric does not make it so.

- Tantra is not polyamory, polyfidelity, open marriage, or about having multiple partners. There is no moral judgment here. A person can be Tan-tric regardless of love-style or relationship style—celibate, single, monoga-mous, or polyamorous.

- Tantra is not for thrill-seekers. It requries patience, self-discipline, and regular practice of non-sexual solo exercises. It may not offer immedi-ate gratification, so it is likely to disappoint anyone looking for a new kind of kick. We do not discourage anyone from seeking new and in-tense forms of sexual pleasure. People who honestly and consciously engage in sexual adventuring can often possess greater integrity and deeper self-awareness than people who go to great lengths to make sex "sacred" to justify engaging in it. In our view, consensual sex is intrinsi-cally sacred.

- Tantra is not an "art," a term that implies it is a skill set or something that you can learn to "do." Since it is a holistic approach to living, it is more all-encompassing than any art form.

- Tantra is not sacred prostitution. Indian society, like many other ancient cultures, had a tradition of temple prostitution, but this tradition was at best peripherally related to Tantra. While we respect the contemporary movement to reclaim the spiritual role of the prostitute, it is not accurate to call prostitution, however sacred, Tantra.

- Tantra does not have a central doctrine. The written texts are primarily practical manuals, and no one text or group of texts can be considered authoritative.

- Tantra is not an easy answer. In fact, practicing is likely to inspire more questions.

Tantra is everything we have said it is not, and more. Truth can only be touched by embracing the paradoxical.

EXERCISE 1. **What Is Tantra?**

Open your spiritual journal and record any thoughts and ideas, no matter how random, that you had while reading the passages "Tantra Is" and "Tantra Is Not."

A Message from Swami Umeshanand and Devi Veenanand

We first met our beloved guru, Dr. Jonn Mumford (Swami Anandakapila Saraswati) at a McDonald's on West Fifty-seventh Street in New York City. He was on an American book tour, sadly perhaps his last. He is now retired from public teaching, except for a yearly guest lecture series at Ananda Ashram in Tamil Nadu, South India.

We went to that first meeting unsure what to expect, but the man we encountered was jovial, energetic, and vibrant, despite his years, and intensely curious about us. At the same time, nothing about Swamiji's outward appearance suggested that he is a Tantric master. He is a small, heavyset man with a high voice and an unprepossessing appearance, and that day he was dressed in business attire. Nothing visual set him apart from any other customer in that McDonald's.

We suspect that most Western spiritual seekers would not have given him a second look, as none of the trappings were there, and yet it was clear to us from the moment we met him that he was exactly what we were looking for in a teacher. He has remarkable powers—physical, intellectual, and spiritual. Those familiar with the Lakota tradition would likely recognize him as a *heyoka* or contrary, and he is a constant source of surprises. Our experiences with him have encompassed both the extraordinary and the most mundane, sometimes simultaneously, but had we been unable to embrace his paradoxical nature in that very first moment, the opportunity would have slipped by. We would not be who we are today, and this book would not be in your hands. Swamiji is a living embodiment of the Path of Paradox. But aren't we all?

Hari Om.

Nyasa

Consider the following questions. Record your thoughts in your spiritual journal:

1. How would you define Tantra?

2. Describe a Tantric experience you have had.

3. What is it about Tantra that attracts you?

4. Are you comfortable with paradox and ambiguity? How does it make you feel to entertain conflicting ideas or a feeling of uncertainty?

5. Describe something paradoxical about yourself.

6. What do you hope to gain from reading this book?

Sexuality

To practice sexual meditation one requires a very strong and stable mind. It is said in the tantra shastras that only those who have eradicated all psychological fears are likely to have success in this practice.

—Paramahansa Satyananda Saraswati,
Sure Ways to Self-Realization

This dala examines the role of sexuality in Tantra and in society in general. You will explore what the word sexuality means to you, look at your own sexuality from several perspectives, consider the nature of attraction, and review your own sexual history. This dala is designed to give you some intellectual grounding and deeper self-knowledge as a prelude to working in the physical realm. Erotic empowerment requires knowledge of every aspect of your being.

As you work through dala 3, read the reflection on the opposite page every day. Then practice tratak on a candle flame for three to five minutes. Do not try to understand or interpret the text. Instead, let yourself absorb the passage on multiple levels and give your intellect a rest. Record your experiences and observations in your spiritual journal. Do this daily for a minimum of seven days.

Sexuality in American Society

In American society, and generally in cultures shaped by Christianity, attitudes toward sexuality are deeply conflicted. Sex is a subject that inspires something bordering on obsessive interest, and it is universally employed as a marketing tool. People are constantly seeking better sex, and this book itself is an expression of our society's fascination with sexuality. At the same time, the subject inspires guilt and shame. Truly open and frank discussion of sexual matters is frowned upon, and enormous cultural and legal pressures inhibit open dialogue about and exploration of sexuality.

If anything, the pressure to remain silent about sexuality has intensified in recent years. Radio announcers are subject to fines of several hundred thousand dollars for using forbidden words. During a recent pre-interview for a radio appearance, we were informed that we should avoid using the word "ejaculation" and that the host had been subjected to a torrent of outraged correspondence after a previous guest said "labia" on the air. (And this was no bible belt venue; it was a health-oriented show on a progressive New York City station.) On national television, the mere exposure of the female breast has led to public outcry and the imposition of heavy fines, while graphic depictions of murder are commonplace. Heaven forbid that the public be exposed to a couple having sexual intercourse!

Sexuality as a Tantric Tool

From the Tantric perspective, sex is one of the most powerful tools available for expanding consciousness, so cultivating and expanding your capacity for sexual pleasure can be a central element in this work. There is some risk involved in this undertaking because it is so culturally frowned upon. By consciously exploring your sexuality and seeking to free yourself from social constraints, you put yourself at odds with the mainstream. This freedom may make others uneasy or worse, so it is wise to be discreet about your sexual exploration and your attitudes. Such discretion is in keeping with the ancient tradition of refusing to be bound by cultural taboos, while maintaining a certain measure of secrecy about the details of Tantric practice and indeed one's involvement in the practices at all.

Maintain a keen sense of awareness as you explore this territory; be scrupulously honest with yourself. Many Tantric scriptures, as well as many contemporary traditionalist works, take pains to distinguish Tantric sexual practices from mundane pleasure-seeking or mere acts of gratification.[1] In the highly charged and emotionally complex realm of human sexuality, there is great potential for self-delusion. Following the Tantric path has been likened to dancing on a razor's edge. Thus, it is important to examine yourself continuously, to try to understand what you are doing and why. If you are

---

1 These reflect an ongoing effort to legitimize Tantra, which has been vilified for centuries. Indian society is puritanical, for the most part. Nevertheless, there is a kernel of truth in these warnings, and they appear in many classical texts, most notably the *Kularnava Tantra*, that predate the Islamic invasion, not to mention the British colonial period.

Figure 10. Yantric depiction of the expanding universe. Note the interplay between the masculine (upward pointing) and feminine (downward pointing) aspects.

merely seeking gratification, be aware of it, and this awareness is likely to produce a subtle change in you.

In Tantric cosmology, sexuality is the power that continually creates the universe. The ebb and flow of creation is a manifestation of sexual energy. You do not need to accept this metaphysical understanding to recognize that sexuality is what makes life possible, but that is only the most basic way of perceiving it. As humans, we have the capacity to understand and explore our sexuality. As we do so, we gain the ability to use it more expansively, in a conscious and directed way.

Defining Sexuality

Most of us tend to take sexuality for granted, as a given. We have probably never even tried to define it. Some think of the word sexuality as referring only to basic orientation, but this is, at best, a starting point. To approach this subject Tantrically, let us undertake an in-depth exploration of sexuality in both its personal and social dimensions.

EXERCISE 2. **How Do You Define Your Own Sexuality?**

Think carefully about your sexuality, what it means to you and what you think about it. Record your impressions in your spiritual journal, working toward creating a definition of sexuality for yourself. You will likely find that your personal definition extends beyond what gender you are attracted to or what kinds of sexual acts you enjoy. Ask yourself:

- What turns me on superficially?

- What turns me on at a more fundamental level?

- What stimuli do I prefer?

- What situations make me react sexually?

- How much of my sense of self is tied up in sexuality?

- Do I use my sexuality solely as an expression of love?

- In what contexts do I recognize that my sexuality is engaged?

. . . .

Many people define sexuality simply in terms of orientation and tend to create ironclad categories, whether gay, lesbian, heterosexual, or even bi-sexual. But it is far more useful, at least from the perspective of consciousness about sexuality, to view orientation as something more flexible and at least potentially more fluid, depending on time and circumstance. The well-known Kinsey Scale shows such a continuum.[2]

2 This scale was devised by Alfred Kinsey as part of his pioneering study of sexuality in America. The results were published in the late 1940s and early 1950s and were widely known as "The Kinsey Reports."

EXERCISE 3. **Place Yourself on the Kinsey Scale**

The Kinsey Scale rates a person's orientation from 0 to 6, with 0 representing an exclusively heterosexual orientation and 6 representing an exclusively homosexual one. According to Kinsey, most people fall somewhere in the middle of this range.

Place yourself on the Kinsey Scale and note the number in your spiritual journal. You can consider any number or combination of factors—your experience, the nature of your attractions, your fantasy life, your dreams, and so on. This is not an absolute statement about your sexual identity; it merely reflects where you are sexually at this particular moment.

The Kinsey Scale is a useful starting point for thinking about this subject, but it has its limitations. Regardless of your current orientation, you can learn from experiences that may not match it. Such experiences may be challenging but are often highly rewarding because they can produce greater awareness and flexibility. The Tantric approach is to maintain an experimental attitude. Exploring areas that might seem unappealing can lead you to a deeper understanding of your sexuality and your psyche in general.

Understanding Your Sexuality

What excites you? The process of answering that question is another step toward understanding your sexuality. This is extremely personal, and there are no wrong ways to become aroused (except if you are engaging in nonconsensual behavior). It is unfortunate that the mass commercialization of sexuality has homogenized what is generally perceived as "sexy." The popular media—from magazines to billboards to mainstream film and television to pornography—have had a profound influence not only on ideas about what constitutes physical beauty but also on beliefs about how to behave in sexual encounters. Many Hollywood depictions of "hot sex" involve virtually no foreplay and last all of thirty seconds. We are shocked by some of what we see, not because of its explicitness, but because it looks so unpleasant. We suspect that this commercialization of sexual imagery has imposed many artificial limits on people's erotic lives and has stifled the expression of the true sexual self by many who live in this culture.

Authenticity is something to strive for. Here, that will require resisting imposed ideas and behavior patterns and engaging in a systematic and conscious exploration of your true sexual self. You may discover that some mainstream sexual stereotypes indeed appeal to you, but you will have arrived at this discovery through a process that renders your attraction more truly your own.

Your sexuality is defined by the acts that you do, at least to some degree, but you are likely to discover that it has both internal and external manifestations. These may or may not be the same, and the degree to which they are congruent varies from person to person. To take ourselves as an example, one of us has a rich fantasy life that encompasses changing genders and acts that are physically impossible, while the other tends to fantasize about past experiences or future possibilities.

EXERCISE 4. **Fantasies**

Describe three of your favorite fantasies in your spiritual journal:

- Do they have a recurring theme?

- Do you have so many that it is difficult to choose only three?

- Do you have one tried and true scenario?

- How does it feel to think about this subject and answer these questions?

You may find that your fantasy life includes activities that are outside your sexual repertoire in the real world, and possibly acts that you would never dream of doing. There is absolutely nothing wrong with an active fantasy life that does not mirror your external behaviors. Problems can emerge, however, when there are feelings of guilt about the fantasies, when one feels compelled to act them out, or when the gap between fantasy and reality is a source of dissatisfaction. Again, bringing conscious awareness to this realm is the key to leading a balanced sexual life.

EXERCISE 5. **Your Sexuality Scale**

Rank the following in terms of their importance to your understanding of your own sexuality. Use a scale of 1 to 10, where 1 means not at all important and 10 means highly important.[3]

1. Orientation

2. Frequency

3. What specific acts you do

4. Social standards

5. Overall drive

6. Fantasy life

7. Emotional/relational

Fantasy and Reality

A sense of mutuality is important in a relationship, but we have met many couples who are unable to support each other as sexual beings. Frequently, in these situations, one or both partners escapes into a private world of fantasy at the expense of being present in the relationship. This urge can be damaging, but the problem does not lie in the fantasy life itself. Rather, it lies in the desire to avoid reality and intimacy. If your fantasy life is not leading to a sense of greater satisfaction with yourself and your relationship, then it probably behooves you to find a way to harmonize the internal and external aspects of your sexuality.

For some couples, the idea of fantasizing about someone other than a partner is tantamount to infidelity or betrayal. Fidelity is a very complex and delicate subject, and it is almost forbidden to question conventional beliefs about it. The Tantric approach to sexuality demands that we examine received wisdom so that we can choose whether to accept it.

---

3 We are indebted to Nina Hartley. Her ideas on this subject have been an inspiration.

People in most societies are conditioned to deny the full scope of their sexuality. In America and throughout most of the West, adults who are in a "committed" relationship or marriage are expected to limit their sexuality to that relationship. In many cases, this limitation encompasses mental as well as physical activity, and the mere act of looking at another person or experiencing even a mild feeling of attraction can produce guilt or shame in one partner and jealousy or anger in the other. As a consequence, many people in relationships restrict their sexual feelings, often unconsciously, and thereby limit themselves. This can frequently have the unintended effect of diminishing desire (including for a partner) because sexuality as a whole is being curtailed.

Conventional Monogamy and the Tantric Approach

For this reason, we take the somewhat radical view that conventional monogamy, as it exists in twenty-first-century America, is incompatible with the Tantric approach to sexuality. According to the popular model of monogamous relationships, it is optimal—indeed morally and psychologically correct—to feel desire for and gain fulfillment from only one other person: fulfillment in all aspects. There may be rare individuals for whom such a singular focus is both possible and satisfying, but for most of us it is impossible, and the effort to achieve it, stifling.

We are not suggesting that one must engage in non-monogamous sexual *activity* in order to explore Tantric sexuality. But a certain degree of sexual openness is necessary, a willingness to experience a full spectrum of sexual feelings, including those that are not entirely comfortable and may not be socially acceptable. The decision whether to act on those feelings is something else entirely, but you cannot truly make a decision when you are trying to deny or suppress them. In our experience, integrity, openness, a sense of devotion or reverence, and solidarity are the key elements in sustaining a fulfilling and dynamic relationship. It is possible to cultivate these qualities, whatever your relationship style.

EXERCISE 6. **Understanding Attraction**

One key aspect of sexuality is attraction. As you examine your sexual self, observe how attraction functions for you. What draws you to people? Consider people for whom you feel an immediate sexual attraction and people who may appeal to you in other ways. Try to define the nature of the attraction in as much detail as possible. Is what triggers it:

- Physical?

- Intellectual?

- Responsiveness to you?

- Socioeconomic status?

- Charisma?

- Power?

- Other qualities?

Record your observations in your spiritual journal over the course of several days. Examine your attraction to others close to you—such as friends and colleagues—as well as people you find overtly sexually attractive.

. . . .

Consider the extent to which the past has shaped your current sexuality, and how that past continues to manifest for you. These questions are worth ongoing consideration. In Vladimir Nabokov's novel *Lolita*, Humbert Humbert's obsessive attraction for "nymphets" is presented as a consequence of an intense, pubescent romance that stopped short of consummation when two older men stumbled upon Humbert and his girlfriend. The young lovers parted and the girl died several months later. Describing the impact of these events on him, Humbert tells the reader ". . . the poison was in the wound, and the wound remained ever open."[4] Nabokov's novel illuminates

---

4 Vladimir Nabokov, *Lolita* (New York: Vintage International, 1989), 18.

how profoundly our first sexual experiences can shape the course of our sexual lives. While these words come from the pen of a character who is trying to justify his own criminal behavior, they reveal a broader human truth. We may never free ourselves entirely from the influence of these formative experiences, whether positive or negative. At the same time, by bringing awareness to the ways in which they have shaped us, we can loosen their grip just a little, so that we are freer as sexual beings. Some wounds may remain ever open, but they need not rule our actions as they ruled Humbert's. Consciousness is the key.

Thus, for many if not most of us, early erotic experiences retain great power throughout adulthood. For some, that power can limit their possibilities in the present, and one need not be as obsessive as Humbert Humbert (an extreme and pathological example) for this to be the case. The more deeply and honestly you examine past experiences, the greater the chance you won't be ruled by them—and you may open a door to a whole new range of pleasures.

EXERCISE 7. **Formative Experiences**

Take some time to recall the three most formative experiences in your erotic life and consider how they influence you in the present. Record your impressions in your spiritual journal. (You will examine your sexual history in greater depth in dala 5, "Pleasure.")

. . . .

In this dala, we have given you some tools for understanding your sexuality. It is up to you to deepen that understanding, and we encourage you to do so. It is not always easy to be honest about sexual matters, and sometimes being honest with ourselves is the biggest challenge of all. Many of the more extreme practices of classical Tantra require the aspirant to face what can be described as demonic forces. Try to bring a similar fearlessness to this more internal challenge.

A Message from Swami Umeshanand and Devi Veenanand

The intrinsic power of sexuality is recognized and highly revered in the Tantric tradition. Like anything that is intrinsically powerful, sex, when engaged in unwisely or unconsciously, can be dangerous. It is important, therefore, to approach it respectfully and with as much awareness as you can muster.

"Sexual addiction" and the compulsive "use" of pornography are hot topics on television talk shows, and we are struck by the judgmental and profoundly sex-negative ways in which these topics are usually discussed. Of course, compulsive behavior of any kind can be damaging, and in some instances, therapeutic interventions may be necessary. Sex, however, is an essential part of human life, and we are wary of attempts to medicalize it and define new pathologies related to it. The problem is in the compulsion, not in the sex, and compulsion is often driven by shame and secrecy.

In our experience, the key to developing a balanced, healthy attitude toward your own sexuality lies in understanding what sexuality means to you, exploring yourself honestly and fearlessly, and striving for greater consciousness. The more we examine ourselves, the more we discover that our individual sexuality, as well as our sexuality as a couple, is fluid and evolving. Since each of us has the space to explore what sexuality means on a personal level, and each of us feels safe to communicate honestly about it, we also have the power continually to discover what it means interpersonally.

Hari Om.

Nyasa

Consider the following questions. Record your thoughts in your spiritual journal:

1. What did you learn about sexuality from your family?

2. What did you learn about sexuality outside the home?

3. What new information have you discovered about yourself by examining your sexuality?

4. How can sexuality be used as a tool?

5. To what degree do your inner fantasy life and real-world activities match?

6. In what contexts or situations do you feel free as a sexual being?

DALA 4
Spiritual Sexuality

I remember again and again the dark primeval Devi
    swayed with passion,
Her beauteous face heated and moist with the sweat
    (of amorous play),
Bearing a necklace of Ganja berries, and clad with
    leaves.

—HYMN TO BHUBANESHVARI
FROM THE *TANTRASARA*

In this dala, we will examine the relationship between sexuality and spirituality and ask you to consider how culture and organized religion may have shaped your attitudes toward both. You will think about what spirituality means to you and arrive at your own definition-in-progress. We encourage you to bring an attitude of reverence into your sexual life and to recognize that the dichotomy between sex and spirit is, in fact, artificial.

As you work through dala 4, read the reflection on the opposite page every day. Then practice tratak on a candle flame for three to five minutes. Do not try to understand or interpret the text. Instead, let yourself absorb the passage on multiple levels and give your intellect a rest. Record your experiences and observations in your spiritual journal. Do this daily for a minimum of seven days.

What Is Spirituality?

People use the word spirituality very freely, apparently without giving much thought to its meaning. The term has become a popular one in recent years and is frequently embraced by those who are uncomfortable with traditional religion. The rejection of orthodoxy is salutary, but only if it is based on clear thinking and rigorous inquiry. It is easy to think we are escaping a rigid ideology only to find ourselves embracing an equally inflexible way of thinking, another form of received wisdom cloaked in a different rhetorical guise. Since we believe it is essential to discover your own truth, we see it as extremely important to arrive at a nuanced understanding of what spirituality means to you.

Figure 11. The Sri Yantra is a tool for meditation that represents all aspects of both Shakti and Shiva. It is a geometric symbol for the entire universe, including the human body.

The Random House Dictionary's definition of spirituality, unfortunately, sheds little light on the term.

> 1. The quality or fact of being spiritual. 2. Incorporeal or immaterial nature. 3. Predominantly spiritual character as shown in thought, life, etc.; Spiritual tendency or tone.[1]

As the popular saying goes, "Religion is for people who are afraid of going to hell; spirituality is for people who have been there." This is perhaps a little more helpful, to the extent that it rejects the punitive model and captures one contemporary cultural understanding of spirituality. But it is still locked into a view that tends to deny the body and negate the possibility that the physical, indeed the carnal, can function as a gateway to the spiritual—right here, right now. Tantra embraces this notion and does not deny the body. Instead, it emphasizes that the body lies at the very heart of spiritual experience.

---

1 *Random House Unabridged Dictionary, Second Edition*, Stuart Berg Flexner, ed. (New York: Random House, 1993), 1840.

EXERCISE 8. **Your Spirituality: A Working Definition**

Since the word spirituality is a bit amorphous, developing your own understanding of it is essential. This may take some time, and your perspective is likely to evolve as you think about it. As a first step, reflect on what spirituality means to you and write a working definition in your spiritual journal. It can follow a dictionary-entry format, or it can be a statement. Be as specific as you can. Then answer the following questions.

- In what context have you had experiences that you consider spiritual?

- Describe in detail one of your most spiritual experiences.

- Do you believe that the body and spirit (or soul, if you prefer that term) are separate? Why?

- How did your beliefs evolve?

- How do you behave in a spiritual way?

Experiencing Connection

For us, spirituality encompasses our recognition that everything is interconnected, our commitment to living with as much integrity as possible, and our dedication to enriching the lives of others. Our own relationship is an integral part of our spirituality, and the honor and respect we show each other is, in microcosm, the way we strive to be in the world. In our view, spirituality is also experiential. The recognition that everything is interconnected is not simply an intellectual premise. It can be directly experienced, perhaps most viscerally when one is in high states of bliss but potentially at other times as well. This kind of visceral awareness can be profound and life-changing.

The knowledge that everything is connected and the capacity to experience it in an array of circumstances—from simple conversation to lovemaking to looking at a tree—are what we mean when we use the terms sacred and divine. These qualities are present in all experience, however mundane, and while we all forget this fact on a regular basis, Tantric techniques can increase our capacity to remember and connect.[2] While it does not mean we are free from judgments, prejudices, opinions, or feelings of alienation or resentment, maintaining at least a little of this awareness in daily life can produce a sense of reverence—something sorely needed in the world today.

We offer our own perspective not as dogma but as one example of an evolving personal definition. This is a deeply individual process, and there is no single right answer. Listen within and find out what resonates.

Religion, Spirituality, and Sex

The idea that sex is sinful is linked to the emergence of religious orthodoxy, of whatever variety, and the institutions that accompany it. Evidence for this argument can be found, for example, in Tibetan Buddhism. The older orders, which formed before monasticism came to dominate Tibetan culture, permit *lamas* (monks) to marry. Conversely, the Dalai Lama's order, which is of more recent origin, is strictly monastic and celibate and quite sex-negative and homophobic.

A similar pattern can be seen in the West. Judaism, while not matriarchal, is matrilineal, and sexuality is celebrated in the Jewish tradition, albeit with a variety of taboos surrounding menstruation, non-procreative sexual activity, and intermarriage. The roots of Judaism are tribal and polytheistic, and some of the fairly tolerant tribal attitudes toward sexuality persist in the Old Testament. Yahweh and the Old Testament prophets worried far more about the first three Commandments, which define the duties of the Jewish people to their God, than about the remaining seven. The greatest sins were not sexual. They involved backsliding into polytheism.

The Book of Kings, for example, describes King Solomon as having "loved many foreign women." The Lord of the Old Testament grew angry with Solomon not for his sexual activities but because relationships with foreign women

---

2 In fact, some of the most extreme Tantric practices, such as those engaged in by the *Aghora* sect—*aghora* means "without fear"—involve identifying oneself with and immersing oneself in the most horrifying and "impure" aspects of the physical world as a way of achieving this sense of oneness, this awareness that all is sacred. For an in-depth discussion of the Aghora tradition by an initiate, see Robert E. Svoboda's trilogy *Aghora: At the Left Hand of God, Aghora II: Kundalini*, and *Aghora III: The Law of Karma*.

would "turn away your hearts after their Gods."[3] And in fact, the Jewish tradition has never glorified celibacy. Rabbis are expected to be householders, to marry and have children, for the very sensible reason that one is ill-equipped to give practical and spiritual guidance to others without direct personal experience of life's complexities.

As Christianity gained power in the West, Jewish and Pagan attitudes toward sexuality were eclipsed. It is by no means clear that Jesus himself had much to do with this development, the Sermon on the Mount notwithstanding. Some early Christian sects practiced group marriage, engaged in sexual rituals, and did not view sex as sinful. Saint Paul (who was not a direct disciple of Jesus) had harsh and judgmental attitudes about sexuality. One of his most famous statements on the subject, "It is better to marry, than to burn *with passion*," implies that celibacy is a spiritual ideal and that the only sound reason for marrying is the inability to control one's sexuality.[4] Paul may have been referring to desire when he talked about burning, but the evocation of hellfire is implicit nonetheless. It is worth considering why Paul's attitudes toward sexuality triumphed, when other ways of understanding the concept of "sin" and interpreting the teachings of Jesus are equally, if not more, reasonable.

We are not historians of early Christianity, and much of that history is highly contested in any event. As we look at the history of religious attitudes toward sexuality, however, we are tempted to speculate and identify certain trends that seem common to many cultures. While most religious traditions draw distinctions between "pure" and "impure" and impose a variety of sexual taboos, there seems to be a link between the rise of organized hierarchical religious institutions and the belief that sex is per se sinful. In many historical instances, this correlates with the consolidation of male power and the placement of spiritual authority into the hands of celibate men. Typically the sexual autonomy of women is simultaneously suppressed, while male sexual energy is directed either into a monastic discipline or into a life of militarism and war—not the warfare of the community or tribal culture, but rather the

3 1Kings 11:1–13 (New King James Version).
4 1Cor. 7–9.

more structured forms of militarism in which the warrior is no longer fighting for his people or his community, but for his king, his God, or his country.

In the West, harsher attitudes toward sexuality emerged after the Reformation. Indeed, some forms of Protestant Christianity elevate questions of sexual "morality" above virtually any other issue. While monasticism is not central to most Protestant traditions, the Reformation paved the way for the modern nation-state and probably for the Industrial Revolution as well. We suspect that the anti-sexual attitude that characterizes so much of Protestant Christianity has served as a tool to redirect the energy of the masses into military service and factory work. These attitudes about sexuality have retained their power and have taken on new forms, even as the clergy's influence has declined.[5]

We point to this association not to claim a causal link but to highlight the historical relationship between social control and the condemnation of sex as sinful. The willingness to embrace sexuality as truly sacred and spiritual can be a powerful force for personal liberation. Things were not always as they are today, and certain types of ancient wisdom may have particular value in the modern world.

Tantra: An Experimental Approach

Unlike most other religious or spiritual traditions, Eastern or Western, Tantra embraces sexuality and the energy that inspires it. Even many celibate practitioners use sexual visualizations as meditative tools. Tantra is probably not a religion, at least in the conventional Western sense. Instead, it is a current within the Hindu, Buddhist, Jain, and Tibetan Bön religions, and it has no clearly defined canon. Each school or lineage relies on its own group of texts, and direct transmission from teacher to student—including both spiritual ini-

---

5 As the power of religious institutions waned in Europe, new anxieties about sexual desire and activity emerged. Masturbation became a serious concern in the early 1700s, and for the most part, those who condemned it did not do so on a religious basis. They were far more worried about the private nature of the activity and attacked it in language that mirrored the economic ideas of the time. It was wasteful and unproductive, sapping the energy of both men and women, energy that could be directed toward work. Thomas W. Laqueur, *Solitary Sex: A Cultural History of Masturbation* (New York: Zone Books, 2004).

tiation and practical knowledge—is generally more important than textual or theoretical understanding.

Faith plays a very limited role in Tantra, just as it does in indigenous and shamanic traditions. This sets Tantra apart from most modern religions, especially Western ones. Except for faith in the guru or teacher, the concept is a nonissue. Generally, the word faith implies a belief in something that can be neither verified nor directly experienced. In Tantra, faith in the guru implies a high level of devotion and confidence that the guru can direct the student toward self-knowledge. Beyond that, truth is gleaned from experimentation and careful observation. As our friend Paul Skye (Swami Ajnananda Saraswati) has succinctly observed, "The Tantric yogi is both experimenter and experiment." (We like to add that the Tantric yogi is also the laboratory.)

This experimental attitude is a core characteristic of the Tantric approach. It is perhaps best summed up in the oft-quoted aphorism from the Buddhist *Ratnasara Tantra*: "The person who knows the truth of the body will come to know the truth of the universe."

Tantra is a path to direct personal experience of the divine, achieved by taking an experimental and scientific approach to one's own consciousness. This process can lead to a state of reverence and worship for all that is, an attitude that can only be described as religious. In Tantra, all experience, including (perhaps most dramatically) sexual experience, can awaken this sense of reverence in each and every one of us.

Is Tantra Amoral?

Although amoral is a neutral term meaning without morals, it has strongly negative implications in the minds of many, connoting an attitude that is almost "anti-moral," self-serving and unprincipled. For this reason, we prefer not to describe Tantra as amoral; however, morality is of no concern to most Tantric practitioners, nor are moral questions a preoccupation of Tantric philosophy. While this idea may seem shocking at first, it is worth considering the concept in some depth. The original meaning of the word moral was "custom of the place," and most of what we define as morality, and especially sexual morality, is little more than that.[6]

---

6 For more about morality and Tantra, see *The Essence of Tantric Sexuality,* chapter 5.

Most human societies throughout history have displayed remarkable flexibility in defining what constitutes moral behavior. Most often, moral strictures have applied only to conduct within one's own group, so that, for example, the biblical injunction "Thou shalt not kill" clearly did not apply in times of war or crusades and was subject to numerous other exceptions.

Within the realm of human sexuality, virtually all societies tend to see their own cultural norms as moral and any behavior that deviates from them as immoral. It is worth remembering that the ancient Greeks, revered by many contemporary conservatives, practiced behavior that our society classifies as pedophilia—which it deems to be both pathological and criminal and condemns as utterly immoral.

Sex between adult men and teenaged boys was not only commonplace in ancient Greece, it was celebrated as one of the highest forms of love. We point this out not to suggest that this type of sexual expression is healthy or desirable, particularly given our contemporary values, but to illustrate how ideas about morality and cultural norms are inextricably entwined.

So the Tantrika aspires to an open approach to life, one that recognizes morality as little more than convention. Even so, there may be times when it is best to abide by conventional moral standards—but one can make that decision consciously, not reflexively or solely because society demands it.

There is an important distinction between morality and ethics. (This is our personal view; as far as we know it is not specifically addressed in Tantric literature.) Remember that the original meaning of the word moral refers to custom. Moral judgments tend to be little more than that, judgments shaped by custom. Most often morality is received wisdom, rather than insight gained through experience and personal exploration. For this reason, morality is a limiting idea, at odds with the exploratory Tantric approach.

The original meaning of the word ethics (from the Greek *ethos*) also implies custom. In fact, Cicero coined *moral* as a Latin translation of the Greek *ethos*. But the Indo-European roots of *ethics* relate it to the Sanskrit *sva*, or "one's own," also the root of the word *swami*. Ethics implies character, suggesting a code that is personal, rather than culturally determined or dictated by custom. Thus, it is useful to think of ethics as principles arrived at on one's own.

So we might describe the open-minded Tantric approach as non-moral but centered on personal ethics. Indeed, it affords an opportunity to discover a deeply personal ethic that is both authentic and integrated. This may not conform to prevailing cultural norms, but Tantrics have never been bound by convention.

Sex: The Spiritual Dimension

Cultures around the world and throughout history have recognized that, at the very least, sex has a spiritual component. In the Old Testament, for example, the Song of Solomon contains some richly erotic passages, and in the Jewish tradition, having sex on Shabbat is considered almost a spiritual duty. As already noted, certain early Christian sects practiced various forms of sexual ritual.[7] It was primarily with the rise of the hierarchical church, which needed to establish authority and control, that sexuality was stripped of its spiritual dimension and equated with sin. Of course, even Christianity in its current form recognizes the sacred dimension of sexuality, but only within the context of marriage. In most Christian traditions, sex itself is not sacred, even if marriage is a sacrament. Instead, it is something profane that can be sanctified in certain contexts.

For this reason, the traditions of sacred sexuality may seem mysterious and alien in modern times. They have been systematically suppressed for millennia, and we have been conditioned to view sex as dirty, nasty, and sinful. (Something you should only do with someone you love.) It is no coincidence that the murder of sexually active young people is a common motif in popular horror films.

But we believe that within each of us is a more primal sense that the very act that makes life possible is the most spiritual act there is. Tantric sexual rituals are intended to deepen this recognition, to make it more visceral. It would be a mistake, however, to view the techniques and trappings of Tantric practice as the elements that make sex sacred. Many contemporary Neo-Tantrics rely on rituals to create "sacred space" in which sexual activity can

---

7 For a discussion of early Christian sacred sexuality, see Nik Douglas, *Spiritual Sex: Secrets of Tantra from the Ice Age to the New Millennium* (New York: Pocket Books, 1997), chapter 4.

occur. And yes, ritual can be a valuable tool, a reminder that we are entering a sacred realm; however, we caution against becoming dependent on ritual or confusing the ritual with the act itself. The sex, not the ritual, is paramount. As David Gordon White observed in his book *Kiss of the Yogini*, modern Neo-Tantra is concerned with ritualizing sex, while classical Tantra was historically concerned with sexualizing ritual—an important distinction.

It is all a matter of how you approach sexual activity. Once you start to embrace the idea that sexuality is sacred and cultivate this awareness, you can begin to experience that sacredness directly. The change takes place in your mind, and what begins as an intellectual understanding can gradually filter into your whole being. If you learn to approach your entire sex life with an attitude of reverence, you have accomplished something extraordinary. It is not easy; our cultural conditioning can be very difficult to shed.

It is possible to think of something as dirty, shameful, and bad and also recognize that it is sacred. If seeing it as dirty, shameful, and bad turns you on, so be it. You can still bring in the awareness that on another level, "all acts of love and pleasure are my rituals"—to quote a modern Pagan approach to worshiping the Great Goddess. Our only caveat is that non-consensual activity, or an extreme lack of parity between or among partners, will negate the sacredness of the acts.

A Message from Swami Umeshanand and Devi Veenanand

In our classes, our students often ask us how to integrate the divine into sexual activity, how to unite sex and spirit. The question seems to arise from the human need to create categories and binary oppositions. As Tantric practitioners, we recognize that sexual energy is intrinsically sacred and that arousal is a physical manifestation of that divine energy. Many people perceive this intuitively, particularly when they are coming of age. Such was certainly our experience as adolescents, and that early sense of possibility is what inspired our initial interest in Tantra.

There is no need to believe in Tantric or occult energetic anatomy to see that arousal is a powerful psychological and physiological phenomenon. From the Tantric point of view, when people are sexually aroused, all the channels of the body are open, and energy flows throughout the entire human system.

This energy, or *shakti,* is a kind of fire ignited by the divine spark that resides in every human being. Thus, in Tantra, there is no need to integrate sexuality and the sacred. There is nothing to reunite, nothing to heal, no gap to bridge. The connection already exists. It has always been there. We only need to bring our awareness to it and pay attention.

Hari Om.

Nyasa

Consider the following questions. Record your thoughts in your spiritual journal.

1. How do you define divine?

2. What does "experiencing the divine" mean to you?

3. Why do you think Tantric ideas might exist in most, if not all, the world's religions?

4. How is sex spiritual for you personally?

5. Have you ever recognized something spiritual in a sexual context? If so, describe how it felt.

6. How do spiritual experiences affect you—physically, emotionally, intellectually, sexually?

DALA 5

Pleasure

Thus the body should be seen as full of all the paths, filled with the varied operations of time, and seat of all the movements of time and space. The body seen in this way is, in itself composed of all divinities, and thus must be made an object of contemplation, of adoration and of the rites of fulfillment. He who penetrates in the body achieves liberation.

—ABHINAVAGUPTA, *TANTRALOKA*

In this dala, you will identify what gives you pleasure and examine the nature of what you find pleasurable, delving a bit more deeply into your sexual responses and personal history. Now that you have a foundation in some theoretical principles, you will begin to connect with your body and explore the way it responds. Anyone seeking erotic empowerment must become aware of the body in order to truly inhabit it and embrace pleasure in all its manifestations.

As you work through dala 5, read the reflection on the opposite page every day. Then practice tratak on a candle flame for three to five minutes. Do not try to understand or interpret the text. Instead, let yourself absorb the passage on multiple levels and give your intellect a rest. Record your experiences and observations in your spiritual journal. Do this daily for a minimum of seven days.

The Role of Pleasure in Tantra

Where you are in your life is perfect. To know this, you must truly comprehend where you are. Through the exercises in the first four dalas you have been developing this understanding, at least in more abstract and intellectual terms. Now it is time to begin examining your sexuality in its present state, and to seek a more embodied and physical understanding of yourself.

Tantrikas are primarily concerned with exploring inner mystical states. Many traditions see body and spirit as antitheses, but in Tantra, the body and the senses are useful tools in the search for mystical experience. All mundane activities are opportunities to encounter the divine, when they are approached with consciousness and intention. While Tantra is a personal path in this sense, the inner journey also generates the awareness that everything is connected. In fact, the word Tantra can be translated as web or weaving, implying an interweaving of the individual self with the fabric of the universe. Moments of intense pleasure are opportunities to feel this sense of interconnection.

In Tantric cosmology, the entire universe vibrates with pleasure. Tantrics view the ever-unfolding process of creation in explicitly erotic terms—the attraction and union of male and female polarities, Shiva and Shakti in the Hindu tradition. Thus, in Tantra, pleasure on an individual, microcosmic level evokes the universal process. At peak moments of pleasure, the practitioner can reach a state of union (*yoga*) with all that is.

This attitude toward pleasure is made explicit in the *Vijnanabhairava Tantra*, an eighth-century Kashmir Shaivite text that is one of the most important Tantric scriptures: "On the occasion of great delight being obtained . . . one should meditate on the delight itself and become absorbed in it, then his mind will become identified with it."[1]

American culture in particular is permeated by an extraordinary ambivalence about pleasure and desire. Desire drives consumerism, and marketers promote the idea that pleasure can be found in the next purchase. Of course, that pleasure is fleeting. As it recedes, it is replaced by desire for another item in a never-ending cycle. Sexuality is one of the main lubricants that keep this wheel of consumerism in motion. We are conditioned to believe that we will be healthier, happier, more beautiful, that we will attract that gorgeous man or woman in the ad, if we just make the right purchases.

At the same time, our society tends to view the body and its pleasures as suspect at best, evil at worst. In spite of the success of marketing that relies on sexual imagery, America remains largely a sex-negative, anhedonic culture that values work and material "success" above all else.

As we have noted in general terms, Christianity and other social and political factors have strongly influenced prevailing attitudes toward sexuality. This subject is worth studying in more detail, and we will return to it from time to time, from slightly different perspectives.

1 Jaideva Singh, *The Yoga of Delight, Wonder, and Astonishment: A Translation of the Vijnanabhairava* (Albany: State University of New York Press, 1991), 68.

In the United States, our Puritan heritage still shapes our social mores. The Puritans saw wealth as a sign of God's favor. They also viewed any form of nonmarital sexual desire or activity as a path to damnation, since Satan could exploit the body and steal the soul. Modern European societies may accept the pursuit of pleasure more readily than Americans do, but there, too, religion's sex-negative legacy is hard to escape. Such attitudes are not exclusively Western. Eastern religious traditions have their own sexual taboos and pleasure-denying attitudes (albeit without the belief in a judgmental deity who punishes with eternal damnation). Many Theravada Buddhists, for example, believe that sexuality must be "transcended" before enlightenment can be attained.

Denial of the body correlates with the rise of institutional religions that define human nature, including human desire and sexuality, in negative terms. As we noted earlier, such definitions can operate as a means of directing men into the monastery or the military and can help create a compliant work force. When people are imbued with a sense of their innate sinfulness or inadequacy, they begin to view themselves as flawed or worse. This negative self-image makes them more willing to surrender autonomy and obey the demands of an institutionalized system—religious, social, political, military, or economic. This completes a wheel of dependence on the values of that system.

Where is the possibility of freedom? We are caught between the conflicting messages of hedonism as a marketing tool and the omnipresent cultural theme that tells us enjoyment leads to damnation. Some people may overreact, convincing themselves that self-indulgence is a form of resistance, but they often remain caught on the wheel. Others may capitulate and snuff out their desires in any of a myriad of ways or fall into a depressive state in which they cannot feel pleasure at all.

There is a way out of this dilemma. By bringing awareness to desire, by studying what truly makes us feel life's vibration within us and around us, we can begin to free ourselves from the cultural constructs that confine us. We may never find total autonomy, but if we bring awareness to our actions and commit ourselves to exploring pleasure, deliberately and consciously, we can find ways to get off the wheel.

In practical terms, this means developing new approaches to pleasure, so that its pursuit can become a truly spiritual practice. This requires cultivating awareness. People generally understand pleasure either in purely instinctual terms, or as it is culturally constructed. Few of us give much thought to what truly brings us pleasure, both erotically and in more general terms. By seeking, discovering, and cultivating the true sources of our pleasure, we can begin to free ourselves from limiting ideas and conditioned responses. The exercises in this dala are designed to help you do just that.

EXERCISE 9. **Your Pleasure Palette**

Open your spiritual journal and quickly list at least twenty things that bring you pleasure, assigning each to one of the following categories:

- sexual

- intellectual

- spiritual

- physical

- social

- other

This is a spontaneous process; don't censor yourself or stop to think about each item. You may discover that your list includes unusual or surprising things, possibly ones that might be thought of as "guilty pleasures"—winning a debate, the rush of adrenaline that accompanies getting out of a dangerous situation, or reading trashy novels. There are no right or wrong answers, and we encourage you not to associate guilt with pleasure. Whether the items on your list are commonly considered pleasurable matters not at all. Look within and find your own truth.

EXERCISE 10. **Qualities of Your Pleasure Palette**

Now that you have identified some sources of pleasure, you can start to go deeper. This initial list will serve to give you perspective and will inevitably change and grow as you work through this book, and beyond.

- Did your list include experiences such as dancing, eating, or playing sports?

- Did you find pleasure in nonparticipatory activities such as seeing children play or watching a sunset?

- Did the list include thinking or meditating?

- Did it include particular physical settings such as your home, the beach, or the mountains?

- Was it full of variety or was it heavily weighted toward a couple of categories?

- How would you like to expand your list?

Now notice how your categories overlap. For example, you might list dinner with friends as a social pleasure, but of course this pleasure has a physical dimension (the act of eating) and, at least potentially, an erotic component as well. How might each of your items cross categories? You may be surprised at what happens when you start to think about pleasure this way.[2]

Pleasure and Reverence

Now that you have started to identify what gives you pleasure and why, you can begin to explore pleasure more deeply and cultivate a sense of reverence. There is nothing intrinsically wrong with seeking pleasure for its own sake, but any pleasure is richer when it is understood and fully appreciated, from eating ice cream to feeling a breeze across your skin. In the context of sexuality, awareness of what brings you to the peak of ecstasy enhances

2 Thanks to our student Y. R. Davis, who helped us develop this exercise.

your reverence for your partner(s), yourself, and for the experience itself. If you truly understand and recognize what brings you pleasure, you will be compelled to appreciate anyone who is involved in sharing it with you. Reverence begins with appreciation.

Awareness and observation are central to developing an attitude of reverence. *People often have pleasurable experiences but barely notice them because they are overly focused on what may be coming next.* Focusing on the future makes it impossible to appreciate what is happening right now, and every moment is an important opportunity. The fewer such opportunities we miss, the better. Each one can rekindle our sense of wonder.

EXERCISE 11. Exploring Your Body and Its Responses

In this exercise you will treat your body as a new, uncharted region to be explored both viscerally and visually. You will acquaint yourself with your entire body, including the genitals, so first let's consider genital touching in general. People usually touch their genitals for a narrow set of purposes, primarily masturbatory and hygienic. They may also cup them before sleep or in certain stressful situations. This is a common, primal gesture of self-protection, and it is also relaxing because it stimulates the parasympathetic nervous system. Because most genital touching is more reflexive than conscious, it can be very interesting to treat your entire body, including your genitals, as virgin territory, to discover its texture and experience a range of non-arousing sensations.

Start by standing nude in front of a full-length mirror. Take your time, and move your hands around your entire body, touching and caressing. Sexual arousal is not the goal. Observe your bodily sensations and notice any visible reactions you may see in the mirror.

- Which parts are most sensitive?

- What touch do you like?

- Do you prefer light caresses?

- Strong stroking?

- Gentle pinching?

Now experiment with a variety of objects—a feather, a butter knife, an ice cube. Try stroking your skin with a wooden spoon. Explore your entire body. The touch that is pleasing on your calf may not have the same effect on your forearm. Work gradually toward your genitals. When you reach them, examine them closely and notice the sensation of touching your genitals in this new, exploratory way.

This exercise can be done alone or with a partner or partners, in which case you take turns doing the exercise, watching and listening while the others explore. Describe your sensations to each other.

You can then touch each other's bodies in the same spirit of curiosity and exploration, without trying to excite the receiver. Notice the responses, including your own. There can be great power in getting to know your partner's body in this way. Some people may do this when they are first falling in love, although not so methodically. And with familiarity, this more inquisitive and playful form of intimacy is often neglected.

When you have finished, describe your experience in your spiritual journal.

EXERCISE 12. **What Is Your Sexual Response Palette?**

The following questions will help you refine your understanding of yourself as a sexual being. The answers are for you alone, not for an audience, real or imagined. If you are not doing these exercises alone, agree in advance whether you will share your answers, in whole or in part. We encourage open exchange between partners, but there is also a place for private and personal exploration. In a healthy relationship, each partner is sensitive to the complex and dynamic interaction between the shared and the private.

- What is your sexual history?

- What have been your most significant sexual experiences? (These may not be the same as the formative experiences you identified in dala 3.)

- What was the best sexual experience you have had?

- What was the worst?

- What turns you on?

- What turns you off?

- How do you define erotic?

- Is there an external situation that may not be commonly considered sensual/sexual but that you find exciting?

- Do you have a habitual pattern of sexual activity? What is it?

- How aware are you of your sexual response?

- Which parts of your body are most sexually responsive?

- Through which stimuli, physical and/or mental, do you commonly reach orgasm?

- What aspects of sexuality have you not explored?

- What would you like to do sexually that you have not done?

- What would be your ideal sexual self?

As you think about your sexuality and write your answers, try to remain objective and avoid making judgments about whether any aspect is good or bad. You are finding out where you are now sexually and what varieties of sexual response you are accustomed to. Later you will learn some techniques that will help you cherish yourself and expand as a sexual being, but right now you are taking the first step toward erotic empowerment by accepting where you are. In Tantra there is no judgment about the way one experiences sexual pleasure, provided that no one is injured or abused. There is no normal, good, or bad when it comes to your sexual response. It is simply yours, nothing more and nothing less.

A Message from Swami Umeshanand and Devi Veenanand

Pleasure can be a slippery subject, especially in a society so structured around reward and punishment. The carrot and, especially, the stick are powerful motivators. The process begins in earliest childhood and continues with our formal education, which relies heavily on criticism. It later pervades our adult lives, including work and our sexual relationships. We are conditioned to think that suffering and pain lead to learning, while pleasure has little or nothing to teach us.

We have seen this attitude manifest itself in many ways, both in our teaching and in our own lives. We often hear couples talk of wanting to "work on" their relationships. We've always felt that this is a dangerous trap. Yes, there are times when relationships demand attention and some measure of effort, but playfulness and creative engagement are far more helpful. Try bringing this sense of play with you into even the most difficult situations. Not only will laughter lighten the mood, it will serve to open your mind just a little, making you more available, flexible, and able to grow.

Like many people, we both have had periods when we we felt compelled to "work on ourselves." But for some, this form of work seems to be a life-long project—one that seems to produce little joy or reward. There is great value in taking stock, in making changes. Sometimes this takes effort, but doing so need not be and should not be tedious and relentlessly grim. There may be good reasons for going through a "dark night of the soul" or two, but that shouldn't make you a nocturnal creature. If working on yourself is breeding unhappiness and not much else, then we suggest you stop doing it. Go out and discover what makes you feel good instead—not the false pleasure of the tormented soul but the genuine pleasure that makes you sing inside, the beauty that reduces you to joyful tears, or the simple sense of satisfaction in doing something well—and you are likely to experience a dramatic change. Pleasure is not only a great teacher; in our experience, it's the best healer there is.

Hari Om.

Nyasa

Consider the following questions. Record your thoughts in your spiritual journal.

1. What is the most important thing you discovered about yourself in working through this dala?

2. What surprised you when you were exploring your body and physical responses?

3. What was your experience as the one who was touched?

4. What was your experience as the one who touched?

5. What aspects of your sexuality are you most comfortable with?

6. What aspects of your sexuality are you uncomfortable with?

7. Did the exercise "What Is Your Sexual Response Palette?" generate any surprising insights? If so, what were they?

DALA 6

Desire

A Sadhaka [practitioner] certainly will perceive the presence of his Devata [deity] in the work, the doer, and the work done; in whatever things—such as dance, music, and the like—he sees or hears; in whatever dresses and ornaments he wears; in whatever animals and things, be it elephants, horses, carriage, bedstead and so forth, on which he goes and rests; in whatever he eats, and in short, in whatever he does. When in possession of those objects of desire which a worldly man enjoys for his own gratification, a Sadhaka will perceive the divinity within them for the gratification of the Devata dwelling in his heart.

—GANDHARVA TANTRA

In this dala, you will begin to explore desire. You will learn some techniques for expanding your awareness in sexual contexts and connecting consciously with the sexual energy within you. You will gain some tools for approaching desire with awareness, helping you transform it into an ally, something that will empower rather than enslave you.

As you work through dala 6, read the reflection on the opposite page every day. Then practice tratak on a candle flame for three to five minutes. Do not try to understand or interpret the text. Instead, let yourself absorb the passage on multiple levels and give your intellect a rest. Record your experiences and observations in your spiritual journal. Do this daily for a minimum of seven days.

Desire in Tantra

Desire is a useful tool, and this perspective distinguishes Tantra from most other spiritual traditions—including most Eastern ones. The Tantric approach does not encourage the suppression of desire. In Tantra, desire is seen as an essential component of life, indeed as the energizing force in the universe. Thus, desire is not something to be ashamed of, avoided, suppressed, or indulged in guiltily—all of these tend to make people slaves of desire and thereby disempower them.

By understanding that desire is an aspect of Shakti, the primordial energy of the universe, Tantrikas can use it skillfully. Desire should be celebrated and embraced. And this embrace should not be confused with the consumerist urge to possess, gain status from, or feel completed by an external object. Desire is not impulsivity, nor is it mere self-indulgence. To use desire skillfully, we must feel its energy without surrendering to unconscious and habitual behaviors and satisfying desires in order to numb, distract, or console ourselves.

In many if not most Eastern traditions, renunciation of the world is the highest spiritual goal. The Tantric approach to renunciation is an inner, esoteric one, so it is said that Tantric practitioners both renounce and enjoy. This is a challenging concept to understand intellectually, let alone experience directly. The key to this inner approach involves experiencing desire without being consumed by the need for a particular result. Central to this approach is developing the capacity to be aware.

EXERCISE 13. **Exploring Desire**

This exercise may extend into the coming days or weeks, but the idea is simple. First think of something you desire but have hesitated to pursue in the past. Now act on this desire consciously and note your responses. Be reasonable and safe. We don't condone any illegal or dangerous activity.

Then, by contrast, think of a desire you gratify habitually, and over the next week or two consciously choose *not* to do so at least a few times. Observe your experiences and feelings and record them in your spiritual journal.

- What changes, if any, did you notice in yourself when you gratified your desire?

- What happened when you denied yourself?

- Was it easy or was it a challenge?

- Did denying your desire require active resistance, or did making the decision to deny it cause it to dissipate?

- Which was more difficult, indulging or denying yourself?

Reclaiming Desire

Contemporary Western culture is filled with mixed signals about sexuality, as noted earlier. Sex and sexual desire are forbidden and secret. At the same time, sex is everywhere as a marketing tool and as entertainment. In this cultural climate, there is little opportunity to approach sexuality with awareness. We are not supposed to think about it at all, and yet we are supposed to think about it all the time, because sexual bliss will be ours if we just buy one more product. Sexual desire is thus transformed into the urge to consume.

Many of us are led to believe that since sex is a natural function, it is unnecessary and even undesirable to approach it deliberately and with awareness. Our sexual education frequently comes from movies, both mainstream and pornographic. Neither type of film has much to do with reality, and each is likely to create false impressions and expectations. All of these factors interfere with our capacity to experience desire authentically. Reclaiming desire can be a powerful way to free oneself.

The key to reclaiming desire lies in perceiving its power and bringing your awareness to all its aspects. The erotic spark is kindled wherever pleasure and desire are found. It reminds us that everyone is divine. Recognizing and cultivating this reverence can transform you. People feel it and reciprocate energetically. The benefits come back to you and multiply, leaving you more open to others, more creative, confident, and sexy, and less constricted by mental boundaries, whatever their origin.

EXERCISE 14. **Discovering Divinity in Desire**

When you feel an erotic charge, a jolt of desire, gaze with awe upon the person who awakens it and mentally repeat a mantra of gratitude and praise such as *Om Namah Shivayah* (Praise Shiva) or *Jai Ma* (Victory to the Goddess). These mantras come from the Hindu tradition, and they are valuable because they require you explicitly to identify a person as divine. We received this teaching from Bhagavan Das, the great American master of *Bhakti Yoga* (the Yoga of devotion) and *Kirtan* (chanting).

In the coming days and weeks, try this practice whenever it is appropriate. If you feel awkward using the mantras, you may use whatever form of praise feels right, but do make a conscious effort mentally to honor that person's divinity. If you don't believe in divinity, or you come from a tradition that considers worshipping another human being idolatry, you can still find your own way to be awed by and appreciative of the person and the feelings that have been awakened in you.

Awareness

By bringing awareness to your own sexuality, you can turn your whole body into an erogenous zone. To put it another way, the entire surface of the skin can respond as if it were a massive genital. The mind is the key. It is often said that the brain is the biggest sex organ of all, and by intensifying your awareness of sensation, you begin to recognize increasingly subtle forms of pleasure. Contrary to many of the myths, the Tantric approach is less about peak sexual experiences than it is about expanding awareness so that even the smallest sensation can be charged with erotic pleasure. As André Van Lysbeth has observed, "A Tantrist . . . must be able to satisfy his/her partner, even in a so-called normal embrace."[1] By normal embrace Van Lysbeth meant conventional intercourse, but we prefer to extend the implications of this aphorism to include a kiss, hug, or light caress. The satisfaction, of course, is likely to be somewhat different, but it is no less profound.

One way to understand awareness is to think of it as focused attention. Many advanced traditional Tantric techniques involve focusing one's attention on various parts of the body. Thus, in Tantric sexuality one strives to be fully engaged with and attentive to one's partner while maintaining acute awareness of one's own physical and emotional state. This may be difficult at first. We have all been conditioned to "go through the motions"—in life generally, not just the sexual realm. It is also easy to become engulfed by sexual excitement and lose awareness of everything else. With practice, however, it becomes possible to remain attuned to your own state while simultaneously focusing on your partner. Herein lies one secret of Tantric lovemaking. It is less a matter of finding new pleasures to be experienced

---

1 Van Lysbeth, *Tantra,* 132.

than it is of noticing pleasurable experiences as they happen from moment to moment. Thus, training ourselves to notice is crucial.

According to a common romantic ideal, sexual experiences should be totally spontaneous. Love and sex should just happen, and if things are right there is little or no need for communication. The mere existence of shared but inchoate and unexpressed desire should naturally lead to mutual satisfaction. Without a foundation of true understanding—including self-understanding—it is easy to lose direction, to feel you are on different pages. When this happens, you may find yourself fumbling, hoping to land on a wonderful encounter. While you may be fortunate enough to have a few, relationships often founder in the absence of self-knowledge and clear communication.

Through Tantric practice, you can dramatically improve your odds of having more satisfying encounters and more fulfilling relationships, both sexual and otherwise. Awareness of yourself and the other, a deep connection with your own desires, and the ability to express that awareness honestly and kindly are the keys to enhancing your experiences.

Not long ago, we participated in a discussion among "experts" about scheduling sex. We were surprised by the controversy the subject provoked. Some people believe that sex should always be spontaneous, and that something is lost when you plan for it. As we see it, planning some of your sexual encounters can be a very valuable part of your repertoire, not only because you are making a decision to be sexual, but also because this type of planning can be a powerful aphrodisiac. Anticipation, another word for desire, can be very exciting. After all, what is dating, for most contemporary adults, but scheduled sex?

EXERCISE 15. **Make a Date**

Set aside at least two specific dates and times, and plan to use them to be sexual with yourself or your partner(s). Pay close attention to how this affects your experience, and note any feelings of anticipation or desire prior to your "dates."

Is Complete Awareness the Goal?

According to some traditions, enlightenment entails living each moment with complete awareness, a state that only the greatest spiritual masters can attain. Whether or not you agree with this outlook, it points to the fact that living with complete awareness is extremely difficult. It may not even be desirable for those of us concerned with the rigors of everyday life, family matters, and economic survival. Moreover, hoping to achieve such a state is a potentially dangerous form of goal-orientation, a hindrance to useful practice.

Complete awareness would be overwhelming for most of us. Imagine if, at this moment, you were aware of every sound, every subtle change of temperature on your skin, the feel of your clothes, your heart rate, your breathing, your digestive processes, the conversation at the table next to you, the TV, the siren in the street, and so on. Living in a state of such extreme awareness would soon paralyze anyone. Tantric practitioners become facile with consciousness, choosing to focus when necessary, opting to function in the normal semi-conscious state, and developing the ability to withdraw entirely and become completely still.

Thus, the point is not to strive to be fully aware at all times. Becoming facile with your consciousness will refine your ability to live with awareness. This will help you recognize that divine spark within yourself and others, and it may well transform the way you experience desire. You may find that the more you practice, the more aware you will become, albeit with periods of contraction as well as expansion.

EXERCISE 16. **Counting Stars**

On a clear night, look into the sky and begin counting stars. Do this a few times, and take note of the highest number you reach before another thought enters your mind. Identify the thought as well.

What did you notice during this practice? Were you able to count higher with each try? Record your results and observations in your spiritual journal.

Discovering Your Pelvic Floor

As we have noted, one of the aims of Tantric sexual practice is to transform the entire body into a massive genital. In other words, pleasurable sexual sensations can be experienced throughout the body, not just in the genital region. This capacity is generally more common in women, but both women and men can develop it. The "full-body" orgasm is but one manifestation of this principle. The ability to spread sensations throughout the body can be learned, although it may take some practice. You may have to expand your concept of what constitutes an orgasm and be open to new possiblities.

Let's begin by focusing awareness on the genital region and the pelvic floor. Most of us neglect this area, noticing it only when we are directly engaged in sex or when we are relieving ourselves (and possibly not even then). We will now bring our full attention to the pelvic floor and ultimately to other parts of the body as well. The brain is the biggest sex organ in the body, so we can consciously stimulate both sexual desire and sexual responsiveness by bringing awareness to the pelvic region.

EXERCISE 17. **Awareness of Your Pelvic Floor**

This exercise is an adaptation of a traditional Tantric and Yogic training method. You will need a timer and a tennis ball, or a tightly knotted cloth, which is the traditional tool. You can do the exercise fully clothed or nude, whichever you prefer.

Set the timer for five minutes and sit cross-legged on the floor. Raise your buttocks off the floor and place the tennis ball or knot at the perineum—the point between the anus and the genitals. Remain still and focus your attention on the contact point. Notice the pressure and any other sensations that may arise. This may be slightly uncomfortable, but it will help train you to bring your awareness fully to the genital region.

Do this two or three times over the course of the week. Then try it without the tennis ball and see if you can hold your awareness at the perineum. Record the results in your spiritual journal.

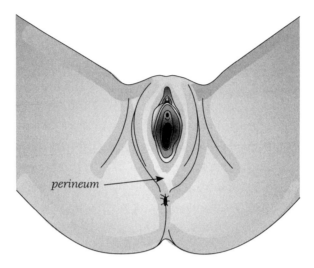

Figure 12. Bringing your focus to the perineum
will help you connect with your sexual energy.

Libido, Desire, and Arousal

Libido, desire, arousal have different meanings, but people often seem to con-
flate them, for example by complaining about "low libido" and "lack of desire"
as if the two were the same. Each term relates to the state of our sexual energy, and each has a specific definition and role to play in our erotic lives.
Let's take a closer look at what each word means.

Libido, a technical term that was popularized if not invented by Freud, is
the broadest of the three. It relates to one's general interest in sex—one's sex
drive—or, more generally and psychoanalytically, all the drives that emanate
from the id. Thus, the libido is unconscious and to some degree innate. We
would suggest that libido is also shaped by other factors—mood, age, culture,
and environmental stresses, to name a few. While strict Freudians might not
agree, we think that libido can and does change over the course of a lifetime
and can even fluctuate from week to week. Nevertheless, in discussing libido, we're focusing on the big picture.

Desire is a state of feeling, of immediate sensation. In the context of sex,
desire is the experience of wanting to have it. Desire may last minutes, hours,
or days, but it is transient, focused, and likely to be directed toward specific

individuals. It can be quite intense, whereas libido is more generalized. A lowered libido is likely to dull desire and reduce the frequency with which you experience it.

Arousal is your physical state in the moment. It is a somewhat more objective phenomenon, since it can be measured physiologically. Desire, in particular, is subject to one's emotions at any given time, but arousal can happen even with a low libido and no palpable experience of desire. People seldom realize this and are reluctant to become sexual in the absence of a subjective feeling of desire.

To return to the question of "scheduled sex," one reason it is valuable is that arousal can occur quite easily even without any noticeable desire. The desire may be hidden from you, or it may be absent, but if you have committed to being sexual at that time, you can still have a pleasant experience. If you do this regularly, you may boost your libido and thereby create the conditions for feeling more desire. Remember the concept of "use it or lose it." If you don't remain sexually active, or if your desire starts to wane and you don't address it, then your libido is likely to diminish. With time, your capacity to become aroused is likely to decrease as well.

It is worth stepping back and examining this from a slightly broader perspective, to see beyond libido, desire, and arousal. If you wish to be a sexual person, as opposed to a person who feels desire for something sexual from time to time, you can take action. You can take the steps necessary to keep your sexual energy flowing. Once you take these steps, the question of libido, indeed the concept of a "sex drive," becomes moot because you are in a position of actively choosing.

EXERCISE 18. **Awareness of Your Breath at Climax**

Just as you bring awareness to desire, bring awareness to its fulfillment too. In some respects, orgasm can be seen as the ultimate fulfillment of sexual desire. In this exercise, you will focus on your breath in that moment of fulfillment. Breathwork is an important aspect of Tantric practice, both sexual and non-sexual. The best way to begin is by honing your ability to notice your breathing at the point of orgasm (either through self-pleasuring or lovemaking). It is very easy to lose awareness at the moment of orgasm, and it may take some practice before you can retain awareness while you're in the throes of passion. It is well worth the effort.

Notice how you breathe as you come.

- Do you hold your breath or breathe rapidly?

- Is your breathing shallow or deep?

- Through your nose or through your mouth?

- Is your basic pattern the same?

- Does it vary depending on the circumstances or type of sexual activity?

Note your observations in your spiritual journal.

A Message from Swami Umeshanand

In the summer of 2000, I had the good fortune to attend a weeklong intensive workshop led by Daniel Odier, one of the most knowledgeable Westerners teaching Tantra. (Odier's works are referred to throughout this book.) The retreat took place at a magnificent home on the Northern California coast and was based on meditations from the *Vijnanabhairava Tantra*. The meditations were incredibly simple yet profound, and practicing the sense-based meditations of this classical Tantric text in such a glorious environment was a remarkable experience.

Daniel Odier's teachings continue to resonate with both me and Devi Veenanand, and although we did not pursue further study with him, we continue to draw on what he shared during that retreat. He has an interesting way of working with desire, and I offer a version of it here for you to think about, as a supplement to this dala. It is my own interpretation based on my memory of Odier's teaching. It may not accurately reflect Odier's thinking, and I wouldn't dream of speaking for him, although we both want to acknowledge his influence and inspiration.

One way to refine your understanding and experience of desire is to reverse figure and ground. Instead of thinking of desire as something within you, think of it as an external energy, something that pervades the environment or even the entire universe. Imagine that desire is all around you, not inside you, and allow yourself to believe that the entire universe desires you.

If you take this idea one step further, you may find it useful for shifting your own attitudes. First bring your awareness to something specific that you desire: it can be a material thing or a change in your life but preferably not a specific person, since that might create some confusion. Now imagine that the object of your desire—that ice-cream cone or brand new car or better job—actually desires you. You may discover that a very interesting shift takes place. By putting yourself in the position of the object of desire, rather than the one who desires, you have given yourself a kind of veto power. The exercise may lead you to feel freer. This is yet another way to use desire skillfully, and if you'd like to explore the subject of desire and the Tantric approach in more depth, Odier's book *Desire: The Tantric Path to Awakening* is a great place to begin.

Hari Om.

Nyasa

Consider the following questions. Record your thoughts in your spiritual journal.

1. What is your understanding of desire? How did the exercises affect the way you feel about it?

2. Why is it important to notice habitual behaviors and choose to break habits from time to time?

3. Why is it important to fulfill desires?

4. What was your experience while doing exercise 14, "Discovering Divinity in Desire"?

5. How did it change your interactions with people?

6. Describe how it feels to focus on the perineum.

7. What did you observe about your breath pattern at climax?

8. Do you have a few different breath patterns, or just one?

Energy

It is Shakti (power) which creates, Shakti which sustains, and Shakti which withdraws into Her fathomless womb innumerable worlds in infinite space. Indeed, she is space itself, and every being therein.

—Shri Yukta Barada Kanta Majumdar,
Introduction, *Principles of Tantra*

Developing the capacity to work consciously with the energies of the body is a core component of Tantric sexual practices. In this dala, you will learn some concrete ways to understand the concept of energy. You will also experience energy in several different contexts and learn some techniques for activating and directing your own inner energies.

As you work through dala 7, read the reflection on the opposite page every day. Then practice tratak on a candle flame for three to five minutes. Do not try to understand or interpret the text. Instead, let yourself absorb the passage on multiple levels and give your intellect a rest. Record your experiences and observations in your spiritual journal. Do this daily for a minimum of seven days.

Energy

From the Tantric perspective, everything that exists is imbued with energy, or Shakti. There is a Tantric maxim, "Shiva is *shava* (a corpse) without Shakti." In this context, Shiva can be thought of as inert matter or pure consciousness, and for all practical purposes, neither of these exists without energy. A similar concept also lies at the core of modern physics. Even a rock, which we perceive as inert matter, is in fact vibrating with energy at the atomic level, so the existence of matter as we know it is an energetic phenomenon.

In Tantric practice, we seek to enhance our awareness of energy both within and without our bodies. Indeed, we sometimes define Tantra as "the intentional use of the body and its energies for spiritual evolution." This is one of our favorite definitions, and it reveals something significant about the role of sex in Tantric practice. In Tantric sexuality, you develop and refine your awareness of the energies of your own body, using tools to work consciously with that energy and/or exchange it with a partner. Because the body and its energies are ever-changing, this process of refining the awareness is never-ending.

If these concepts seem abstract and confusing, that's no surprise. The word energy is so widely and sometimes so vaguely used that its meaning can be elusive. There is no substitute for experiential knowledge, and it only takes a little practice to begin developing an awareness of energy. Before moving into the practical realm, however, let us consider a few applications of the word "energy" in a Tantric context.

Initiation and the Guru Principle

Although lineage-based initiation is not widely available in the West, at least outside of Tibetan Buddhism, we are among the many who see it as integral to any authentic form of Tantric practice. Those who study with a traditional teacher or guru may go through one or more initiations, creating a connection with a chain of practitioners that often spans centuries.

It may seem counterintuitive to talk about the guru principle here when the subject is energy, but there is good reason for doing so. Transmission creates a profound connection and empowers the physical practices that the student has learned. The energy of the lineage is thus passed on from generation to generation. Within that context, individual teachers are free to fine-tune techniques, but this transmission or empowerment provides an energetic link with the past even as practices and traditions evolve.

Initiation, or *diksha,* is almost always given by an "outer guru" who is authorized to transmit it in the traditional way.[1] The term guru does not necessarily mean "great spiritual master." Rather, it means a person who has been authorized to teach by his or her own guru, who carries the shakti of a lin-

---

1 Some prominent Indian saints have become gurus in their own right and established lineages, without having either an "outer guru" or going through the traditional process of initiation. These rare individuals are widely recognized for their spiritual accomplishments. Some report having received initiations in visions or in other indirect ways. We feel it is wise to be wary of anyone who proclaims his or her own enlightenment, who tells you to "follow your inner guru," or who has received astral empowerments of whatever sort.

eage, and who is devoted to carefully monitoring the student's practice and growth. This close teacher-student relationship is a powerful form of love, and it is a mutual love that nurtures the student's development and freedom. At its best, the Guru-Chela relationship is one of the deepest forms of friendship. Although mistrust of gurus is commonplace in the West, this is the unfortunate by-product of cultural misunderstandings and a number of highly publicized scandals.

According to Georg Feurstein:

> The Tantric authorities stress the importance of acquiring a guru who is part of an established teaching lineage. The deities, states the Kula-Arnava Tantra (14-5), provide protection only to those teachers who preserve a lineage (parampara). The Sanskrit word 'Parampara' means literally 'one after the other', referring to the unbroken succession of teachers, all linked by the empowered teachings passed down the line from teacher to student . . . A lineage is like an uninterrupted electric current that does not diminish in power, at least not unless there is a weak link.[2]

Indeed, many feel that these techniques are imbued with the energy of those who practiced them in the past, so that they actually grow more and more powerful as they are transmitted from generation to generation.

Thus, Tantra is all about energy, and in ways that might seem unexpected at first, but you may still be wondering how this relates to Tantric sexuality.

For one thing, in some Tantric schools, diksha can be given through sexual ritual. Daniel Odier's beautiful book *Tantric Quest* includes an account of one such initiation. In her fascinating, scholarly treatise *Passionate Enlightenment: Women in Tantric Buddhism*, Miranda Shaw describes similar initiations within Tibetan Buddhist Tantra Interestingly, Odier's account evokes the ancient Tantric tradition in which men were sexually initiated, and thereby empowered, by women who were possessed by wrathful female deities. While the practice of sexual initiation persists in Tantra to this day, in the Western world it is virtually impossible to find an authentic teacher who conducts such initiations, and we caution you to be very suspicious of anyone claiming to offer them.

---

2 Georg Feurstein, *Tantra: The Path of Ecstasy* (Boston: Shambhala, 1998), 97.

Nevertheless, with practice, you can experience some of the power of Tantric sexuality and serve as your own (or your partner's) initiator, albeit in a limited, metaphorical way. Your practice will not have the power that lineage-based transmission bestows, but you can still benefit. Exploring this energetic dimension will enhance your experience of sex. All you have to do is master a few skills.

Energy and Sex

So what exactly do we mean by energy? This can be confusing at first, especially if you don't have a background in Yoga, Tai Chi, or other Eastern practices. Books on Tantric sex with diagrams depicting the exchange of energy can seem incomprehensible to beginners. Some of them certainly did to us. We were both puzzled by what we read about Tantra before we began practicing ourselves. Ultimately, we found that energy really isn't all that complicated, and those diagrams are road maps. At this stage, though, let's start to understand what energy is and begin to feel it.

When you stop and consider what has made your best sexual experiences so good, it may be hard to identify any concrete external factor. But when you recognize the energetic element you can start to unravel the mystery. Energy is a dynamic current. When you are in the throes of falling in love or the grip of intense sexual anticipation, you are merely more open to that current. That's why you can feel chills when your beloved enters a room. It also helps explain those instances when things seem perfect on the outside—you are well rested, you have spent a pleasant evening with someone, the mood is right—and yet, the lovemaking leaves you unsatisfied or even disappointed. This is often due to a subtle lack of attunement between the partners, an energetic disharmony.

Learning to have great sexual experiences depends less on external factors or technical skill than it does on cultivating the capacity to experience this energy, to recognize it in your partner, and to use techniques that harmonize your energies. Such skills lay a foundation for the more advanced practices, such as working with chakras and Kundalini, that are often taught and depicted in books on Tantra.[3]

EXERCISE 19. **Eye-Gazing**

This practice is widely taught in Neo-Tantric groups. It is an adaptation of the classical form of tratak that is part of your sadhana for each dala. We have added an enhancement we learned from Dr. Jonn Mumford (Swami Anandakapila Saraswati), which makes the technique both more powerful and subtler.

If you have been practicing alone, you can either recruit a friend for this exercise or simply gaze at your reflection in a mirror—which can be a profound experience in its own right. In fact, we highly recommend eye-gazing in a mirror regularly, whether you are in a relationship or not, as a powerful way to develop love and reverence for yourself.

Sit cross-legged on the floor facing your partner or your reflection in a mirror. Position yourselves so your knees are touching, and place cushions under your buttocks to avoid stress on the knees and back. If this is uncomfortable, try sitting in chairs with your feet propped on a footstool or phone book. Slightly elevating the feet can ease back strain and adds stability. Keeping your spine straight, face your partner with hands palm down, fists gently closed. Now, without lifting your hands, extend both your index fingers and close the circuit by touching your partner's index fingers. If you do not have a partner, bring your left and right index fingers together to create a circuit within your own body. You might want to experiment with the other fingers, too.[4]

---

3 Kundalini is the life force energy represented as a serpent coiled at the base of the spine. One central purpose of classical Tantric practice is to awaken this energy. There has been much hype and mystification about Kundalini. In our view, it is active whenever you are sexually aroused. See also chapter 4 of *The Essence of Tantric Sexuality*.

4 The index finger has the largest psychic output. It is the guru or Jupiter finger used ritually, the pointing imperious finger, the ring-bearing king's finger. The little finger is the most sensitive, the thumb the most phallic: in fact, the words thumb and tumescent share the same root, giving new meaning to the thumbs-up gesture. Both thumbs and little fingers are tertiary *kama marmas* or erogenic zones, so keep that in mind. (See *The Essence of Tantric Sexuality*, chapters 10–13.)

Figure 13. Eye-gazing with your own image in a mirror is a tool for deepening your love, self-awareness, and self-esteem.
(Photograph by Teresa Ambrose)

Figure 14. Partnered eye-gazing produces greater harmony between partners, and the physical contact creates a direct energetic connection.
(Photograph by Teresa Ambrose)

As you sit, gaze into each other's eyes while observing your own physical and emotional state. Maintain this gaze for at least three minutes. You are likely to become absorbed by the experience, but do your best to maintain awareness. Keep your eyes engaged but relaxed; this is not a staring contest. It is okay to blink, but try to limit the blinking reflex as best you can.

Bring your full attention to your right eye and focus on your partner's left eye. At the same time, try to be receptive to the energetic flow. This will let your gaze soften, enabling you to melt deeply into union with your partner or yourself. If your gaze is diverted, keep coming back to your partner's left eye.

Conclude with an embrace or expression of appreciation for your partner. If you are doing the practice alone, express appreciation for yourself verbally. It may feel somewhat awkward at first, but there is great power in it. We will revisit the practice of eye-gazing, and share some powerful ways to conclude it, in dala 9.

EXERCISE 20. **Noticing Energetic Flow**

After practicing eye-gazing, record your experiences in your spiritual journal. At some point in the practice did you feel your consciousness was altered? Make a note of when you noticed an energetic shift and how that felt. Cultivate the ability to recognize this kind of change.

The Purpose of Eye-Gazing

The purpose of this practice—at this stage—is to develop one-pointed attention (*ekagrata*) and enhance your ability to be fully present in a relaxed and open state. When people first fall in love, they may spend long periods gazing into each other's eyes. By practicing eye-gazing, you are consciously recreating the experience of falling in love with another and/or yourself.

Eye-gazing may not be easy, especially at first. Some couples find it challenging and are prone to laughter as a way of coping with the discomfort. But know that you are producing profound changes within your system, and that staying with the practice will be hugely rewarding. Eventually you will be able to keep more still and enter into a deeply relaxed but concentrated state.

Tratak has other benefits, too. Developing one-pointed concentration in this context is likely to improve your general ability to focus. In addition, we suspect that eye-gazing has a positive effect on brain function. Disruption of the gaze is often the first sign of significant problems in bonding between mothers and infants. Since all infant-mother bonds are imperfect and disrupted to some degree, we believe that making eye-gazing a daily practice can effect a repair at a very deep, pre-conscious level. There is a substantial body of psychological research on the importance of mirroring, which is how humans interact in nonverbal ways to regulate and harmonize both emotional and physiological states. We suspect that this practice facilitates a form of mirroring for couples and thereby creates an added level of harmony.[5]

The Pubococcygeal or PC Muscles

One of the most effective ways to build your capacity to experience sexual energy is to exercise the pubococcygeal muscles regularly. (Pronounced "pyu-bo-kok-*sij*-e-ul," these are more commonly known as the PC muscles.) You may or may not be familiar with this part of your anatomy. The PC muscles comprise the pelvic floor, running from the base of the spine to the pubic bone. During sexual arousal and plateau, the PC muscles reach a high state of tension, then go through a series of rapid releases during orgasm. By strengthening and gaining voluntary control over these muscles, men can enhance their ability to regulate ejaculation, strengthen their erections, and possibly improve prostate health. Similarly, women can become more sexually responsive, more orgasmic, raise their potential for ejaculatory and/or "G spot" orgasms, and reduce the risk of incontinence late in life.

Many women learn about these muscles during pregnancy when they are taught to do Kegel exercises, so-named for Dr. Arnold Kegel, the gyne-

---

5 The importance of mirroring and the role of the gaze in the infant-mother relationship are discussed in detail in Beatrice Beebe and Frank M. Lachmann, *Infant Research and Adult Treatment: Co-Constructing Interactions* (Hillsdale, NJ: The Analytic Press, 2002). Beebe and Lachman explore how human relations are co-creations, relying on scientific research and clinical observations. The authors are primarily concerned with the co-created nature of the analyst-patient relationship, a radical re-imagining of the psychoanalytic process and a perspective that is evocative of the Tantric view of the universe as relational, a manifestation of the interplay between Shiva and Shakti.

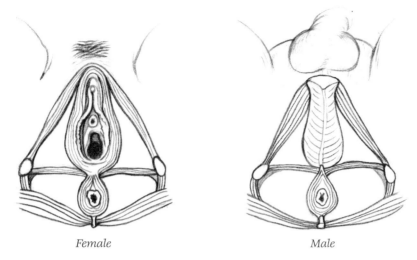

Female   *Male*

Figure 15. Exercising the pubococcygeal muscles benefits physical
health and builds sexual energy.

cologist who "discovered" them in the 1940s. In these exercises the PC muscles are contracted and flexed repeatedly, an action that can help prepare
for childbirth, and speed postpartum recovery. Some women have told us
that in their childbirth classes, the other benefits of PC flexing were never
mentioned. Other women learn about PC exercise as a way to prevent age-
related urinary incontinence. Many men are entirely unfamiliar with these
muscles, or they mistakenly believe that exercising them is for women only.
In fact, exercising the PC muscles has important benefits for people of all
ages and both sexes. This has been known for centuries in the Tantric and
Yogic traditions.

It may surprise you to learn that exercising the PC muscles is actually an
ancient Tantric technique. You may think of Kegels as a physical exercise,
but there is a deeper Tantric and energetic benefit to developing the PC
muscles. Many Tantra and Kriya Yoga practices depend on either tightening
or flexing these muscles. *Mulabandha,* or the "root lock," involves contracting and gently maintaining tightness of the anal sphincter, and is used to

contain energy within the body. *Ashwini Mudra* is a rapid pulsing of that sphincter, moving energy from the pelvic floor into the rest of the body.[6] At advanced levels, specific regions of the PC muscle system can be isolated and moved independently of the others, but for now we will concentrate on the basics.

Some years ago, Devi Veenanand attended a class in which Kegel exercises were taught. One student shared her past experience working with the PC muscles. She once believed that a multi-orgasmic woman was "someone who had two in her lifetime." She explained with a grin that learning to do Kegel exercises had transformed her entire sexual experience. We can't guarantee that your results will be quite so dramatic, but we are confident that if you practice, you will benefit.

The easiest way is to locate these muscles is to interrupt the flow the next time you urinate. Then you can start to exercise them consciously.

EXERCISE 21. **Locating Your PC Muscles**

Even if you are already familiar with your PC muscles, try the following exercise. It will intensify your awareness and help you work with them more effectively.

Drink two large glasses of water. After about a half-hour, you should start to feel your bladder is full. Go to the bathroom and urinate, and when you do, release it in five to ten spurts, stopping and starting the flow of urine. The muscles you are using are your pubococcygeal muscles.

EXERCISE 22. **Range of Motion**

Experiment with your PC muscles, contracting and then relaxing them. Early on, you may need to engage the muscles of the buttocks and the lower abdomen, too, as you contract. That's fine at first, but ultimately you should strive to isolate the PC muscles and work them independently. Now explore the full

---

6 For other techniques for becoming adept at Mulabandha and Ashwini Mudra, see chapter 14 in *The Essence of Tantric Sexuality*.

range of movement, not only contracting and relaxing, but a slight pushing out or bearing down. For women, this bearing down should be accompanied by a slight parting of the labia. Men generally have the sensation that the testicles have dropped slightly.

Working the PC muscles keeps them from atrophying, but it is important to use the full range of motion. Too much contraction may result in hypertension or muscle spasms, and this can make sexual intercourse painful for some.

· · · · · · · · · · · · · · · · · ·

In their groundbreaking 1982 book *The G Spot and Other Discoveries About Human Sexuality*, Alice Ladas, Beverly Whipple, and Thomas Perry emphasized the importance of exercising the muscles through their entire range of motion, including bearing down—a technique many teachers overlook. Fully exercising the muscles should produce a dynamic, energized feeling, possibly including sexual arousal, and a sensation of openness in the pelvic region.

The bearing-down action is also a key to female ejaculation. This is a real phenomenon that has been well documented, although there are still people who doubt it, many of them male gynecologists. Female ejaculation usually occurs after stimulation of the G spot—not really a spot but an area of erectile tissue along the urethra. Because the G spot responds to stimulation only during high states of arousal and, for most women, there is nothing erotic about a gynecological exam, it is unlikely that any of these "experts" would encounter female ejaculation, at least not in a clinical setting. No one who has experienced or observed the phenomenon firsthand can doubt that it is real or claim that female ejaculate is just urine.

This is yet another instance in which Western medical science is just beginning to catch up with ancient Indian knowledge. Female ejaculation is described in erotic texts such as the twelfth-century *Koka Shastra*:

From allaying of this itch by the vigorous thrusting of the penis and the flowing of their love-juice, women experience the need for visrsti, which is the female counterpart of ejaculation. At the outset, this sensation is unpleasant and brings them little satisfaction, but at the climax, they experience a discharge like that of a man, which renders them practically senseless with pleasure.[7]

This medieval Indian sex manual raises an important point. In many women, the initial sensations that lead to ejaculation may be slightly unpleasant, and the onset of the ejaculatory response may be mistaken for the need to urinate. Bear this in mind when exploring this kind of stimulation, since attempting to stimulate the G spot prematurely can be painful or irritating at best. With time, practice, and a sufficient level of arousal, any uncomfortable sensations have the potential to evolve into pleasurable ones. It is also important not to become overly goal-oriented with respect to ejaculation. It is not the be-all and end-all of female sexuality. Contrary to popular myth, it is not the *sine qua non* of the Tantric woman, and it is not entirely clear that all women are physically capable of ejaculating, although any woman who has access to the orgasmic response can probably discover pleasurable sensations in this part of the body. We suspect that dehydration may be a factor when ejaculation seems elusive. More research remains to be done on this subject.

EXERCISE 23. **PC Muscles—Putting It All Together**

But to return to the practice of working with the PC muscles—take a moment and become aware of the pelvic floor, then practice flexing, releasing, and bearing down. Do this in three stages, taking about a second at each stage. Do twenty rounds, exercising the full range of muscular motion.

7 Alex Comfort, trans. *The Koka Shastra and Other Medieval Indian Writings on Love* (New York: Stein and Day, 1964), 111–112.

The Secret Language

Some people familiar with Tantric sexual practices describe conventional genital intercourse somewhat dismissively, as "friction sex." As the term suggests, friction sex is the familiar piston-like thrusting that relies on rubbing and rapid tension buildup to intensify excitement. Tantric lovemaking is generally slower paced, relying more on muscle contractions and energetic exchange as the building blocks of erotic experience. While there is nothing wrong with friction sex, and indeed it can be very pleasurable, there are many other possibilities. If you limit yourself to one approach, you will not discover the range of sensations and the subtleties that can enrich your erotic life. Exploring Tantric practices should enable you to expand your sexual repertoire without sacrificing the pleasures of more conventional methods. Using the PC muscles during lovemaking, while otherwise remaining still, can be a subtle but gratifying way of adding new textures to your erotic encounters. Known as the secret language, this technique offers the opportunity to slow down and enjoy making love in a way that can be surprising for those who have never experienced it.[8] The secret language introduces a subtle yet powerful energetic aspect into your sexual life.

EXERCISE 24. **The Secret Language**

If you are practicing as a couple, pause during penetrative intercourse and take some time to explore pulsing your PC muscles back and forth. You can devise patterns: for example, one partner pulses three times, then lets the other respond. Improvise and play around with various rhythms, too. The secret language can be an utterly delightful addition to your repertoire, both in the context of slow, meditative lovemaking and interspersed with more conventional, vigorous activity. Tantric sexuality is often more about stillness than motion. The secret language is one way to explore that stillness. Pausing to speak the secret language can also offer a chance to incorporate the eye-gazing practice into your encounters.

---

8 This "secret language" is not to be confused with "twilight language" or *sandhabasa*, a Sanskrit term for the hidden meanings in Tantric texts, many of which were written to be obscure or incomprehensible to the uninitiated.

Figure 16. Yab Yum: The quintessential Tantric sexual posture is a very good one for speaking the secret language.

If you are practicing alone, you can explore a variation on the secret language in the context of self-pleasuring. Of course, you will be talking to yourself, but this can be interesting in its own right. When masturbating, see how it feels to stop and work your PC muscles at various stages of arousal. People with partners, too, can benefit from this exercise, experiencing how the body works, on its own.

- Does the secret language help you get aroused more quickly?

- Does it sustain your arousal longer?

- Does it push you over the edge?

- Do you notice anything different if you stop and work the PCs just before orgasm?

- What happens when you pulse after orgasm?

Record your observations and experiences in your spiritual journal.

A Message from Swami Umeshanand and Devi Veenanand

We suggest that you start by doing a series of ten to thirty simple pulses three times a day. There is no harm in doing more, within reason. You will only be strengthening the muscles and enhancing your responsiveness. (Once you have mastered the flexing and are very familiar with the PC muscles, you may wish make further refinements, distinguishing Mulabandha from Vajroli Mudra. If so, we recommend the routine described on pages 42–45 of Dr. Jonn Mumford's *Ecstasy Through Tantra.)*

We have found that the easiest part of this practice is learning it. The challenge lies in remembering to do it, making it a habit. We often exercise our PC muscles to amuse ourselves when we have some time to kill. Try associating PC pulsing with some other regularly occuring stimulus in your life, perhaps using one or more of these situations as triggers:

- getting stuck in traffic

- stopping at a red light

- standing in line

- riding the bus or train

- brushing your teeth (although this may take some coordination)

- doing the dishes

- listening to music (try rhythmic pulsing in this context)

After you're familiar with the practice, challenge yourself by pulsing as many times as possible in thirty seconds. These exercises are only beneficial if you do them consistently. And no one needs to know why you are walking around with that secret smile!

Hari Om.

Nyasa

Consider the following questions. Record your thoughts in your spiritual journal.

1. How do you define energy?

2. How does the traditional concept of diksha relate to energy?

3. Why do you think that eye-gazing can have such powerful benefits?

4. What was it like for you to do the eye-gazing exercise, and did your experience change over time?

5. Were you able to locate your PC muscles?

6. How does exercising the PC muscles relate to experiencing energy?

7. What is the value of slowing down during lovemaking?

8. How did it feel for you to speak the secret language, with a partner and/or in the context of self-pleasuring?

DALA 8

Meditation

At the commencement and end of a sneeze, in terror, in sorrow, in the condition of a deep sigh or on the occasion of flight from the battlefield, during (keen) curiosity, at the commencement or end of hunger, the state is like that of Brahma.

— *VIJNANABHAIRAVA TANTRA*

This dala will explain meditation in terms that might surprise you. You will take an inventory of the ways you achieve altered states of consciousness in your everyday activities. You will learn two basic forms of Tantric meditation and some methods for using your fantasy life to expand consciousness and increase sexual flexibility.

As you work through dala 8, read the reflection on the opposite page every day. Then practice tratak on a candle flame for three to five minutes. Do not try to understand or interpret the text. Instead, let yourself absorb the passage on multiple levels and give your intellect a rest. Record your experiences and observations in your spiritual journal. Do this daily for a minimum of seven days.

Practice

Developing a daily meditative practice is essential for anyone with a serious interest in Tantra. Meditative techniques have value to the extent that they inform or enrich every moment of daily life, and, from the Tantric perspective, all of one's experiences in life can be gateways to meditative states. Develop a personal practice that blends easily with your lifestyle, and find a balance between following a rigorous schedule and doing what comes naturally. The highest teaching in Tibetan Buddhist Tantra is that there is nothing at all to do. We are already enlightened beings, but we can only return to the natural or *sahaja* state through diligent practice. "Diligent" may sound effortful and demanding, but consider the Latin root, *diligere*, which means "to esteem" or "to love." In the absence of a sense of value or love for the practice, you probably will not stay with it for long, reap any significant benefit, or intuit even a hint of what sahaja truly means.

The same principle applies in the realm of Tantric sexuality. There are many techniques that can be employed to heighten and prolong arousal and to develop the capacity to experience full-body orgasm. Some teachers advocate non-ejaculatory sex for men, while others emphasize transmuting sexual energy prior to ejaculation. Ultimately, these techniques are nothing but techniques, and they all have one goal—if there can be any goal in Tantra—and that is to lead us back to our natural state, so that we can choose to be fully present in lovemaking and in life. Attaining this state of presence can be very difficult, and it is harder still to sustain it for an extended period. Therefore, in meditation and in sex, techniques provide a much-needed foundation.

Meditative practice will help you participate more consciously in sexual activity, refine your sensory capacity, bolster your awareness of your inner states, and enhance your ability to be present and aware in all aspects of your life. It is up to you to find the form of meditation that suits you and to cultivate the habit. You will discover that your life is enriched as a result.

What Is Meditation?

Meditation is the deliberate performance of a mental or physical act that creates a change in consciousness. According to the *Yoga Sutras* of Patanjali, "Yoga is the cessation of the fluctuations of the mind-stuff."[1] Different scholars and different Tantric and Yogic schools translate and interpret this axiom in a variety of ways, but the important point, for our purposes, is that in a meditative state the consciousness is altered and a certain calm and stillness of mind ensues.

People often think that in order to meditate, you must rise at dawn, sit silent and motionless, counting breaths or mentally repeating a mantra while keeping your mind free of all chatter. Although such practices are indeed forms of meditation, they can be difficult, if not impossible, for many people. Preconceptions about what it means to meditate can lead people to repeated failure when they find they cannot sit still or cannot focus for protracted

---

1 The original Sanskrit is usually transliterated as "Yogaschitta vritti nirodaha." This translation is Dr. Jonn Mumford's.

periods. It may take months, years, or even a lifetime to develop the ability to meditate effectively in this way, and we suspect that some people are simply unsuited for such inactive forms of meditation, although steady practice can be productive for most of us. According to the classical texts, Tantra is appropriate for active people, those with a heroic temperament. With this understanding and with the pragmatism characteristic of Tantra, the practitioners of old devised a wide variety of meditative techniques suitable for those with more active natures.

If you think you cannot meditate, you probably haven't found a suitable form of meditation, or you may actually engage in some form of meditative practice without defining it as such. Whatever the case, it is important to find methods that work for you, something that can only be accomplished through trial and error.

The more you practice, the more skillful you will become. At first, two minutes of seated meditation can seem like an eternity, but with time, patience, and experimention with other forms of meditation, even this technique may become much easier. Tratak is a classical form of meditation in both the Hindu and Buddhist traditions, so you have already been building a foundation.

Experiment with the practices in this book. Find the ones that are enjoyable and fun for you. Approach meditation with a sense of playfulness and flexibility. As you become more skillful, you will discover that you can use different techniques to respond to different life circumstances and external conditions. For example, you may find that guided relaxation practices are most effective during stressful periods, and that Tratak is beneficial when you need to enhance your ability to focus.

There may be times when you feel the urge to stop doing a practice merely because it is difficult, but this feeling alone should not make you give up. If the practice causes significant physical discomfort, is emotionally upsetting, is consistently boring, or if you think it is not fruitful, discontinue it and try something new. Exercise judgment, and focus on the practices that work for you. The guidance of a skillful teacher can be very helpful when these problems arise, but so can your own self-knowledge.

Two Classical Tantric Meditations

At this stage, we'll introduce you to two simple forms of traditional Tantric meditation. One involves rotation of consciousness through the body, which is important in the context of Tantric sexuality because it refines your ability to bring your full attention to different parts of your body. It is the basis for classical Tantric nyasa and also for *Yoga Nidra* and our modification of that technique, *Ananda Nidra*, which you will explore in dala 11, "Bliss." In the other, you will withdraw your consciousness as completely as you can and turn your focus inward. This can be a very effective way of exploring the interplay between the inner and outer worlds. Withdrawal of consciousness is one of the stages of meditation described in the *Yoga Sutras*, and it is an integral part of a number of practices, including *Antar Mouna* (inner silence).

EXERCISE 25. **Rotation of Consciousness**

Do this exercise lying down in *shavasana* (the corpse pose), on your back, legs straight, feet eighteen to twenty-four inches apart. If this is uncomfortable, you can place pillows under your knees to support your back. Relax your ankles, allowing your feet to point outward. Keep your arms six to eight inches away from your body, palms upward or, if this is awkward, rest your hands upright on their edges.

Close your eyes and bring your attention to your left foot. Move your consciousness up your body to the left leg, then the left hip, left side of the torso, your left arm, left side of the neck, left side of the jaw, left ear, left eye, to the the top of your head. Then start down the right side: right eye, right ear, right side of the jaw, right side of the neck, right arm, right side of the torso, right hip, right leg, and right foot.

Repeat this rotation of consciousness as many times as you can. You may drift into a deeply relaxed state, on the border of sleep and wakefulness, even before you complete the first round. It may be helpful to imagine someone with a large feather fan making a sweep around your body. Mentally repeat *left foot, left leg,* and so on as you move your awareness around the body. Try this practice several times this week as you work through dala 8, recording your experiences in your spiritual journal.

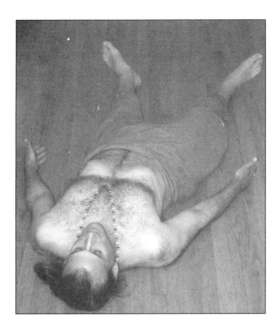

Figure 17. Shavasana,
the corpse pose
(Photograph by Teresa Ambrose)

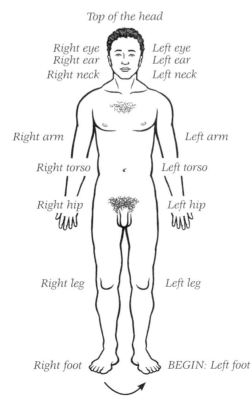

Top of the head

Right eye   *Left eye*
Right ear   *Left ear*
Right neck   *Left neck*

Right arm   *Left arm*

Right torso   *Left torso*

Right hip   *Left hip*

Right leg   *Left leg*

Right foot   *BEGIN: Left foot*

Figure 18. Rotation
of consciousness
through the body
produces a state of
deep relaxation.

EXERCISE 26. **Withdrawal of Consciousness**

The first stage of this technique is similar to the practice of tratak, but you are not fixing your gaze on a particular object, and there is no interplay between the inner and outer worlds. In tratak, you are internalizing the flame. Here, you are focusing outward as completely as you can. In the second stage of this practice, you turn your attention away from the external world and draw it inward.

This calls for a more conventional meditative posture—kneeling or seated erect in a chair with your spine straight. If you use a chair, place a phone book or cushion on the floor to elevate your feet. You will also need a timer. Set it for three minutes. Start with your eyes open, and focus on whatever you see before you. Do your best to bring your full awareness to your sense of sight and to externalize your consciousness as completely as possible. Imagine you are projecting yourself out through your eyes. Looking out a window should make it easier for you to do this. When the timer rings, close your eyes and withdraw your consciousness into the center of your head, again as completely as you can. It can be helpful to imagine that you are a turtle and that you are retreating into your shell. This may take a little practice, but once you get the hang of it, you should have no trouble replicating the experience. Do this practice several times and record what you observe in your spiritual journal.

How Do You Meditate?

Many of your daily activities probably alter your consciousness in some way. Although these activities may seem mundane, we suggest you think of them, at least potentially, as forms of meditation. Consider making coffee or tea in the morning, for example. This daily activity creates a change in consciousness that can prepare you for the day—and the ritual is often more central to this change than the consumption of caffeine.

Physical activity can also alter consciousness, although it is often overlooked because we tend to imagine that stillness is a prerequisite for meditation. While the famous "runner's high" is usually described in terms of neurochemistry, it is an altered state of consciousness that is at least akin to a meditative state. According to John Douillard, the experience of runner's high can precede exhaustion and collapse, or it can be a state of flow, what Douillard calls "The Zone," in which the athlete performs at peak levels for prolonged periods in a way that seems virtually effortless.[2] Thus, physical activity can be a very powerful form of meditation.

Repeated physical action can have the same effect as repeating a mantra. Activities such as knitting and quilting, or simple household chores such as ironing or doing dishes, can create an altered state. The trick is to identify these activities and begin to make use of them in a conscious and intentional way.

EXERCISE 27. **How Do You Change Your Consciousness?**

Make a list of everyday activities that change your consciousness and record them in your spiritual journal.

The Erotic Gaze as Meditation

In his book *The Soul of Sex*, Thomas Moore, a Christian psychotherapist and religious scholar, suggests that the erotic gaze is inherently spiritual, and the sexual arousal it produces can lead to deep meditation. Thus, it is possible to enter a meditative state when looking at pornography, erotica, or erotic performance, even though commercial pornography is usually poorly made and is often designed to exploit both the performers and the consumers. It may well be that the enduring power of pornography lies not only in its capacity to titillate but also in its consciousness-altering properties. From the Tantric perspective, this idea makes sense, provided one approaches the material with reverence and the awareness that the erotic gaze is sacred. This Tantric attitude is manifest in the erotic temple art of India and Nepal and also in *thankas,* Tibetan, Nepalese, and Mongolian religious paintings, usually done in lavish colors on silk, that make use of sexual imagery to inspire contemplation.

---

2 John Douillard, *Body, Mind and Sport: The Mind-Body Guide to Lifelong Health, Fitness and Your Personal Best*, rev. ed. (New York: Three Rivers Press, 2001), 11–20.

Figure 19. This Tibetan *thanka* depicts deities in sexual union. *(Yogambara; Tibet, 17th century; Collection of Rubin Museum of Art, C2001.1.2. Used with permission.)*

It is not only the erotic gaze that is sacred, it is the state of sexual arousal, and the more prolonged the arousal, the more profound the alteration of consciousness. On a physiological level, this is due to the release of various hormones and endorphins that flood the system during extended periods of excitement. A similar alteration of consciousness takes place at the moment of orgasm, when a sense of merger, ego loss, and suspension of time often are manifest.

The ancient Tantrics had the profound insight that sexual activity is probably the easiest and most pleasurable way for people to access meditative states. This is one of the main reasons for the emphasis on prolonged arousal and extended, full-body type orgasms in Tantra. Tantric sexual practices did not evolve for the sake of sexual athleticism, staying power, or for their health benefits. They evolved because prolonging sexual activity and expanding the experience of orgasm are gateways to the divine.

Remember: Meditation is the deliberate performance of a mental or physical act that creates a change in consciousness.

EXERCISE 28. **How Else Do You Change Your Consciousness?**

Using the above definition, list some additional ways in which you achieve changes in your consciousness. Include as many activities as possible. The results may surprise you.

Habitual Behaviors

"Deliberate" is a crucial word in our definition of meditation. Do not confuse reflexive, habitual, and addictive behaviors with meditation. As noted above, certain kinds of habitual behavior can induce an altered state, but these are by definition not conscious. Bringing consciousness to such behaviors is often the most effective means of changing them, either by transforming them into something altogether different or by depriving them of their power. This is not always easy to do, since many habitual behaviors serve to dull awareness, but it can be a very effective approach to changing habits you view as negative.

Take smoking as an example. Trying to "quit" can be self-defeating. Instead, we suggest bringing full awareness to every aspect of the smoking process—the amount of money it costs, the actual sensation of inhaling the smoke (which can be pleasurable), the feeling in your lungs when you wake up in the morning, and so on. This can be a very effective way to break the grip of the addiction. We can't claim this approach will always work, but personal experience suggests that this method can be very useful.

EXERCISE 29. **Changing Your Consciousness—A Closer Look**

As you did with the Pleasure Palette in dala 5, examine the list of ways in which you change your consciousness (exercise 27). Notice whether it has variety or is limited to a few categories. Did your list include:

- physical activities such as athletics?

- rituals such as a morning routine?

- pastimes like sitting in a park or watching the stars?

- particular physical settings such as your home, the beach, or the mountains?

How would you like to expand your list? Record your answers in your spiritual journal.

Visualization

Many forms of meditations involve visualizing, and in advanced Tantric practice, these visualizations can be quite complex. People often think that visualizing is difficult, if not impossible. We will now show you that virtually anyone can do it.

Close your eyes and think of your favorite sexual fantasy, the one you use most frequently to bring yourself to orgasm. In all probability, it has a visual component. It is likely that almost all sighted people employ visualization in sexual fantasy. In our eight years of teaching, we have met only one person who claimed not to. We tend to doubt the claim and suspect it was based on a poor understanding of what it means to visualize, a belief that one must see clear pictures in one's mind. If you create even a vague mental picture or visual impression in the context of a sexual fantasy, or any other context for that matter, you are visualizing. With practice, you may find that your capacity to paint mental pictures increases.

Humans are perhaps unique in the animal kingdom because we are able to have sexual responses to a wide variety of stimuli. While certain predispositions may be hardwired and others may be shaped by early experiences, virtually anything can be eroticized. What few people realize is that erotic tastes can be manipulated and redefined intentionally. Armed with this knowledge, you can choose to expand your capacity for sexual response. It is as simple as deliberately developing new neural pathways.

EXERCISE 30. **Fantasy Expansion**

Now you will use visualization as a meditative tool by employing sexual fantasy as a form of Tantric practice. In other words, you will use visualization and self-stimulation to create an altered state of consciousness—arousal—while simulaneously expanding your sexual response.

Pleasure yourself several times during the coming week, relying on fantasies that you've never used before. You might fantasize about a new location, partners of the gender that is not your preference, or something a little kinky. As you do this practice, observe how you respond.

If this seems too difficult, you may choose to begin with a fantasy that works for you, then, at a heightened state of arousal, either change or expand it. Explore your ability to enrich your sexual life, but you need not go beyond your level of comfort or feel you should suddenly begin fantasizing about extreme forms of sexual behavior.

Fantasy and Reality

Some people find it very difficult to fantasize about a beloved, while others may feel it is wrong to fantasize about anyone but a beloved. We believe that becoming locked into a single type of fantasy can limit your capacity for erotic response and expansion. Your mind is your playground. Feel free to use your imagination as you choose. In the words of Dr. Jonn Mumford, "Tantra is an organized system that rejects nothing as a means to an end," the end being spiritual evolution, with the proviso that "use not abuse is the key."[3]

People frequently ascribe excessive power to their thoughts, but thoughts are just thoughts—the firing of neurons. Unless we invest them with energy and intention, they have no more effect on the external world than dreams.

---

3 Dr. Jonn Mumford (Swami Anandakapila Saraswati), *Ecstasy Through Tantra*, 51.

Sexual fantasies of any kind are neutral in and of themselves. It is what we think about them and the emotional charge we attach to them that makes all the difference. We will examine intention and attention in considerably more depth in dala 13, "Transformation," but for now, simply recognize that your inner world is yours, and that giving free rein to your imagination without shame or fear can be a very liberating experience.

Note that we are *not* advocating acting on any of these fantasies. There is an enormous difference between imagining something and actually doing it. Some may fear that fantasizing will lead to infidelity; however, it is not the fantasy that brings about the act. The underlying issues in the relationship itself are usually the primary cause. There is a big difference between acting out and having a limitless fantasy life. One characteristic of contemporary Japanese culture illuminates this distinction. While Japan is one of the safest countries in the world, violent imagery is more pervasive in popular graphic novels and comic books there than it is in America.

Nevertheless, we strongly discourage you from indulging in fantasies that involve minors, abuse, or criminal activity. Some people with particularly active fantasy lives can picture virtually anything and even play out scenes that incorporate some extreme behaviors. We have no moral judgment about this type of exploration. We know people who engage in it consciously, in a safe and intentional way, but they are extraordinarily clearheaded, thoughtful, and knowledgeable about what they do and where they draw the line. As a general rule, compulsive fantasies about children, nonconsensual and abusive behavior, especially when accompanied by an urge to act, may indicate psychological problems that should be addressed with the help of a mental health professional. If you have compulsive, violent, abusive fantasies, you probably are not suited to the practice of Tantra.

EXERCISE 31. **Broadening the Fantasy Spectrum for People with Partners**

Take some time to discuss your fantasies together. This topic can be emotionally loaded, so be sure to treat each other kindly and respectfully, and maintain a playful attitude. Do not use the discussion of fantasy as a forum for expressing dissatisfaction or to push anyone into an activity that seems uncomfortable.

One way to start the discussion safely is to play Fantasy Tennis. One person takes thirty seconds to describe a fantasy while the other listens, then you reverse roles. These need not be your actual fantasies. Use anything you can dream up. This exercise can make the discussion of fantasy fun, creative, and less challenging. You may come up with some new ideas in the process.

After playing Fantasy Tennis for at least five minutes, each of you now selects a fantasy from the other's repertoire—one that both of you are comfortable borrowing and sharing. Then, over the course of the next week, you pleasure yourself using your partner's fantasy. Polyamorous people may find it particularly interesting to make Fantasy Tennis a doubles match. At the end of the week, take some time to discuss your experiences.

A Message from Devi Veenanand

I have found that my favorite ways to meditate are often kinesthetic in nature. I suspect this is due in part to my training as an opera singer. Despite the fact that the physical act of singing is quite complex—or perhaps because of that fact—I have often experienced heightened states of consciousness during performances. Building on this awareness about myself, I began experimenting with rotating my consciousness through my body while working out at the gym. The results were extraordinary. I enjoy my workouts far more and have had some very interesting experiences in the process. These have included feelings of weightlessness, a sense that my body had increased in density, and both a quickening and a slowing of my perception of time. I have also been able to increase my strength by adding visualization to my lifting routine. I like to meditate and work out regularly, and combining the two has increased my enjoyment of both practices. I might easily have started to think of either or both of these activities as a chore had I treated them as separate tasks.

Hari Om.

Nyasa

Consider the following questions. Record your thoughts in your spiritual journal.

1. Name three of your favorite ways to alter your consciousness.

2. What about them do you enjoy?

3. Was it easier for you to rotate your consciousness through your body or to withdraw it into your head?

4. Did exercise 30, "Fantasy Expansion," enhance your ability to visualize?

5. What is the difference between seeing with the eyes and visualizing?

6. Describe any changes you may have experienced as a result of doing exercise 30 and/or 31.

7. Did you find exercise 30 challenging? Why or why not?

8. What is your understanding of the purpose of exercise 30?

DALA 9

Expansion

According to Tantra, sexual life has a threefold purpose. Some practice it for procreation, others for pleasure, but the tantric yogi practices it for samadhi. He does not have any negative views about it. He does it as part of his sadhana. But, at the same time, he realizes that for spiritual purposes, the experience must be maintained. Ordinarily this experience is lost before one is able to deepen it. By mastering certain techniques, however, this experience can become continuous even throughout daily life.

—Paramahansa Satyananda Saraswati,
Kundalini Tantra

This dala addresses the role of taboo breaking and social transgression in the Tantric tradition. You will engage in a conscious exploration that involves breaking your own taboos in a gentle way. We will discuss the concepts of enlightenment and liberation and what they mean in Tantra. There is a link between breaking taboos and liberation, and this exploration will guide you toward an evolving understanding of these terms and their relevance in your life. You will also learn more about the role of breath patterns during high states of arousal and how working with the breath can be a tool for consciousness expansion in those states.

As you work through dala 9, read the reflection on the opposite page every day. Then practice tratak on a candle flame for three to five minutes. Do not try to understand or interpret the text. Instead, let yourself absorb the passage on multiple levels and give your intellect a rest. Record your experiences and observations in your spiritual journal. Do this daily for a minimum of seven days.

Expansion—Taboo Breaking

Taboo breaking is related to fearlessness. It is an important practice with deep roots in the Tantric tradition. Refusal to be bound by cultural norms was an important element in classical Tantra, and modern Neo-Tantric teachers including Bhagwan Shree Rajneesh (Osho) have also emphasized freeing oneself from social constraints.[1]

---

1 The history of Rajneesh and his movement sheds much light on both the benefits and the perils of striving to free oneself from social constraints and the risk of replacing one form of orthodoxy with another.

In classical *Chakra Pujas* (sexual rituals), the traditional restrictions of caste do not apply, and these rituals generally involve the deliberate violation of a number of social taboos—eating foods that are normally forbidden, particularly meat, drinking alcohol, and/or having a sexual partner selected at random. Engaging in any of these acts would shock most orthodox Hindus, and especially Brahmins. The most extreme and notorious Tantric practices include meditation in cremation grounds and *Shava Sadhana,* which involves protracted nocturnal seated meditation on a corpse. Leaving aside the implications related to facing the fear of death and the supernatural powers usually associated with it, these activities entail the conscious transgression of powerful Indian taboos against uncleanness and impurity.

These practices serve a twofold purpose. On one level they were originally believed to make possible the acquisition of *siddhis* or powers. In this sense they are closely related to the initiatory ordeals of many shamanic traditions, although it is unclear whether Tantra and the shamanism of the Indian subcontinent followed separate evolutionary tracks or whether they are one and the same. On a more esoteric level, siddhis can be understood as metaphorical. It is very hard to know how many people actually believed they would develop the ability to fly, for example, by meditating on a corpse overnight—and many scholars would argue that most eighth-century Indians believed just that. But there is little doubt that such an experience would significantly change a person's psyche. From this perspective, the purpose of the practices is to acquire inner power: in other words, to effect a transformation of consciousness in the practitioner—one triggered in part by shocking the system and in part by overcoming fear.

This taboo breaking behavior was and still is practiced in a strictly controlled ritual context under the guidance of a spiritual teacher. Provided the teacher is competent, this structure serves to protect those who are unprepared for the ordeal and to create a safe container for the participants. Ideally, the teacher or guru keeps the participants focused on the sacredness of the activity, since focus can be lost in the throes of any intense experience, sexual or otherwise, particularly a socially transgressive one.[2]

---

2 Note that we do not intend you to understand the word transgressive in its more Christian sense, which implies sinfulness or acting against the rights or welfare of another person in some way. We use it to refer to the intentional breaking of social and personal taboos.

For all the apparent freedom that exists in modern society, Westerners remain as bound by social convention as people were in ancient India—or modern India, for that matter. Western conventions are different and less governed by rigid social categories and ideas about purity and impurity, but they are strong nonetheless. Sexual roles and what constitutes appropriate sexual behavior are constantly being codified and recodified in the media. Ironically, the codes seem to be growing more rigid rather than less, despite the ever-increasing access to information, including offbeat erotic material.

Personal habits and self-imposed taboos can be equally limiting, whether they are a product of upbringing or of our own preconceptions or ideals. Becoming a truly free person requires you to break through these formulaic restrictions on behavior and beliefs about yourself. If you then choose to return to your normal routine, you have done so freely and knowingly—and perhaps some of your certainty and reliance on habit will have loosened just a little. Similarly, your knowledge of who you are as an individual will be deeper and more authentic, based on lived experience rather than on abstractions.

Pushing past limits, whether self-imposed or cultural, can be a powerful tool for growth, partly because you can shock yourself and thereby open yourself to new possibilities, expansion, and evolution, although it may be difficult to appreciate this in the moment. Needless to say, there are risks involved in this approach to personal growth. You have to prepare yourself for the consequences of the social transgression, both internal and external, and that requires groundedness and considerable self-awareness. Sometimes people push themselves into situations believing they are ready, only to find themselves filled with regret or worse when they discover that they have gone beyond the comfort zone. Going too far is a particular peril in the realm of sexuality, at least for some people, given that sex can be so highly charged emotionally. For others, going to sexual extremes can simply function as a form of escapism. Also bear in mind that you are not working within the strict confines of the Guru-Chela relationship and the ritual structure characteristic of classical Tantra, so the ultimate responsibility lies with you.

For these reasons, while we suggest you challenge yourself, we also encourage you to know your limits. Examine them and yourself thoroughly before you try to expand them. Remember, this is the path of pleasure, and we do not subscribe to the "no pain, no gain" philosophy. Compare the process to a physical stretch. The ideal is to find the point that is just at the edge of discomfort but not beyond it. If you push too far, something will tear, but if you don't push at all, your body will not feel the benefit of the stretch. The same principle applies to the exercises in this dala.

EXERCISE 32. Conscious Transgression of Social or Personal Constraints

Think of something that you forbid yourself to do or that you consider socially unacceptable. Then do it, deliberately and with awareness. For example, if you are basically shy, think of an environment or situation in which you might be reticent, then deliberately be forward and outgoing in that context. If you habitually eat breakfast in the morning, skip it for a couple of days. If you eat meat, try a vegetarian diet for a week or two.

As partners, too, think carefully and identify your habitual ways of engaging sexually. Most people tend to have a pattern, a dance of give and take, that they go through unconsciously. Start noticing the pattern or patterns, and take the time to examine how well they work for you. Discuss the way you habitually interact, then deliberately alter it in a mutually agreed-upon manner for at least three consecutive sexual encounters. It might be as simple as trying a different position, deciding not to ejaculate, or trying something you've never done before.

We are not suggesting you go to extremes in order to violate social norms or personal boundaries. Nor are we suggesting you take undue risks or do anything illegal. Instead, we are enouraging you to push beyond habitual behavior and self-imposed restraints to discover what lies beyond the border, something that may turn out to be very interesting. Be mindful of your safety, and take care not to harm others, but try to stretch yourself. Observe how this feels for you and describe it in your spiritual journal.

Liberation, Enlightenment, Consciousness Expansion

The Hindu and Buddhist traditions emphasize seeking liberation or enlightenment. This usually refers to breaking free from the cycle of death and rebirth, freeing oneself from one's *karma,* the law of cause and effect, and merging with all that is. A number of Sanskrit words describe this, but from the Tantric perspective the key word is *jivanmukti,* or liberation while in this body. In Tantric Buddhist terms, *nirvana,* or liberation, exists within *samsara,* the cycle of death and rebirth. These concepts are worthy of careful consideration.

It is difficult to discuss words such as liberation and enlightenment because they are alien to the Western spiritual worldview, in which salvation is the paradigm. Moreover, they are translations, and there is disagreement as to their exact meanings. Tantric and Yogic scriptures describe the great powers that can be gained through sadhana, and sometimes these powers are seen as evidence of liberation. Some examples of these siddhis are clairvoyance, clairaudience, omniscience, great longevity, and even immortality. Siddhis also include superhuman abilities to control one's own body, the environment, and the actions of others—shape-shifting, levitation, telekinesis, and the capacity to hypnotize others at will. The rewards of sadhana are indeed significant but not necessarily as dramatic as the texts suggest.

People of all cultures seem to have a deep-seated need to believe in stories of miraculous happenings and the extraordinary powers of certain highly evolved individuals. In the West, we need look no further than the Judeo-Christian tradition for examples. Jesus, after all, is said to have raised the dead, walked on water, and produced food for multitudes, and to this day the Catholic Church requires miracles of its saints. The Puritans believed that worldly success was a sign of God's blessing. Some Western traditions relegate miracles and revelations from God to the past. Others contend that they continue to this day.

This emphasis on supernatural powers and "perfection" is also a strand in many Eastern traditions, including Tantra. Tibetan Buddhist lore, for example, is replete with accounts of great yogis and their magical powers. Devotees of Paramahansa Yogananda believe that his body did not decompose after his death. In India, the hagiographies of many spiritual masters describe apparently supernatural accomplishments. In the modern era, some skillful conjurers have been embraced as great spiritual masters, even after their trickery was unmasked.

Miracle stories are very alluring, but they can also function as a trap. Many Western spiritual seekers have been deeply disappointed to discover that their revered Eastern teachers are all too human. This humanness frequently involves sexual scandal. In our view the real problem in many of these scandals has not been sexual activity, it has been hypocrisy—pretending to be celibate and imposing a rigid standard on students that the teacher himself cannot or will not meet. The issue is honesty, and it is appropriate to expect it from a teacher. Perfection is something else again.

One ancient Tantric maxim can be paraphrased as "The guru is God," but then, from the Tantric perspective, so are you. As our beloved guru has told us many times, "The more imperfect the student, the greater the need for a perfect guru." We see miracle stories and "perfect teachers" as valuable metaphors and appreciate their ability to inspire, but please consider that nothing is more miraculous than your very existence.

Another way of thinking about these powers is to recognize that we have all experienced some of them at one time or another, and through practice we can enhance our ability to notice them. This is the concept of flow, and it is akin to Joseph Campbell's idea that you should follow your bliss. When you follow your bliss, when you are in touch with your truest self, it is much easier to recognize extraordinary events when they take place. (More on Campbell and this famous aphorism in dala 11, "Bliss.")

Consider the possibility that many of these powers are experienced subjectively, in meditation or other altered states of consciousness, and that the magical powers described in the classical texts have to do with changing one's inner state. Sometimes little or nothing will happen when you practice, but on some occasions, you may have extraordinary experiences—time stopping or bending in surprising ways, clairvoyance, visions, or sensations of growing large or small, to name a few. With practice you may find that extraordinary things happen more frequently and that your sense of reality undergoes a gradual transformation. From an esoteric perspective, these miracles all occur within our own minds, and we suspect the great Yogis could recreate these inner changes at will, while for most of us such events are more random.

In any case, regardless of what we believe about them, powers or siddhis are not to be confused with spiritual accomplishment. In fact, as Tantra evolved, acquiring such powers came to be seen as a mere by-product of practice, and seeking them as a dangerous trap. If you explore the deeper aspects of Tantra, you may have some uncanny and inexplicable experiences. (We certainly have.) The challenge is to notice these extraordinary happenings without attachment and without seeking to recreate them. Otherwise, the ego will take charge with potentially disastrous results.

We think that liberation implies a reduced need to find fulfillment in external things. To put it another way, a liberated person has an enhanced ability to find pleasure in what is at hand, without having to seek out heightened sensations. We are conditioned to desire new and better experiences and more, bigger, better things. Although this state of craving may be a fundamentally human one (and remember, as we discussed in dala 6, we view desire as a good thing), it is artificially intensified by the forces of consumerism that surround us, forces with which the ancient yogis did not have to contend. We think that liberation might mean a loosening of compulsion, a more relaxed attitude in life.

You may find that Tantric practice generates a certain internal equilibrium that can actually heighten your experience of pleasure because you no longer need the pleasure quite so much. Your definition of pleasure can change, so that you no longer seek it but still experience it all the time. You can enjoy life more fully when pleasurable experience is chosen, not chased after. Pleasure and desire are intimately entwined. Again, recall Daniel Odier's advice: Think of both pleasure and desire as external forces that are drawn to you like bees to a flower.

EXERCISE 33. **What Do Liberation and Enlightenment Mean to You?**

Take a few minutes to write about this topic in your spiritual journal. It may be a new concept for you. What is your understanding of liberation? If you were to have liberation in your life, what might be different, if anything?

If you tend to associate these terms with great saints or high-ranking clergy, try to look beyond that. In most schools of Tantra, it is understood that the common practitioner can experience liberation in this lifetime. If we understand enlightenment as a process, rather than a state, then we never become enlightened. We find moments in which we have the experience of enlightenment.

We have presented our thoughts on liberation and enlightenment for your consideration, but we want you to arrive at your own definition.

. . . .

This dala has been heady so far, and now we'd like to bring things back to the body. We have already discussed the Tantric understanding that the orgasmic state is a state of union with the divine, and by now you should have a fairly good grasp of the concept that Tantric sexuality is a tool for consciousness expansion.

EXERCISE 34. Changing Your Breathing Pattern at Orgasm

Deliberate use of the breath is one way to expand your consciousness, and working with the breath during heightened sexual arousal and orgasm can have a synergistic effect. In dala 6, "Desire," you observed your usual breathing pattern during orgasm. Here you will take that approach a step further and explore the effects of consciously changing your breathing during heightened states of sexual arousal.

There are no right or wrong ways to do this. While Tantric practitioners use a variety of specific breathing techniques to expand consciousness or direct energy during lovemaking, we would like you to undertake a personal exploration and discover what happens in the laboratory of your own body. In dala 13, "Transformation," we will show you how to work with one basic technique for using the breath to direct energy, but in general, such specifics are best taught in person.

During this week, try one or more of the following during a self-pleasuring or lovemaking session.

- Slow your breathing at orgasm.
- Quicken your breathing at orgasm.

- If self-pleasuring, notice your normal pattern of self-stimulation and how it relates to your breath, then change the ratio of movement to breath. If you are working with a partner, you can apply the same principle to intercourse.

- Breathe more deeply than normal.

- Pant as you approach orgasm and as you go over the edge.

- Vocalize as you exhale.

Describe what you experience in your spiritual journal.

A Message from Swami Umeshanand and Devi Veenanand

We have touched on some philosophy in this dala and have discussed complex and difficult topics. We have shared some of our thoughts on these subjects, and we encourage you to formulate your own because there are so many purveyors of enlightenment out there. If you go any further on the Tantric path, or any other spiritual path for that matter, you are sure to encounter them. For this reason, it is very important to have a strong inner sense of what the term enlightenment means to you. Otherwise it is easy to be deceived by false teachers or to compromise yourself in your quest for spiritual development.

Our own experience has been one not of linear progress but of development and change by fits and starts. We may have the most elevated and elevating experiences in our meditations and in our lovemaking, but we still have to take out the garbage and clean the catbox. We may spend days or weeks in bliss. But sudden reversals or disappointments may still leave us depressed and immobilized. We still get sick or get stuck. We still slack off in our sadhana and lose our focus. For us, it is all part of the process, and the challenge in Tantra is to embrace it all and recognize it as, at once, human and divine.

Hari Om.

Nyasa

Consider the following questions. Record your thoughts in your spiritual journal.

1. What do "purity" and "impurity" mean to you?

2. What fears would you personally like to vanquish?

3. Why do you think breaking taboos is important in Tantra?

4. What was your experience of expanding a personal boundary? If it was in a social setting, how did others react to you?

5. How do you define enlightenment and/or liberation? Is there a difference? Do these terms have any relevance to you?

6. How does the statement "Light is insignificant without darkness, and life is meaningless without death" relate to the concept of enlightenment or liberation?[3]

7. Why do you think changing your breathing pattern during sexual arousal can change consciousness?

---

3 Mumford, *Ecstasy*, 102.

DALA 10

Reverence

Actually, Shiva is already present in the world, but people ignorant of this fact do not see Shiva when they look at the world. Kaula (Tantric) sadhana is a way to see Shiva in the world and the world as Shiva. Kaulism 'transforms' the world into Shiva. It is a divine alchemy that turns everything into gold. When someone worships an object or person as if it is God, that object or person becomes God for the worshipper.

—KAMALAKAR S. MISHRA,
KASHMIR SAIVISM: THE CENTRAL PHILOSOPHY OF TANTRISM

In this dala, we return to the subject of reverence and the intrinsic divinity of all beings. You will gain some tools for cultivating reverence in all your interactions and finding the divine in unexpected places. We will also introduce you to the principles of giving and receiving genital massage sessions that align this Neo-Tantric practice with more traditional concepts.

As you work through dala 10, read the reflection on the opposite page every day. Then practice tratak on a candle flame for three to five minutes. Do not try to understand or interpret the text. Instead, let yourself absorb the passage on multiple levels and give your intellect a rest. Record your experiences and observations in your spiritual journal. Do this daily for a minimum of seven days.

The Divine Is Everywhere

All is sacred in the eyes of the Tantric practitioner. All beings are divine incarnations, and the entire universe is similarly a manifestation of the divine. Everyday experience separates us from this awareness because we are unavoidably caught up in the process of evaluation, judgment, and decision-making. As long as we are living in the world it is neither possible nor desirable to abandon the capacity to judge and evaluate; however, the Tantrika strives to live as nonjudgmentally as is possible and prudent, understanding that "good" and "bad," "like" and "dislike," "attraction" and "repulsion" are relative—the by-products of limited human consciousness.

The idea that everything is sacred is often easier to accept in the abstract than it is to embrace in concrete, everyday experience. Everyday life often seems remote from the sacred. We are faced with inconveniences, annoyances and mundane demands that can leave us feeling irritated, angry, or disconnected—out of alignment with ourselves. Most of us who live in the modern world are cut off from nature. The pace of modern life is hundreds of times faster than it has been for almost all of human history. Consider that Lewis and Clark took over a year to reach the Pacific Ocean from Illinois, a journey that can be completed in several hours today. Everything moves more rapidly, and we are bombarded by stimuli—especially visual and auditory stimuli—that are utterly unnatural in volume and intensity. As creatures of the twenty-first century, we are unavoidably both addicted to and overwhelmed by the pace and intensity of modern life and its sensory input. This sensory overload can cause us not only to lose touch with nature but also to lose the ability to appreciate anything very deeply, since there is always another stimulus coming our way.

The best way to alter this pattern is to slow down and cultivate a sense of reverence—not only for those things that are conventionally revered, but for people and things that are often disdained. This approach is, at least in part, what Jesus meant by "love your enemy," and it is by no means an easy thing to accomplish. Indeed, it is a lifelong effort, because we cannot avoid being governed by our tastes, our personal preferences, and our moral, political, and esthetic values. These attitudes cannot simply be discarded, and it would be very unwise to do so, since effective functioning in the normal realm of human experience depends on making such distinctions. Nevertheless, as you develop flexibility, you are likely to find greater enjoyment in your interactions with the world.

EXERCISE 35. **Finding the Divine in Unexpected Places**

Do this practice daily for a week, keeping the same person in mind each day. Choose someone you mildly dislike, for whatever reason, but with whom you interact regularly. Each morning as you start your day, visualize that person for a moment and find some divine spark in him or her, some quality you can honor. Mentally bow to the person, then return to your daily routine. Each time you encounter the person, remind yourself of the visualization and the quality you are honoring. This act of intentional remembering will become a valuable tool for slowing down and appreciating many things in your life. It directly relates to Tantra's sexual aspects. The Tantric approach involves developing and refining your ability to slow down, become aware, and honor yourself and your partner(s), a far easier task than developing the ability to honor someone you dislike.

Observe yourself carefully in this process of honoring someone you dislike and pay close attention to how you feel in each encounter. At the end of the week, take some time to examine yourself. What, if anything, has changed? Write your answers in your spiritual journal.

- Has your attitude about the other person shifted?

- Did you gain any new insights into your own personality and attitudes?

- Did the quality of your interactions with the person seem different?

- Were your interactions with others affected in any way?

- Were there any shifts in your emotional state that you can attribute to the practice?

Your Very Being Is Divine

Believing that divinity exists within yourself may have been an alien concept when you began reading this book. This way of thinking sets Tantra apart from many other systems of belief, although in most mystical traditions it represents one of the deeper secrets. You may need some time to become fully comfortable with this idea. In Tantric ritual, we are both invoking the external divine and evoking the internal divine, which helps transform an intellectual construct into a viscerally experienced reality. Through diligent practice, you will become more familiar and comfortable with the sense of yourself as a divine being. This concept of evocation, too, may seem strange at first, but it is shared by many of the world's religions, at least in their esoteric aspects: "The kingdom of heaven lies within you" is but one expression of this transcultural esoteric truth.

If embracing your innate divinity seems like a big leap, take a moment to focus on the life coursing through your veins right now, on the vital energy coming into your body with every breath. Focus on the miracle of your life. Focus on the sweet mystery of this divine existence. See it in yourself and in others. If you have a beloved, strive to see it in him or her, even in the midst of a difficult conversation or a moment of conflict. Such times can provide the richest opportunities for intensifying your sense of reverence. You won't always succeed. You may feel silly at times, and you may forget more often than you remember, but if you stay with it, this new awareness will gradually become integrated into the core of your being. As this integration happens, you may notice some unexpected benefits, and others will probably notice a subtle shift in you.

All aspects of life can become sources of wonder. Your very existence is miraculous. For a Tantrika every moment is an opportunity to feel awe. It is all a matter of taking the time to observe and training oneself to notice. As we noted in dala 9, "Expansion," one way of understanding siddhis is to consider that the real power lies not in the realm of the supernatural. It lies in the capacity to recognize the miraculous that is happening at all times and all around us. Magic occurs in that moment when you know exactly what your beloved is going to say before he says it, in that moment when you really see the beauty in the landscape, in that moment when everything just seems to fit together. You stop and see it, and you are thunderstruck. These moments occur incessantly, but most of the time, most of us are too caught up in mundane concerns to notice. When we do, we are experiencing siddhis that are more profound and glorious than mere telekinesis. The capacity to notice and appreciate these moments is an ability that you can develop. All it takes is practice.

EXERCISE 36. **Cultivating Awe**

To cultivate your sense of awe, find the wonder in seven everyday occurrences. It is up to you to select them. They can be natural miracles: birdsongs, flowers, stars, the workings of your own body. They can be emotional miracles: your feelings about someone, great acts of kindness or self-sacrifice. They can even be technological miracles: consider how extraordinary it is to flip a switch and light up a room. The miraculous truly has no limits, and the potential to discover the awe-inspiring is infinite. Each day for the next week, choose something that fills you with awe, take a slow deep breath, and imagine you are taking the sense of wonder into your body deeply. Record your observations in your spiritual journal.

Veneration of the Lingam and Yoni

Many religions and societies see the genitals as dirty and shameful, things to be hidden, but in Tantra they are the most sacred of symbols. The *lingam* is a symbolic representation of the penis. It is found in seated in a *yoni* base, which represents the vulva, in temples dedicated to Shiva—the most important male deity in the surviving Tantric traditions.[1] Shiva is often called the god of destruction, but it is more apt to call him the god of transformation or change; the generative organ is one of his main symbols, after all. In many Shiva temples, the lingam resides in the central shrine, where the most sacred pujas, or rituals, take place.[2]

In Tantra, the great union of the lingam and yoni represents the source of all creation. This is the deeper symbolism behind the Yab-Yum images that are so common in Buddhist and Hindu iconography. In monotheistic traditions, the male God creates the universe, but in Hindu Tantra, the male deity is inert, indeed lifeless, in the absence of his energizing feminine counterpart. It is only through the union of male and female, of Shiva and Shakti, of energy and consciousness, or wisdom and compassion (to use the Buddhist terminology) that creation occurs. Thus, the entire process of creation is understood in highly sexualized terms. The moment of sexual bliss that creates life mirrors the continual ecstatic pulsation that is the universe. This univeral pulsation goes on continually within and around us, manifesting in our very breath and heartbeat.

---

1 During the medieval period, when Tantra truly flourished, there were many different sects whose worship focused on different Gods, including Ganesh, Lakshmi, and Vishnu. Modern Tantrics tend to worship Kali or another form of the Divine Mother and Shiva. The Tantric embrace of these fiercer and "destructive" deities is in keeping with the tradition's transgressive elements and its emphasis on transcending fear and taboo.

2 For the symbolism of a South Indian Shiva Lingam Puja, see *The Essence of Tantric Sexuality,* 5–7.

Figure 20. The Shiva Lingam Puja is replete with erotic symbolism.

What Is Puja?

Puja means ritual, worship, or offering. A core practice in virtually all branches of Hinduism, it may be conducted in a temple or any sacred place, around a fire pit, or before an altar in the home.

Hindu ritual, like any good ritual, is designed to awaken the participants on all levels of consciousness, including and perhaps especially those beyond the realm of normal perception. The early stages of the ritual send a message to the unconscious, alerting it to the fact that something special is about to take place. The senses, rather than the intellect, are the primary avenues for this awakening.

In Hindu temples and homes, a puja is usually conducted before an image or statue of a deity, but the ritual can take many forms. In traditional Tantra, group sexual ritual is called a Chakra Puja. Many Neo-Tantric groups incorporate a non-sexual variant of this ritual in their programs. In this modern version, participants form two concentric circles with the outer circle revolving. The pattern allows people to exchange energies and do simple (usually non-sexual) practices or exercises with others, often with all the participants of the opposite gender. This ritual can raise a great deal of energy and lead to profound experiences, often ecstatic for some and occasionally difficult for others.[3]

But puja is not necessarily a group undertaking, and in fact it can be an entirely internal process, with the ritual performed and offerings made through visualization alone. This is generally a very advanced form of practice. Still, even when one has mastered the ability to go through an elaborate ritual entirely in one's head, the external practice of puja remains very powerful.

During Puja All the Senses Are Awakened

- The sense of hearing is awakened with the sound of music, chanting, or a simple ringing of a bell. Hearing is associated with the element ether or space.

- The sense of smell is awakened with perfumes and incense. Many religious traditions the world over use incense as an integral part of ritual.

---

3 We have not identified the origin of this practice. It may be a modification of Sufi dancing, a derivation from Gurdjieff, or one of Osho's innovations.

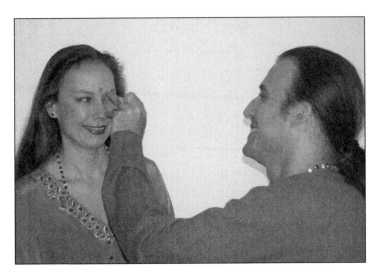

Figure 21. As a puja ends, worshippers receive a *tilak,* a mark in the center of the forehead just above the eyebrows at the "third eye" or ajna chakra. It is often red and made with kum-kum powder, which may symbolize menstrual blood. *(Photograph by Teresa Ambrose)*

In Tantra, smell is associated with the earth element. It is our most powerful and primordial sense. Smell goes directly to the unconscious mind unmediated by other mental processes.[4]

- The sense of sight is awakened with the image of the divine. In conventional Hindu puja, *darshan*, or seeing the image of the deity, is a key aspect of the ritual. Indeed, it is often the climactic moment. Darshan implies not only seeing but also being seen. So in the context of Tantric sexual practices, the act of seeing and being seen by your beloved (or seeing yourself, for that matter) can have great power, if approached with reverence. Sight is associated with the fire element.

- The sense of touch is awakened through receiving a *tilak.* In the closing phase of a puja, the *pujari* (the person conducting the ritual) places a *bindu* or mark on the "third eye" of each participant. The experience

4 See *The Essence of Tantric Sexuality*, chapters 8 and 9, for more on this subject.

of touch is often integral to traditional initiations wherein the energy of the Tantric lineage is transmitted from teacher to student in part by touch. Touch is associated with the air element.

- The sense of taste is engaged at the end of a puja by the consumption of *prasad,* food that has been offered to the deity during the puja, then returned by that deity in an energized state. Taste is associated with the water element.

Each sense corresponds to a chakra and to one of the five elements in the traditional Hindu system, in which earth, water, fire, air, and space are recognized as the building blocks of all that is. Most Tantric ritual involves working with these elements, or *tattwas,* in some way.[5]

Reverence in a Sexual Context

"Tantric massage" has become a popular advertising slogan in the back pages of alternative newspapers. More often than not, this term is a euphemism for genital massage, usually for men. Some Neo-Tantric schools offer training in such techniques, which are often designed to help men learn to control ejaculation and experience multiple and/or full-body orgasms. Today "Tantric massage" for women usually includes stimulation of the G spot and is often aimed at teaching women to ejaculate.

We get numerous requests for "Tantric massage," usually from men who seem to be seeking sexual services and some kind of thrill (even though our website specifies that we do not work "hands on"). At first, such requests irritated and confused us, but we have come to understand that many of these callers are sincerely seeking something more from their sexual experiences, an impulse we both respect and admire. What seems to be missing is an understanding that practicing Tantra requires discipline and personal investment of time and energy. It is not an experience you can purchase or passively receive from someone else. The allure of supercharged "Tantric sex"

---

5 For more on the five elements and the chakra system, see *The Essence of Tantric Sexuality*, chapter 2, and Dr. Jonn Mumford's *Ecstasy Through Tantra* and *A Chakra & Kundalini Workbook.*

is powerful. Sex sells, but often only if it is packaged in a way that makes people feel what they are buying isn't just sex.

The number of ads offering Tantric massage in New York's *Village Voice* has skyrocketed over the last decade, and while we are not personally familiar with what goes on in such sessions, we suspect that many of their purveyors have no training or knowledge and are using the word Tantric as both a euphemism and a marketing tool. We find this troubling, not because we object to prostitution per se.[6] Many of these advertisers may be sincere and committed to the well-being of their clients, but calling something Tantric doesn't necessarily make it so.[7]

In the following exercise, we are reclaiming genital massage as a practice that is—while not strictly traditional—at least in keeping with the spirit of Tantra. While the methods are similar to those taught by many Neo-Tantric groups, the mental approach is radically different. As noted earlier, David Gordon White has observed that authentic Tantra is about "sexualizing ritual" while Neo-Tantra tends to "ritualize sex." We are inclined to agree, but as we see it, worshipping the genitals is a way of simultaneously ritualizing sex and sexualizing ritual. For Westerners who are unschooled in Hindu or other traditional practices, this may be the best way to discover a form of sexual ritual that is deeper and more authentic than merely dressing in caftans and lighting candles and incense.

When making love, people usually engage in a dance between giving and receiving. Set patterns in this dance usually emerge fairly early in a relationship, as partners get a sense of what produces a response. While this is perfectly normal and can be wonderful, there is often much that is left unspoken and assumed, and people frequently end up feeling shortchanged. In addition, most of us are unskilled at fully recognizing our sexual responses and even less skilled at communicating about them.

In Tantra, we seek to explore and expand the boundaries of how much we can give and receive, while we hone our awareness of sensation. Neo-Tantric

6 Sacred prostitution has a long history. We feel there is a place for it in the modern world, and also that prostitution generally should be legal and aboveboard, removed from the netherworld that fosters guilt, shame, risky behavior, and trafficking in women.

7 For a discussion of massage techniques that are in fact Tantra-based, see *The Essence of Tantric Sexuality,* chapter 14.

genital massage can powerfully expand your awareness and your understanding of your sexuality. It can also bring an attitude of worship and service into the sexual realm, and in this sense, it can be a truly Tantric practice, even if it is not a classical one. And for many, this attitude of worship challenges some of the conventional wisdom about how one should approach sexuality.

Worshipping the Genitals

In this dala, the main exercise involves setting aside allotted times to practice genital massage both alone and/or with your partner(s). Before you do the exercise, let's review a few key concepts, technical tips, and practical considerations. If this is something new for you, the experience should be delightful. If you are familiar with Neo-Tantric "giving and receiving" sessions, bringing a more traditional attitude to the practice will probably make the experience a very different one.

Key Concepts

Treat these sessions as opportunities not only to give and receive pleasure but also to learn even more about yourself. Approach each session with a spirit of exploration and experimentation. Feel free to try new things and discover any new sensations that emerge as a result. If you can maintain this attitude, there will be no right or wrong way to give or receive and no possibility of failure. Remaining open and curious will help ensure that you remain focused on the moment and will help create an environment in which a worshipful attitude can flourish.

Points for Receivers

To make the most of this experience, keep the following in mind when you are the receiver: (1) remain passive and receive, (2) be kind, (3) shift your focus, and (4) delay orgasm.

1. Remain passive and receive. If you are receiving the massage, remain passive but receptive and see how deeply you can take in the touch—every stroke, every moment of contact with your skin. Focus on your partner's hands and imagine that the pleasurable current is flowing deeper and deeper into your body. This is your chance to experience being worshipped.

2. *Be kind.* You may choose to guide the giver and indicate what feels good and what does not. This can be tricky, since the role of giver is a very vulnerable one, and you may enjoy being in a position to give direction. Remember that you are receiving, not taking, even though you too are vulnerable. This approach to physical interaction may be new to you, so it may be best to rely on nonverbal communication. Use gestures: a thumbs-up if something feels good, the typical so-so gesture for "not sure about that," raising your palm to say "stop." Try to avoid making negative statements such as:

"Don't do that."

"I don't like what you're doing."

"You never touch me the way I want to be touched."

"Do this . . . Now, do that."

It helps to express appreciation before giving any feedback. Remember to say please when asking for what you want. Your kindness and gratitude can go a long way toward making the giver feel confident about his or her ability to give you pleasure. So say things like:

"That's nice."

"I like what you are doing."

"Your touch feels so good."

"You're doing a great job. I'm not sure I love this sensation—would you try a firmer touch?"

"Thank you."

"That's wonderful."

Remember that anyone who plays the role of giver has truly extended him or herself to take you on this journey.

3. *Shift your focus.* This is also a chance to turn inward and learn about your body's responsiveness. You may wish to close your eyes, yet there may be times when you will want to turn outward and meet the gaze of your beloved. This is not a requirement, however. It can be very interesting to explore the interplay between your inner experience and your connec-

tion with your partner. At the same time, remember that you are receiving. While you can connect with your eyes, try to avoid reaching out to your partner physically or doing anything to give back. Allow yourself to receive and know that this is your time to do just that. Your time to give will come.

4. Delay orgasm. Don't rush to have an orgasm. Delay it instead. Allow yourself to go to the edge and then back off several times. Both men and women can benefit from experimenting with the orgasmic response. Remember that this is a prolonged session. There is no need to hurry. The giver should be monitoring your responses very carefully, but it's up to you to communicate if the stimulation gets too intense. As noted, a simple "stop" gesture may suffice, but if you need to say stop as you approach the point of no return, then do so. The closer you get to the edge, the more you can spread the pleasurable sensations throughout your body, and the more intense your orgasmic response will be.

Points for Givers

Givers should remember these points: (1) revere the genitals, (2) be present, and (3) attend to the quality of your touch.

1. Revere the genitals. When you are giving, focus on the genitals themselves as objects of adoration. Most of us are taught that it is "bad" to objectify, that reducing our beloved to a body part is dehumanizing. After all, most pornography fixates on the genitals and fetishizes them, and people often condemn pornography for that very reason. Nevertheless, we can reclaim the sacredness of this objectification. We are all the products of the human genitalia, and these body parts are worthy of reverence and worship. Make your giving and receiving session a ritual in which you honor the divine power of the genitals as the source of human life and of sexual pleasure.

Herein lies a subtle difference between the way we're asking you to approach the giving and receiving session and what is suggested in most Neo-Tantric versions of the practice. We are asking you to honor the genitals instead of asking you to honor each other as God or Goddess. You can, of course, incorporate the latter attitude, but try to focus your reverence on the body parts themselves. You may also find it valuable to explore both approaches and see how they differ for you.

2. Be present. See how fully you can be present while maintaining an attitude of love and service. Stay in physical contact with the receiver to the best of your ability, and say something in advance if you need to break the connection even for a moment. Keep your focus on the receiver's state. You can gain insight by noticing changes in skin tone, breath patterns, and perspiration. Do your best to gauge the level of the receiver's arousal. It can be helpful to synchronize your breathing as you observe your partner. The secret of becoming a truly great lover lies in cultivating attentiveness and the ability to read your partner. This is a perfect opportunity to refine these skills. The more attentive and loving you are, the more pleasure your partner will experience. And the more you are able to give, the greater your capacity to receive will be when your turn comes.

3. Attend to the quality of your touch. Try to discover as much as you can through your own exploration and experimentation, and remain acutely aware of the quality of touch. Don't worry about specific strokes for the purposes of this exercise. Be playful. Explore different qualities of touch, both when massaging the body and when stimulating the genitals.[8] The possibilities include light tapping, pinching, rolling the skin, long strokes, and deep muscular massage, to name a few. Be sure to use different types of stimulation, and don't limit yourself to your usual way of arousing your partner. The receiver may find that some forms of touch are simply interesting or calming. Such sensations are worth exploring in their own right. Be sure to check in with your partner—either verbally or nonverbally—to see how your touch is being received.

---

8 For specific techniques and strokes, see Barbara Carrellas, *Urban Tantra: Sacred Sex for the Twenty-First Century* (Berkeley, CA: Celestial Arts, 2007), 176–200.

Points for Solo Practice

By practicing alone, you can be both giver and receiver and thereby honor yourself.

1. Be both giver and receiver. Solo practice lets you explore the boundaries of gender and fuse the roles of giver and receiver. Allow yourself to play both roles in your imagination. Devote the session to a detailed and prolonged exploration of your sexual response, making it a lengthy exercise in honoring and worshipping yourself. Be sure to apply the same principles as above. Take your time. Rather than going directly to the genitals, devote an extended period to caressing your body and pleasing your other senses first, just as you would if you were practicing with a partner.

2. Honor yourself. This is an opportunity to honor and make love to yourself, slowly, tenderly, and with a mindset few people employ while masturbating. Cultivate an attitude of reverence. People seldom masturbate with love and reverence for themselves. This is an opportunity not only to explore but to love yourself.

Genital Massage Tips

Before you begin the massage, it's important to know some facts about feminine arousal, masculine arousal, and ejaculation, both female and male.

1. Feminine arousal. Feminine arousal usually proceeds from the outside in—that is, from the extremities to the genitals. Those with a more "feminine" pattern of response will enjoy genital stimulation only after the rest of the body has been engaged and will only enjoy penetration after a high state of arousal is reached. Most Neo-Tantric teachers advise givers to ask permission before entering the yoni. This request for permission can function as an expression of reverence for some. It may seem artificial to others. You are welcome to decide for yourselves.

2. Masculine arousal. Masculine arousal tends to move from the inside out. Many men are quite happy to have their genitals stimulated immediately and have little interest in other forms of sensual touch. It is valuable for men, or those who respond in a more "masculine" way, to explore and cultivate a more "feminine" form of erotic response, since doing so is likely to create many new possibilities for experiencing pleasure. It may take some time to develop these new erotic pathways, but it is well worth the effort.

3. *Ejaculation: Female and Male.* A form of this exercise is taught at many Neo-Tantric weekend workshops, usually as homework/homeplay. Many of these workshops emphasize G spot massage for women with female ejaculation as a goal. Some teachers contend that female ejaculation is every woman's birthright or suggest that women store sexual trauma in the G spot and must release it in order to own their sexual power. We don't endorse either idea. It is certainly true that digital stimulation is the most effective way to stimulate the G spot, and that many women learn to ejaculate in receiving sessions, but it is better to allow the session to proceed organically. A purely external massage can be just as satisfying as an internal one.[9]

Conversely, many Taoist and Neo-Tantric teachers discourage male ejaculation during these sessions. We suggest that male receivers conclude with ejaculation—after going to the edge and pulling back several times. Playing on the edge is a wonderful way to spread sexual energy throughout the body and is the key to experiencing full-body orgasms, but once you have circulated the energy, there's no reason not to ejaculate. In many classical Tantric systems, ejaculation is an offering, and as such it can be the receiver's thanks for what he has received.

Practical Considerations

These tips may be helpful from a practical standpoint, so consider them in advance: (1) prepare before you begin, (2) do some form of ritual, (3) be comfortable, (4) have supplies on hand, and (5) conclude the massage with reverence.

---

9 For specific instructions on how to massage the G spot, see *Urban Tantra*, 183–185. For more on the G spot, see Ladas, Whipple, and Perry, *The G Spot*, the seminal text on the subject.

1. Prepare before you begin. Setting aside an allotted time in which the roles of giver and receiver are fixed creates a container for a conscious and playful exploration of sexual response. If you are planning a partner session, communicate and decide in advance about the structure and what aspects of ritual you would like to incorporate.

Prepare by cleansing yourself. Bathing before (or during) ritual activity is important in many spiritual traditions. In addition to bathing, brush your teeth, wash your hands and clip your nails—a very important consideration when working with delicate tissues of the body.

2. Do some form of ritual. Ritual is very important. It will help remind you that you are engaging in a sacred activity, so try to incorporate each of the elements we described in our discussion of puja into the practice, stimulating all the senses. We have no wish to indoctrinate you into any particular religion. We are not teaching you to conduct a traditional Hindu or Tantric puja, but bringing ritual elements into the practice in a way that is comfortable for you and creating an atmosphere of sacredness and worship can make the experience more meaningful. This may be as simple as lighting a candle, burning incense, sharing some special food, or taking turns expressing your love and appreciation, but the more elements you can incorporate, and the more senses you can engage, the better.

Use your imagination in creating the ritual. You can then include it in your lovemaking whenever you so desire. The "Tantric Weekend" and "Rite of the Naked Fire" chapters in *Ecstasy Through Tantra* or "The Tantric Mass and the Secret of Amrita," chapter 15 in *The Essence of Tantric Sexuality*, can serve as blueprints for more complex, formal ritual activity, if that is something you wish to explore more deeply.

3. Be comfortable. Make sure that all participants are as comfortable as possible at all times. You should be focused on the experience. Be sure the room is warm and softly lit. Muscle cramps and spasms are a distraction and can interfere with the ability of both givers and receivers to be present and enjoy the experience, so we recommend using a massage table if possible—it's an investment that pays for itself in pleasure very quickly. If you are working on a bed, use pillows to align the spine and allow for free breathing, and do whatever else is necessary to maximize comfort.

4. *Have supplies on hand.* Keep massage oil, lubricant, and a towel within easy reach. (For internal massage, use a high-quality non-oil-based lubricant; Liquid Silk is a personal favorite.) You can almost never use too much lubricant, even when working externally, whether the receiver is male or female. At the same time, it can be very interesting to stimulate the genitals gently before applying the lube. A dish or spray bottle filled with warm water is handy for moistening the lube if needed.

5. *Conclude the massage with reverence.* Conclude the session by bowing to each other (or yourself), taking a warm bath, enjoying a meal, or doing whatever else feels right to extend the afterglow. Remember that sexual arousal changes consciousness and that people are very open and vulnerable during and immediately after lovemaking, so save any discussion of the experience for another time. Use this time to bask in the pleasure you've experienced. You can talk about it later.

EXERCISE 37. **Worshipping the Genitals in Practice**

Set aside a minimum of an hour and a half for this practice, including preparation. Whether you are solo or partnered, be sure to do at least one solo session. If you are working with partner(s), have multiple sessions over several days, so that each of you has the opportunity to give and receive at least once. Review the above guidelines on attitudes and practical preparation.

This is an opportunity for you to worship the lingam or yoni of your beloved. If you are practicing alone, worship your own genitalia and your own sexuality, applying the same principles to an extended self-pleasuring session. It may be difficult to have such a prolonged masturbatory session, and if so, you may take breaks and then resume. The experience of going in and out of arousal for a protracted period can be very interesting, and you may be surprised by the power of the orgasm you experience at the end of the session. This can be a particularly valuable experience for multi-orgasmic women.

Begin with a full-body massage, working slowly toward the genitals first, then exploring them with reverence. Be sure to do this as a solo practitioner as well.

Remember that this is a prolonged session, and there's no need to hurry. With time, you'll discover a rhythm that works for you. Also remember that this isn't foreplay. The experience is an entity unto itself, so avoid having intercourse immediately afterward and allow it to sink in.

A Message from Devi Veenanand

In some Neo-Tantric workshops, the practice of giving and receiving is introduced with warnings about how the sessions are likely to re-evoke trauma and pain, particularly in women. It is certainly true that powerful emotions can be awakened by this exercise (including positive ones, such as love for one's partner), but we believe that these caveats run the risk of creating a self-fulfilling prophecy. If such negative feelings do emerge, we recommend shifting attention toward whatever pleasure can be found in the experience or observing the emotional response without evaluating it. If you can see emotions as just another form of energy and allow that energy to move, the emotions may resolve themselves. If neither of these approaches is possible, it is probably best to stop and try again at another time.

Another emotional challenge can arise in these sessions, and we have some personal familiarity with it. We began exploring giving and receiving sessions early in our relationship, and our first attempt was rather rocky. Swami Umeshanand had recently been through a teacher's training that focused heavily on this technique, and he offered me a session. I slightly misunderstood the process and treated it as more of a "taking" session than a receiving session. I saw it as an opportunity to explore my own responses but did not appreciate his vulnerability as the giver. As a result, I gave a great deal of direction without saying please very often and without expressing much appreciation. By the end of the session, Swami Umeshanand was very unhappy and was left feeling both incompetent and exhausted. We agree that some of these feelings may have been the result of a blow to an inflated ego. He had just taken a teacher training, after all! But we also recognize that anyone would have been very upset under the circumstances.

It took a long conversation to sort out what had gone wrong, and we did not encounter that pitfall again. We share this experience with you to point out the importance of kind communication and expressing appreciation, and also to show just how vulnerable a giver can be. If you approach this exploration with genuine reverence—and with more understanding than we had—you should be able to avoid our mistake and have wonderful experiences as giver or receiver. If you are working solo and are both giver and receiver, celebrate and revere yourself. If you do, it will enrich your own life and any sexual interactions you have with others.

Hari Om.

Nyasa

Consider the following questions. Record your thoughts in your spiritual journal.

1. Describe your experience in exercise 35, "Finding the Divine in Unexpected Places."

2. Why do you think that exercise is included in this book?

3. List three things that filled you with awe this week.

4. What seven everyday things did you choose for exercise 36? What was your experience in doing the practice? Did your perception of the things you chose change for you over the week?

5. Is ritual important to you? If so, why? If not, why not?

6. What were the details of your experience in exercise 37? Document the ritual you created and identify the high points.

7. Has your understanding of your sexuality changed as a result of doing the exercises up to this point?

DALA 11

Bliss

From bliss proceeds the cosmos, it is sustained in bliss and dissolved in bliss.

—AJIT MOOKERJEE, *TANTRA ASANA*

In this dala, we will examine happiness, ecstasy, and bliss from a Tantric point of view and share insights about the deeper meanings of these words. You will revisit your Pleasure Palette and see what changes have taken place. You will also learn a more advanced form of Tantric meditation, one adapted from a traditional technique, and consider life as an ongoing process of expansion and contraction.

As you work through dala 11, read the reflection on the opposite page every day. Then practice tratak on a candle flame for three to five minutes. Do not try to understand or interpret the text. Instead, let yourself absorb the passage on multiple levels and give your intellect a rest. Record your experiences and observations in your spiritual journal. Do this daily for a minimum of seven days.

Happiness, Pleasure, Bliss, and Ecstasy

References to bliss and ecstasy are abundant in Western writings about Tantra, and the words have become a way of marketing the tradition. They have enormous appeal to people seeking extraordinary experiences and transformation of consciousness. The pursuit of happiness is a preoccupation of Western society in general and American society in particular. After all, this pursuit is a fundamental human right according to the document that marked the founding of the United States, so it is only natural that the emphasis on bliss and ecstasy in many Tantric texts would fascinate Western seekers. Let us now examine the meaning of all these words—happiness, pleasure, ecstasy, and bliss—with some specificity.

Sanskrit Terminology

Because Tantra emerged in a vastly different culture and translation is an imprecise art, it is best to begin with the Sanskrit terminology from which these words emanate. According to Monier-Williams's classic *Sanskrit-English Dictionary,* the word *ananda* means "happiness, joy, enjoyment, sensual pleasure." It is also frequently translated as "bliss."[1] All these words have similar meanings, but there are matters of degree involved. They also have deeper, more esoteric meanings that have little to do with the way they are commonly understood. First, note that the dictionary definition of ananda directly connects it to the physical realm. This highlights the Tantric view that physical pleasure and enjoyment are not necessarily distinct from spiritual pleasure and, indeed, that sensual pleasure can lead us to mystical states.

The focus on seeking happiness and bliss is also evident in Sir John Woodroffe's early twentieth-century translations of and commentaries on Tantric scriptures. "There is but one thing which all seek—happiness—though it be of differing kinds and sought in different ways. All forms, whether sensual, intellectual, or spiritual are from the Brahman, who is Itself the source and essence of all Bliss, and Bliss itself (rasovai sah)."[2] While Woodroffe's definition of seeking is quite open-ended, it still seems to reflect the modernity of his approach, since happiness or bliss is implicitly elsewhere, notwithstanding the more Tantric implication that "bliss itself" is everywhere.

---

1 See Sir Monier Monier-Williams, *A Sanskrit-English Dictionary: Etymologically and Philologically Arranged with Special Reference to Cognate Indo-European Languages* (Oxford: Oxford University Press, 1899, repr. 1979), 139. Although Monier-Williams did not include bliss among the words he used to define ananda, that usage has a long history. Avalon, for example, translated Shankaracharya's classic *Anandalahari* under the title *The Wave of Bliss.*

2 Sir John Woodroffe, *Introduction to Tantra Sastra* (Madras: Ganesh and Company, 1952), 150, originally published as the Introduction to Arthur Avalon (trans.), *The Great Liberation (Mahanirvanatantram)* (London: Luzac, 1915), one of Avalon/Woodroffe's earliest works. The translation of "*rasovai sah*" as "bliss itself" is less familiar than *ananda,* the word most commonly linked to bliss and ecstasy in the Western mind.

Ananda Nidra

We have adapted Ananda Nidra from a practice called Yoga Nidra, which was first introduced in the West by Paramahansa Satyananda Saraswati in the 1960s. It has become increasingly popular over the years, and many schools of Yoga teach it in some form. We were initiated in and authorized to teach Yoga Nidra by Dr. Jonn Mumford (Swami Anandakapila Saraswati) who learned it from Paramahansa Satyananda himself. Unlike conventional Yoga Nidra, which can involve a variety of sensations and visualizations, we designed Ananda Nidra to focus your attention on pleasure (including sexual pleasure) to help increase your capacity to experience it in everyday life.[3] As a first step, both Ananda Nidra and Yoga Nidra induce relaxation by rotating the consciousness through the body.

We introduced you to a preliminary form of this practice in dala 8, "Meditation." This form involves a more detailed rotation of consciousness. If you fall asleep during this process, do not be concerned. The contents of the meditation will reach your unconscious. One of the aims of Yoga Nidra (and Ananda Nidra) is to explore the border between sleep and wakefulness.

EXERCISE 38. **Practicing Ananda Nidra**

You can find the script for Ananda Nidra in the appendix. Read it aloud and record it, speaking slowly, soothingly, and with an even tempo, pausing where indicated. Then practice Ananda Nidra by listening to the recording several times over the course of a week, daily, if possible, and note your experiences in your spiritual journal immediately afterward. If you are doing these exercises as partners, you may find it valuable to make separate recordings and allow your partner's voice to take you on the journey. This can be a wonderful experience that deepens your bond in a very subtle way.

---

3 For more on Yoga Nidra, see Mumford, *A Chakra & Kundalini Workbook,* 173–186, and Paramahansa Satyananda Saraswati, *Yoga Nidra* (Monghyr, Bihar, India: Bihar School of Yoga, 1976).

Happiness

The idea that happiness is something to pursue is a modern social construct, and this pursuit is a key component in the machinery of contemporary consumerism. In his important book, *Happiness: A History*, Darrin H. McMahon traces the ways happiness has been perceived in Western society from the time of Socrates to the present. According to McMahon, contemporary beliefs about happiness only began to take shape in the eighteenth century. Over the course of the last two hundred years, early modern ideas about happiness have evolved (or perhaps degenerated) into a kind of empty hedonism that is accompanied by endless disappointment:

> . . . we have steadily added another [burden] since the age of Enlightenment: the unhappiness of not being happy. Collectively, we possess more than ever before, and still we long, expecting to be happy, and are saddened when we are not. And though in some respects this suffering is the ultimate luxury—the indulgence of those whose most pressing needs have been satisfied—it is for that very reason, widespread and acute in the affluent societies of the West. It may be comforting to some to believe that the anxious pursuit of happiness is a peculiarly American affliction, and in some ways, no doubt, this is true.[4]

In modern society, people are socialized to believe that happiness is something "out there" to attain, instead of something inside to discover or something nurtured by living one's life in accordance with the dictates of conscience or duty. These latter beliefs are more characteristic of archaic and non-Western worldviews. Modern, individualistic ideas about happiness are not necessarily wrong, but they reflect a relatively recent evolution in human thought and are the expression of a specific set of social values. In its more extreme manifestations, this externalized understanding of happiness fosters a state of disaffection and restlessness.

As demands on our time increase, our need for instant gratification in this pursuit of happiness intensifies, making our goal even less attainable. We are barraged by messages that encourage us to discover and live our potential and thereby become happy and fulfilled. We are told this can be accom-

---

4 Darrin M. McMahon, *Happiness: A History* (New York: Atlantic Monthly Press, 2006), 473.

plished in ten easy steps or over a weekend. Of course, happiness is seldom attained so easily or so quickly, and as disappointment sets in, another instant cure is there for the purchasing. This "anxious pursuit of happiness" can easily degenerate into a frenetic, obsessive focus on bettering oneself, having more experiences or acquiring more things.[5] Thomas Jefferson undoubtedly had something very different in mind, but happiness, as it is pursued in the twenty-first century, tends to recede, even as the pursuit becomes ever more relentless.

There is a way to discover a deeper and more stable form of happiness, simply by framing the subject in different terms. This dala should help you with the reframing and provide you with some additional tools to embrace this different, more satisfying happiness.

Pleasure

Pleasure is related to happiness, but the word pertains not to a state but to a more immediate experience or sensation. Indeed, the contemporary understanding of happiness conflates it with pleasure. This confusion can be a source of dissatisfaction or worse, since pleasure is ephemeral by its very nature. If we expect to obtain an enduring state of happiness through a never-ending series of pleasurable experiences, the quest is doomed from the start. This is not to condemn pleasure-seeking behavior. Pleasurable experiences, when approached with consciousness, can be a valuable, indeed an integral, part of the spiritual journey. Once it becomes clear that pleasure is not the same as happiness, the anxious or desperate quality of the quest is likely to dissipate.

In Tantra, all pleasures are valuable in their own right, and we recognize them as tools. We seek to broaden, expand, and refine our capacity for pleasure so that we can truly savor it while simultaneously observing how it affects our consciousness. This reduces the need to up the ante in order to achieve the same degree of pleasure or to focus so heavily on external stimuli. Instead

5 McMahon also compares contemporary Western society with the one depicted by Aldous Huxley in *Brave New World* in its shallow fixation on youth, pleasure, and entertainment. For many, it may no longer even be a matter of having experiences. Kurt Cobain's famous line "Here we are now. Entertain us" seems chillingly accurate today.

it helps create the capacity to find pleasure in even the most mundane experiences and also in one's own inner world. It is said that Tantric practitioners can both renounce and enjoy the world, and this view sets Tantra apart from most other spiritual traditions. One key to making this abstract statement a reality is to take a radically different approach to pleasure and discover that it is everywhere for us to use.

EXERCISE 39. **Pleasure Palette Expanded**

Refer back to your notes on "Your Pleasure Palette" in dala 5, "Pleasure." Can you add any new items that fall into the existing categories? Have you thought of any additional categories? Has your Pleasure Palette expanded or changed in the past few weeks? If so, how? Record your observations in your spiritual journal.

Orgasm and the Pleasure Ceiling

For all of our society's emphasis on pleasure, there is an astounding degree of guilt and negativity associated with its pursuit. As noted earlier, America is, in many ways, an anti-hedonic culture, McMahon's argument notwithstanding. Though we modern Westerners are incessantly encouraged to pursue pleasure and instant gratification, we are also assaulted by contradictory messages that treat pleasure as suspect and seeking it as immoral. This harsh, moralistic attitude is perhaps most evident in some of the homophobic and sex-negative rhetoric of the Christian Right, which views non-procreative sex (sometimes even within marriage) as evil and socially corrosive. No one who grows up in American society is immune from internalizing these conflicting messages, and while other Western cultures are somewhat more flexible, a similar ambivalence exists throughout much of the modern world. We have certainly noticed it in our travels to other countries.

This ambivalence manifests itself, perhaps most viscerally, in the context of sexual activity. In our own work, we have observed that many men and women, even those who are open enough to explore fringe and alternative aspects of sexuality, are in some measure disconnected from their own capacity for pleasure. An unconscious inhibiting factor restrains many seemingly liberated people from engaging with true abandon. In many cases, and particularly among men, orgasm can function as a way to curtail or interrupt the pleasurable experience by cutting off that surge before it becomes too intense. While this may not be clinically provable, it is our impression based on observation, and we suspect that cultural influences are the primary cause. This is not to say these individuals are incapable of feeling pleasure, only that they are unable to tolerate it beyond a certain point.

EXERCISE 40. **Deepening Pleasure**

The next time you notice a pleasurable physical sensation, bring your entire awareness to that place in your body where you feel it most acutely. Next, slowly inhale and imagine that you are actually sucking that sensation deeply into your body. With the next breath take it in even more deeply. Continue to inhale the pleasure for at least three or four more breaths, and see how deeply you can allow it to penetrate your being.

Ecstasy

Perhaps no other word is more closely connected with Tantra in the popular imagination. Our own teacher titled his book on sexual Tantra *Ecstasy Through Tantra*. Margo Anand has created a virtual industry based on the word with her books *The Art of Sexual Ecstasy*, *The Art of Everyday Ecstasy*, and *The New Art of Sexual Ecstasy*. One of the most popular videos on Tantra is *Ancient Secrets of Sexual Ecstasy*. Evidently, ecstasy sells, and there is no denying that Tantric and Neo-Tantric practices can lead to ecstatic states. We have experienced these states outselves, but we are ambivalent about the word and its popularization.

When we teach, we seldom talk about ecstasy. If we overemphasized it, we would run the risk of engendering false expectations. Similarly, suggesting that ecstasy is an objective of Tantric practice is not false, but it is lacking in context. Thus, we generally prefer to quote Paramahansa Satyananda Saraswati, who once said people should do practices "because something interesting might happen."[6] Although Paramahansaji was talking about Kriya Yoga, the same principle should apply to Tantric sexual practice or virtually any form of spiritual work. Trying to attain ecstasy is likely to lead to disappointment. Approaching every experience with curiosity and the recognition that it may lead to something interesting leaves us open to the ecstatic potential, without demanding that it be fulfilled. It is in this context that ecstasy may take us by surprise. Our own experience has borne this out.

So what is ecstasy? It is a state of "rapturous delight" and is sometimes considered synonymous with bliss; however, unlike bliss, ecstasy often has a sudden, unexpected quality associated with it, as the second definition makes clear—"an overpowering emotion or exaltation; a state of sudden, intense feeling."[7] Thus, ecstasy often manifests as a sudden sense of elation, a "high" the likes of which has never been felt before. By their very nature, ecstatic feelings are often fleeting, although they may briefly free a person from the emotional confines of mundane life, as implied by the original meaning of ecstasy, "to be driven out of one's senses."[8] At their best, ecstatic experiences can produce lasting changes—expansion into new psychic territory.

Frequently, when expansion takes place too rapidly, contraction will follow. This may be temporary, but it can still take a while to feel that you have regained your equilibrium. For this reason, we generally think it best to explore and expand gradually, with the goal of discovering subtleties, rather than pursuing ecstatic and transformational breakthroughs. If such experiences happen, they can be a blessing, since ecstatic states often open a door to something different and new. For example, when a person suffering from depression has an ecstatic experience, that person can sometimes discover a new range of emotional possibilities. In the best cases, having access to that emotional range creates the potential for significant change, even when the ecstasy is followed by a period of contraction.

6 Swami Anandakapila told us this story. It succinctly describes the Tantric approach to life.

7 *Random House Dictionary*, 619.

8 *American Heritage Dictionary of the English Language*, William Morris, ed. (Boston: Houghton Mifflin, 1976), 413. The word's original meaning implied being driven out of one's wits or "beside oneself." Ernest Weekley, *An Etymological Dictionary of Modern English*, vol. 1 (New York: Dover Publications, 1967), 493.

We have another caveat here, again based on our own observations. Sometimes various forms of mental illness, particularly manic states, can mimic ecstatic ones, and this mimicry can be perilous for people who are mentally unstable. In such cases, chasing the rapturous can have serious consequences.

Episodes of excitation can be valuable, provided they are not followed by a crash in mood. Such elevated states can result in astounding creativity and productivity. Sometimes it is difficult to distinguish among ecstasy, excitation, and the manifestations of mental illness. We would suggest that the difference lies in what happens afterwards. Manic states often occur cyclically, and in general, episodes of mental illness do not lead to greater groundedness and contentment. Truly ecstatic states tend to lack the feverish quality of mania and generally lead to greater integration. They can produce a sense of new possibilities in life, without an accompanying urge to recreate the ecstasy. Peak experiences are only valuable over the long term if they expand one's awareness of what is possible in everyday life.

Bliss

Of all these words, bliss is perhaps the most challenging to understand from the Tantric perspective. People often think of bliss and ecstasy as synonymous or understand bliss either in the context of a cliché—"wedded bliss"—or as a kind of stupor, drug-induced or otherwise. "Blissed-out" is a derogatory term that implies disconnection from reality, a kind of ongoing ecstasy, devoid of intelligent thought or discernment. None of these ways of thinking about bliss approximates what we understand as the Tantric definition.

We have already discussed the dictionary definition of the Sanskrit term ananda, and in examining this term we are moving into a more esoteric realm. We do not deny the validity of the more familiar definitions of bliss that treat it as a near-synonym for ecstasy. But true bliss is far subtler. In some ways, it is more akin to the clichéd phrase "wedded bliss" than to any altered or exalted state. Bliss is right here, right now, quietly waiting for you to notice it and embrace it. There is not much to do except observe.

The phrase "follow your bliss," coined by Joseph Campbell, has become another popular aphorism, unfortunately stripped of its meaning. Many contemporary Westerners trained in the pursuit of happiness focus on "following" and thereby misunderstand Campbell. His meaning was much closer to the Tantric view than it might seem at first glance. Campbell said:

> My general formula for my students is . . . Follow your bliss. Find where it is, and don't be afraid to follow it. Now, I came to this idea of bliss because in Sanskrit, which is the great spiritual language of the world, there are three terms that represent the brink, the jumping-off place to the ocean of transcendence: sat-chit-ananda. The word 'Sat' means being. 'Chit' means consciousness. 'Ananda' means bliss or rapture. I thought, 'I don't know whether my consciousness is proper consciousness or not; I don't know whether what I know of my being is my proper being or not; but I do know where my rapture is. So let me hang on to rapture, and that will bring me both my consciousness and my being.' I think it worked.[9]

While Campbell used the word "rapture," we think that what he meant by bliss is more akin to "flow," those situations or activities in which things just come together and work. This interpretation is, in many ways, closer to the general Hindu concept of *swadharma,* one's own path or way. When you act in accordance with your true nature, which you can discover through both self-exploration and trial and error, things often flow naturally and fall into place in ways that increase your sense of equilibrium and invest your life with the primary quality of effortlessness. Not everything will always be easy; you will not be immune to illness, disappointment, and the vicissitudes of human existence, but the overall course of your life will be relatively smoother. This feeling of flow is true Tantric bliss, and when seen from this perspective, heightened emotional states, however wonderful, are just states of mind that we experience from time to time.

So, while it is true that ananda is often translated as bliss, the Tantric state of ananda is not a heightened state; rather, it is a stable one. Contentment, which is a lesser-known definition of the English word bliss, is closer to what we are describing. Contentment often carries with it an undertone of resignation or complacency, but not from the Tantric perspective. In Tantra, the examination of the inner world is dynamic, a far cry from a passive acceptance of the status quo. Contentment implies that you are living in harmony with your true nature, that you approach life with equanimity,

9 Joseph Campbell with Bill Moyers, *The Power of Myth* (New York: Doubleday, 1988), 120, 149.

and that your inner state is stable. This stability is one of the key indicators of whether you are living your *dharma*.

Of course, life can be very difficult. The sign of true stability and equanimity is not that you are unaffected by events or the vicissitudes of mood, but that you rapidly return to the stable state in the aftermath of a disruption. It is one thing to have truly transcended your emotions and to be perfectly magnanimous. It is quite another to suppress your feelings because you want to be a "good" person and get beyond your emotions and ego, creating a false serenity as a guise to prove how holy or evolved you are.

In the stable state of bliss, your awareness of grosser emotions—such as joy and happiness, disappointment and anger—does not overwhelm or uproot you, and you are simply connected with the vibration and flow of the universe. True bliss settles in on you as a blessing, or it may emerge as the fruit of your spiritual practice. It is not something that can be aggressively pursued or artificially induced. This is the deeper meaning of ananda.

EXERCISE 41. **Expansion/Contraction**

Your life is filled with expansion and contraction, ebb and flow. The more fully you recognize this fact, the easier it is to embrace and accept the conditions of life. While you cannot pursue true bliss, you can prepare yourself for it to happen. It all begins with the breath.

For this exercise, you will need a watch or clock with a second hand.

Step 1. Sit in a comfortable posture with your spine straight. Take in a deep breath, filling your lungs as completely as you can. Lower your chin toward your chest, but do not strain your neck. Glance at the time, then hold your breath for as long as you can, taking a small sniff of air shortly before you exhale, noting the time as you do. Throughout, observe how your body feels, particularly your throat and ribcage. Note your experience and time in your spiritual journal. Relax a moment.

Step 2. Inhale again, filling about two-thirds of your lungs. Repeat the other steps described above, and again, hold your breath for as long as you can.

Notice how your body feels and observe any specific physical sensations. Record what you experienced, and also note how long you held this breath.

- What were your observations?

- What specific physical responses did you have to each way of breathing?

- What do you think the implications of this exercise are?

- How do you think this exercise relates to the philosophical issues discussed in this dala?

A Message from Swami Umeshanand and Devi Veenanand

While we were promoting our book *The Essence of Tantric Sexuality,* we attended a sex industry trade show in New York City. Unlike many trade shows, this one was open to the general public and was also a commercial venture. Several female adult film stars were in attendance, and the event included signings and photo opportunities that were clearly the main attraction, with waits of what looked to be a half an hour for photographs with the biggest stars. The excitement was palpable among the almost exclusively male fans waiting to be photographed with these stars, most of whom were surgically enhanced and what Aldous Huxley would have called "pneumatic." Fully half the crowd seemed to be observing the event through video or cell phone cameras. In this context, a voyeuristic desire to be entertained seemed to have replaced any interest in genuine human interaction, and the emotional energy around this activity struck us as bizarre and disconcerting.

We do not have any moral objections to pornography and indeed have friends in the business. We may have misunderstood what was taking place, but it was disturbing. This tendency to retreat from reality seems to be a product of contemporary culture, and it is not limited to the world of adult entertainment. It may even be threatening our human ability to interact. In Tantra, the inner world is important, but so is the outer world. Your every interaction with another person is an opportunity for bliss. This is engagement, not entertainment, and it is powerful medicine in our atomized, technological world.

Hari Om.

Nyasa

Consider the following questions. Record your thoughts in your spiritual journal.

1. Describe a recent experience that resulted in a sustained feeling of bliss.

2. How long did this feeling last?

3. What was your experience in practicing Ananda Nidra?

4. How do you define happiness, pleasure, ecstasy, and bliss?

5. In what ways do you "follow your bliss"?

6. What does the pursuit of happiness mean to you?

7. When was the last time you experienced contentment, a state of peaceful satisfaction?

8. Can you identify and describe what brought on this feeling?

DALA 12

Imagination

Visualize yourself as Shakti (consort of Lord Shiva),
and with all Her bewitching charm, you too woo
and play with the Supreme (Shiva). When you are in
complete bliss, then only will you be able to unite with
the Supreme and realize "I am one (Brahman) and not
two." This leads to Samadhi.

—GHERANDA SAMHITA

In this dala, we will discuss the importance of imagination in life and its role in Tantra. You will consider the Tantric perspective on gender, a topic we will examine in greater depth in dala 14, "Union." The exercises in this dala are designed to help you examine and expand your imaginative capacities, awaken a new sense of wonder, and open you to new possibilities for interacting reverently with others.

As you work through dala 12, read the reflection on the opposite page every day. Then practice tratak on a candle flame for three to five minutes. Do not try to understand or interpret the text. Instead, let yourself absorb the passage on multiple levels and give your intellect a rest. Record your experiences and observations in your spiritual journal. Do this daily for a minimum of seven days.

Imagination and Magic

Imagination: 1. The faculty of imagining, or of forming mental images or concepts of what is not actually present.

Magic: 1. The art of producing illusions as entertainment by the use of sleight of hand, deceptive devices, etc.; legerdemain, conjuring. 2. The art of producing a desired effect through incantation or various other techniques that presumably assure human control of supernatural agencies or the forces of nature.[1]

And, in the words of Dr. Jonn Mumford:

Imagination (image-in) is not just important—it is EVERYTHING.[2]

---

1 *Random House Dictionary*, 955, 1155.

2 Dr. Jonn Mumford, *Magical Tattwas: A Complete System for Self-Development* (St. Paul, MN: Llewellyn, 1997), 205.

Magic and imagination may not have the same etymological root, but these two similar-sounding words reveal the very core of Tantric theory and practice. When we visualize, we engage the imagination to create changes in our inner and/or outer environments, and many Tantric techniques rely on visualization. Seeing the divine in one's partner is a supremely imaginative act, at least at first. But this very act will ultimately transform a partner into Shiva or Shakti within the mind of the imaginer. We don't accept the popular view that certain thoughts are sinful and by themselves have an impact in the physical world, or that some kinds of fantasies are intrinsically bad. We do believe that by combining imagination and focused attention, you can transform your relationship with yourself and with the world at large.

Many Tantric scriptures are concerned with mundane magic, the casting of spells, various charms for curing ailments, success in business or in battle, attracting a lover, gaining supernatural powers, and so on. The prevailing view of Tantra during the British colonial era was that it was nothing more than "lust, mummery and black magic"[3] or a "black art of the crudest filthiest kind with a rough background of the Shiva Shakti cult."[4] The prevailing stereotype in the modern West, that Tantra is sacred sexuality and nothing more, is a very similar oversimplification, albeit without the negative connotations of "black magic."

As with many stereotypes, these ideas about Tantra contain an element of truth, although it is a distorted one. Tantra includes what the puritanical British of the Victorian era would have considered black magic (some of the magical practices remain shocking even today, and they periodically scandalize the contemporary Indian public), and some Tantric sects practice sacred sexuality. At its most profound level, Tantra is a magical tradition of the highest order, an art of self-transformation. Imagination is the means to an inner union of apparent opposites—between the multifaceted male and female aspects within each of us, among all the elements that make up our physical and spiritual beings, and between the human and the divine.

---

3 In *Principles*, vol. 1, page x, Avalon quotes Brian Hodgson, a nineteenth-century visitor to Nepal. No further details are provided about the source.

4 *Ibid.*, page xii. Avalon quotes a review of his translation of the *Mahanirvana Tantra* without identifying either the reviewer or the publication.

The Imagination Has No Limits

Imagination is an essential tool in the practice of Tantra, and it must be cultivated. We live in a world that values only certain limited forms of imagination. Children are discouraged from daydreaming. Only the practical, goal-oriented forms of imagining are universally recognized as worthwhile. It was not ever thus. Traditional cultures around the world have appreciated the power and the value of imagination since time immemorial. As Native American author N. Scott Momaday put it, the goal of our human incarnation is "to imagine ourselves richly."[5] This modern expression of ancient wisdom is well worth remembering. In Tantra, the imagination—combined with intention and will—enables you to direct your energy and expand your consciousness. Using it in a focused and systematic way will help you discover new ways for invoking, evoking, and experiencing the divine both within you and without you.

EXERCISE 42. Imagination

Close your eyes and take a few deep breaths. Then imagine a bright orange elephant. Open your eyes and, in your spiritual journal, write down what you saw and experienced. Describe the entire process in as much detail as you can.

Now open the palm of your hand. Close your eyes again and imagine the bright orange elephant sitting there. Again, open your eyes and record what you saw and experienced in as much detail as possible. Placing the elephant in the palm of your hand may have produced some physical sensations. Did you notice any? Were you aware of the elephant's scent? The process of visualizing often engages more than one sense.

Even when given specific instructions about what to visualize, some people find this exercise challenging because it involves seeing something impossible (at least in everyday life) in the mind's eye. Remember that visualizing does not necessarily require you to see the image in the same way you would with your eyes, and some people find that using descriptive words in the mind will help create the desired mental picture.

---

5 N. Scott Momaday, "Commencement Address," Hobart and William Smith Colleges, 1980.

You may have found that your rational mind resisted, telling you that it was impossible for an elephant to fit on the palm of your hand, or perhaps imagining bright orange as its color was an obstacle. Then again, perhaps you imagined yourself as a giant with a hand large enough to hold an elephant. If you didn't, try the exercise again and enlarge yourself instead of shrinking the elephant. If imagining the impossible is difficult for you, make a practice of inventing impossible events or creatures and visualizing them in as much detail as you can muster.

Within the realm of imagination, anything is possible. The laws of the physical world need not apply, and the only limits are, ultimately, self-imposed. Even if you were discouraged from using your imagination in the past, now you can start to exercise it like a muscle and expand your capacity to create new worlds for yourself. The imagination is perhaps the most powerful tool we human beings have at our disposal. You are reading this book because generations of people imagined things—not only the various technologies that made it possible to publish this book and bring it to your hands, but its actual content, which is a product of our own imaginations and those of many others both known and unknown to us.

EXERCISE 43. **The Power of Imagination**

Consider the following passage:

> Imagination, which in truth
> Is but another name for absolute power
> And clearest insight, amplitude of mind,
> And reason, in her most exalted mood.[6]

Think carefully about this passage and record your thoughts in your spiritual journal, along with some ideas about how you can use your imagination as a tool for growth. Give particular attention to any ideas you have about how your imagination might help you connect more deeply with your sexuality.

---

6 William Wordsworth, "The Prelude; XIV. Conclusion" (vol. 1) in *The Oxford Anthology of English Literature*, Frank Kermode and John Hollander, general eds. (Oxford, UK: Oxford University Press, 1973), 189–192.

Tantra and Gender

Tantra is often described as having two distinct paths. The Sanskrit word for path is *marga*. In the simplest terms, the left-hand path or *Vama Marga* includes both the visualization and the physical enactment of practices (including sexual ones) that are only visualized by right-hand path or *Dakshina Marga* practitioners (who may or may not be celibate in their daily lives). The reflection that begins this dala is an example of a Dakshina Marga practice taken from a classical source, the *Gheranda Samhita*, a seventeenth-century Tantric/ Yogic text. It is significant to note that texts of this sort were written primarily for male practitioners, and this one unabashedly advises the male Yogi to visualize himself as a female deity.

The distinction between these paths is somewhat arbitrary, and it can be misleading because most Vama Marga Tantrikas engage in Dakshina Marga practices more frequently than they do in practices that are commonly defined as left-handed. Nevertheless, the categories provide a useful framework for understanding two approaches to the practice of Tantra. More importantly, however, both right-hand and left-hand Tantric practitioners understand that we are, all of us, both male and female internally, as the passage from the *Gheranda Samhita* implies. All Tantrics seek to unite these elements within their own bodies. Vama Marga practitioners also attempt to unite these elements externally through ritual, including sexual ritual.

In the West, and particularly for heterosexual men, the idea that we have the other gender within us can be very threatening; however, recognizing, exploring, and embracing the inner female can be transformational for men. The same applies to women and the inner male. Although Sigmund Freud held that "biology is destiny," it is very limiting to think that our genitals alone determine our identity. Carl Jung recognized that within every man is the *anima* or feminine aspect and within every woman is an *animus* or masculine aspect, a somewhat simplistic but significantly more useful insight. We will encourage you to explore the internal aspects of gender more deeply and arrive at a more specific and personal understanding.

One of our teachers, Dr. Rudy Ballentine, has suggested that "gender is a place to play, not an identity."[7] This concept may not seem self-evident,

---

7 We are deeply grateful to Dr. Ballentine. His ideas have influenced us profoundly and have helped shape both this dala and dala 14, "Union."

and some may find that it calls into question some fundamental beliefs about the nature of the self, since many of us are deeply identified with our physical gender. One does not need to embrace Dr. Ballentine's statement as absolute truth to view gender as certainly something worth exploring. Developing a more flexible relationship with your own gender lets you define what it means to you, rather than allowing yourself to be defined by it or by socially constructed beliefs about "masculine" and "feminine" traits.

EXERCISE 44. **Imagination—Gender Transformation**

The following exercise may be something you have never considered, since our cultural conditioning about gender tends to treat it as a strict category, a boundary never to be crossed, but we encourage you to explore it and integrate it into your awareness. All it involves is a simple visualization. Sit down quietly and go within. Take a few deep breaths and center yourself. Begin by visualizing your body as it is now, then slowly morph it into the body of a person of the other gender. Feel the changes in your body, breasts and genitalia, and sense this different body as viscerally as you can. It is up to you to use your imagination and transform yourself in a way that works for you.

Once you have completed the visualization and you feel you truly inhabit this new body, spend ten to fifteen minutes experiencing it. Do some ordinary household tasks. Wash your face and brush your teeth. Try to feel what it would really be like to be you and to be the other gender. It may be helpful to begin by imitating the movements or mannerisms of the other gender, but make this a deeper, more personal exploration. Do your best to avoid lapsing into stereotyping or mimicry, since these are impersonal and reflect distorted, albeit conventional, ideas about gender. Discover your own unique understanding of what the other gender is to you and how you can authentically express and embody those traits, which already exist internally. Discover what works for you and treat these instructions as general guidelines. Do this exercise at least three times over the course of a week, and record your experiences.

If you are doing this as a couple, you can elaborate by applying the visualization in an intimate context. This exercise is designed for dyads, since it involves an exploration of energetic polarities, a union of perceived opposites. Thus, polyamorous people will have to work with a single partner, but the chance to alternate between roles may be an interesting avenue.

For heterosexual couples, one very effective way to explore this is to sit or lie together in any of the classical female superior Tantric postures, but with the man on top instead of the woman, and visualize the transformation together. When you do this, concentrate on the sensation and emotions that this shift brings about.

If you are a same-sex couple, you can trade off, or you can visualize that you are both changing to the other gender. The possibilities are limited only by your capacity to imagine—and that is potentially limitless!

Imagination: Recognizing and Honoring the Divine

In Tantra, it is a given that each and every one of us is a manifestation of the divine. Techniques for focusing our awareness on our own divinity are common to virtually all schools of Tantra, whether Buddhist or Hindu. Unlike most religious practices, which tend to invoke the divine from an external realm, Tantra places more emphasis on evoking the divine from within. The evocation is a preliminary step. In advanced individual practice, the Tantrika merges him- or herself with a personal deity or *ishtadevata*, first by visualizing the deity externally. Since the deity is conjured by means of the imagination, it is actually more of an evocation than an invocation. In the next phase, the practitioner brings the deity near and ultimately merges with him or her. Eventually, with diligent practice, the aspirant will be fully identified with the deity, at which point the visualization becomes superfluous.

Similarly, the famous mantra "So-Ham" ("I am he") is a contraction of "Shivo-Ham" ("I am Shiva"). The feminine "Sa-Ham" ("I am she") also explicitly identifies the self with the divine. In the Judeo-Chrisitian tradition, humans are created in God's image. In Tantra we imagine ourselves as gods or goddesses and thereby reclaim the divinity that exists in ourselves but that we have forgotten. In Vama Marga practice, one worships one's partner as an embodiment of Shakti or Shiva, and in sexual ritual, the partners embody these deities. This process of embodiment is tremendously powerful because we are highly suggestible in states of sexual arousal, and therefore the reminder of our innate divinity reaches the deepest levels of the unconscious mind.

A simpler and more concrete ritual that reminds us of the divinity within is the use of the salutation *namaste* ("nah-ma-stay") coupled with a bow. This single word and simple gesture are a profound expression of honor and reverence. Although the word namaste has a glamorous and exotic aura in the West, it is the standard greeting in much of India and Nepal. It literally means "I bow to you," and often the gesture of bowing alone suffices; the word itself is implicit. Derivations of namaste are used to honor the deities in ritual, so even in its everyday usage, it acknowledges the divinity that resides in all beings.

Many Westerners tend to think of bowing as an act of subservience or submission, as it is usually associated with servility in our culture. There is a much healthier way of understanding bowing—one that is commonplace in Asia and somewhat less familiar in the West, except perhaps among performers who bow to the audience as a gesture of gratitude, humility, and acknowledgement. From this perspective, bowing is an act of reverence and respect, not one of submission, a sign of honest humility, not servility. In bowing to our beloveds and they to us, we are expressing a broad range of emotions—each recognizing the other's intrinsic divinity and each expressing awe and appreciation at the divine manifesting itself before the other. This awareness is truly a humbling one, and humility is a key to maintaining balance as we recognize our inner divinity.

EXERCISE 45. **Recognizing Yourself as Divine**

Stand in front of a mirror. Look deeply into your own eyes and hold the meaning of *namaste* in your mind for several minutes. Take a few deep breaths, and intensify your concentration. See yourself as a manifestation of the divine (or as being created in God's image, if your religious beliefs require it), in whatever form you understand it, and believe it. Let this belief permeate your being all the way into your bones. When you feel it deeply, press your palms together at your heart and bow to yourself, maintaining the gaze into your own eyes, while repeating *namaste*.

Record your experience. Continue doing this every day for at least a week. You may choose to make this a long-term daily practice, for instance after you brush your teeth every morning. It can be a powerful way to fortify a deep internal love for yourself, something few people in this society have learned to do very well. The benefits of doing this single practice on a regular basis can be profound. We recently heard from a student who had attended one of our classes five years before. He told us that honoring himself on a daily basis had changed his life and helped him develop a genuine appreciation for himself.

EXERCISE 46. **Embracing the Divine in a Sexual Context**

Bring exercise 45 into a sexual setting. If you are a couple, practice seeing your partner as divine while you are making love and conclude your love-making sessions with a bow and a namaste.

Treat self-pleasuring as an act of worship and self-honoring, too. You may wish to do this in front of a mirror, but it is not necessary. When you have finished, either bow to yourself in the mirror or visualize yourself as a god or goddess (or vividly visualize that you are created in the image of God), and bow with a namaste.

Many of us are not conditioned to experience sexuality—and particularly masturbation—as a sacred act. You may find it difficult to treat your erotic self with a sense of reverence and wonder, but practice makes perfect, so stay with it. At the same time, some people feel the need to do elaborate rituals in order to make their sexual activity "sacred." While ritual can be very valuable in certain contexts, all consensual sexual acts are sacred by their very nature. Attitude is more important than strict adherence to ritual formulae. The act of bowing and saying namaste serves as a reminder of the sacredness and can help shape your attitude toward future encounters as well.

Innate Divinity and Humility

Some texts suggest that the practice of Tantra can be dangerous and difficult, that it is like "licking honey from the razor's edge." One of the main pitfalls is the ego inflation that may accompany an unbalanced recognition of one's own divinity. You are divine, but you are not different from or better than anyone else. The recognition of your innate divinity, if it is genuine, is accompanied by humility, knowledge of your ordinariness, and greater empathy for others.

Conversely, ego inflation is often marked by a disintegration of character, a sense of superiority, and an overly judgmental attitude toward others, rather than an integration of one's inner being and an identification with all of those around you. It may also be accompanied by manic states and delusions of grandeur, which can be symptoms of more serious problems. The key distinction is that the deeper the recognition of your own divine self, the more you will see divinity in everyone and everything you encounter.

Self-monitoring can be very difficult. The reflections of others around us often tell us when we are losing our way. If you are cut off from others, it can be difficult to see clearly or have any sense of perspective. This is one reason that the Guru-Chela relationship is so central to traditional Tantra. The guru can serve the student by leading him or her to connect with the inner divinity, while monitoring for signs of self-aggrandizement. For many in the modern West, however, the problem is not so much an inflated level of self-esteem as it is the lack thereof, and grandiosity is perhaps more often a symptom of diminished self-esteem than it is of overly inflated self-regard. In any case, the act of conscious bowing can help to maintain a balanced perspective and a sense of reverence for what lies within you and all around you.

A Message from Swami Umeshanand and Devi Veenanand

In our own lives, we bow to each other and offer a namaste virtually every time we make love. By making this practice a routine, we remind ourselves of the sacredness of our shared sexual life, of our every act of loving, of our union, and of the divinity that resides in both of us. This is a small, simple act, but in that moment, it generates a sense of reverence and takes us out of mundane consciousness. It is this sense of reverence—more than any technique or level of sexual prowess—that is central to the Tantric experience. We sometimes feel that the only ritual that is truly necessary is to bow and/or offer a namaste.

While it may feel awkward and artificial at first, you will get used to it, and it is a very beneficial habit to cultivate. We believe it has the power to transform relationships—with self and others. If there is one thing we hope you take from this book and incorporate into your life on a regular basis, it is this simple practice.

Hari Om.

Nyasa

Consider the following questions. Record your thoughts in your spiritual journal.

1. How would you define imagination?

2. In Tantra, everyone is seen as having qualities of both Shiva and Shakti. How do you understand this?

3. Were you successful in the first visualization exercise? What was your experience?

4. What characteristics do you think are feminine?

5. What characteristics do you think are masculine?

6. List three masculine and three feminine traits that are part of your make up.

7. Did you find it easy to incorporate bowing in a sexual context? Did anything change for you when you did?

Transformation

Prepare the rasa (juice)
While there is still passion
Within the body.
If you heat the rasa
With the fire of your passion,
It will surely thicken.

Let me tell you about rasa:
"Uncooked, it becomes sour.
Keeping the mind steady,
Stir the rasa,
So achieving transformation."

Watch carefully.
Passion makes the rasa
Go round and round.
From passion comes
The seed of love . . .

—SONG OF RADHA SHYAM

In this dala, we will examine the role of magic in Tantra in more detail and introduce you to a simple, straightforward form of sexual magic. Then you will undertake a systematic and practical magical experiment and take careful notes about the results of your practice. You may be surprised by the outcome. As a first step, we would like you to arrive at your own definition of the word magic.

As you work through dala 13, read the reflection on the opposite page every day. Then practice tratak on a candle flame for three to five minutes. Do not try to understand or interpret the text. Instead, let yourself absorb the passage on multiple levels and give your intellect a rest. Record your experiences and observations in your spiritual journal. Do this daily for a minimum of seven days.

Magic

As you may remember, one of our favorite ways to define Tantra is: "Tantra is the magic of transforming your consciousness and thereby transforming your entire being." In this dala, you will have the opportunity to put this concept into practice, using a magical approach to transforming yourself and gaining an integrated understanding of how magic works.[1]

Consider these three definitions of magic:

1. *The Art and Science of causing changes to occur in conformity with the Will.* This is Aleister Crowley's famous definition.[2]

---

1 We rely on the basic concepts outlined in chapters 6 and 7 in *The Essence of Tantric Sexuality.*

2 Aleister Crowley quoted in Isaac Bonewits, *Real Magic: An Introductory Treatise on the Basic Principles of Yellow Magic,* rev. ed. (York Beach, ME: Samuel Weiser, 1989), 30.

2. *Magic is the art and science of creating both internal and external changes in conformity with the will.* Here we rephrase Crowley's formulation.

3. *Magic is the deliberate bringing together of intention and attention for the purpose of producing a desired result.* "Intention and attenton" are the words of our friend Sylvia Brallier, who has studied Tantra as well as various shamanic and magical traditions.[3]

EXERCISE 47. **What Is Magic?**

Copy the above definitions of magic in your spiritual journal, then write your own one-sentence definition. Read all four carefully, then write a few more sentences elaborating on what the word "magic" means to you. Consider these questions:

• Do you think magic is something that can be useful for you? If so, how?

• How do you think magic relates to spirituality?

• Is magic a help or a hindrance, spiritually?

You will draw on this initial exploration as you work through this dala.

Magic, Tantra, and Transformation

In ancient cultures around the world, magicians were respected and sometimes feared. They appeared to have abilities beyond those of average human beings, including ways of controlling natural forces that seemed superhuman. In the medieval world, in Europe, the Middle East and India, the line between magic and science was, for all intents and purposes, nonexistent, since astrology and alchemy were both considered sciences. Today it is common to think of magic as antithetical to Chrisitianity. But pre-modern churches, both Catholic and Protestant, not only tolerated certain forms of magical practice but actively embraced them. The Puritan clergy denounced various forms of popular magic, but accepted practices that were in fact

3 Visit her website at www.tantricshamanism.com.

quite magical, including petitionary prayer (an attempt to create changes in conformity with the will by asking God to intercede on one's behalf), divinatory prayer, and casting lots to determine God's will.[4]

Of course, some forms of magical thinking remain popular in the twenty-first century, many of them not far removed from the beliefs of our seventeenth-century ancestors. But as a consequence of the changes that began to take place during the early-modern period, magic has a bad name today, at least within mainstream society. The occult movements of the late 1800s and the New Age movement of the late 1900s reinvented magical practice for the modern era, but its role in society as a whole remains marginal and repressed. Conventional attitudes tend toward the dismissive. For some, magic means entertainment and sleight of hand, mere trickery. For others, the word implies chicanery and fraud, and for yet another segment of the population, including many who engage in petitionary prayer, all magic is "black magic" and therefore evil.

Magical practices are far more common and socially acceptable in modern India than in the Western world, even as India becomes a technological superpower. Magic and alchemy are both far more integrated into India's social fabric and more readily available to the general population, both as textual and initiatory traditions. This may be due, in part, to the absence of a strictly hierarchical church committed to stamping out heresy and witchcraft. India also has an ancient tradition of respect for wandering *saddhus* (holy men) whose spiritual practices were often aimed—at least in part—at developing magical abilities. Saddhus are still ubiquitous and widely revered in twenty-first-century India.

Although Yogic and Tantric scriptures are replete with magical instructions, at its most sublime levels, Tantra is not about creating external changes or the quest for powers. Still, many Tantric scriptures deal with these subjects and provide detailed guidelines for mundane magical rituals—spells for defeating enemies, attracting lovers, acquiring wealth, or curing disease, to

---

4 Keith Thomas, *Religion and the Decline of Magic* (New York: Charles Scribner's Sons, 1971), 117–150. In his definitive study of magic in early modern England, Thomas argues that magic had begun to decline by the 1500s and that this decline was a necessary precondition for the extraordinary changes that began to take place during the Industrial Revolution.

name a few. In many instances, these spells are as crude as those one finds in any folk-magic tradition. Indeed, they can be quite macabre.

The Damara Tantra, for example, includes instructions for Bhuta Sadhana, a ritual for invoking the goddess Kali.

After an initial period of abstinence and dietary restriction, the aspirant must obtain the corpse of a fetus from "the womb of a woman who may have been struck dead by lightning." The corpse is dried and flattened over the course of a month, by which time there will be "no bad odour left in it." At this stage, the corpse becomes the seat for the sadhana, and after days of ritual, the practitioner will start to see "numerous horrible sights." If he gives in to fear or answers any questions from the apparitions, the magical practice will fail, and he may suffer severe physical consequences.

Eventually, a ferocious-looking, foul-smelling, half-naked female figure will appear to him, and he must ask her to sit before him and accept his worship. As the practitioner mentally repeats the mantra of this *Devi* (goddess), she will inquire as to his request. He must reply: "My only request is that you may always remain with me and fulfill all my desires." She will try to dissuade him, but he must not be daunted. In the end, she will give him two objects. One will cause the Goddess to appear and grant his wishes whenever he brings it into contact with fire; the other he should carry with him always to ward off evil.[5]

Taken literally—as it almost undoubtedly was and perhaps still is—this seems a grotesque form of ritual, if not a truly absurd one. It certainly illuminates why Tantra has been seen as a form of black magic by both Europeans and more orthodox Hindus. On a more metaphorical, esoteric level, however, the ritual can be understood as an alchemical process.[6] Through focused practice, discipline, and attention, we can transform those things we find most repulsive, horrifying, and frightening. If we stay with the process and refuse to back down, no matter how terrified we are, through an act of will, these terrible things will become our allies and help us realize our dreams. This is perhaps the most extraordinary magic of all.

---

5 Ram Kumar Rai (trans.), *Damara Tantra* (Varanasi: Prachya Prakashan, 1988), 119–120.

6 The metaphorical interpretation makes sense. It would be virtually impossible to follow these instructions to the letter. How exactly would one go about obtaining a fetus that died in the prescribed manner?

Figure 22. The goddess Kali in her fierce manifestation.
Each element depicted has a symbolic meaning: the
severed head, for example, represents the ego.

In this dala, however, you will explore a kinder, gentler, and altogether more pleasurable form of magic. You need not go down into the depths, face your fears, and transform them. You need not obtain the corpse of a fetus and make it into a seat for meditation. We have never done anything like that, and we don't expect you to either.[7] Instead, you will use pleasure, focused practice, and attention as tools to transform your consciousness. You will decide on a magical objective and practice diligently, all the while maintaining your capacity to observe the results.

---

7 Nevertheless, this is a real aspect of Tantric practice, one often glossed over not only by Westerners who focus on sexuality, but also by Indian scholars who seek to reclaim the more sublime aspects of the tradition and deny its magical components in an effort to harmonize it with more orthodox branches of Hinduism.

The magical technique is simple and practical. It does not require any elaborate ritual. Through direct experience of the practice, you will find out for yourself whether it is effective.

Setting Your Intention

First, look within and choose a project or intention to work with for at least one week as an experiment in transforming your consciousness. Of course, you may find that more time is required or desirable, and you may wish to stay with your intention for months at a stretch, which can be highly rewarding. For the purposes of this exercise, choose a modest and achievable internal change as your intention, so you can observe your results. "World peace" or "global healing" would not be suitable objectives here. You can always conclude your practice by dedicating it to the benefit of all beings as an addendum to the process, as is done in many Hindu and Buddhist rituals. Once you've had a chance to observe your results, you may decide to attempt something more ambitious.

Remember our definition of magic as "the art and science of creating internal and/or external changes in conformity with the will." Please focus on creating internal changes. Projects such as getting a promotion at work, attracting a lover, or achieving any material objective are not what we have in mind. In any case, it often turns out that external changes happen more readily when you have changed your consciousness. The process of altering your internal world can enhance your ability to notice when opportunities arise and prepare you to act accordingly. Find a positive quality or behavior pattern in yourself that you would like to reinforce and work with that. Unless you are very experienced it is unwise to work on serious personal problems or emotionally fraught issues. Making major changes such as breaking bad habits requires great skill. Focusing on negative behavior, even with a desire for change, can tend to reinforce it, so for our purposes, it is best to accentuate the positive.

Choosing this intention should not be an overly intellectual process. You may find it valuable to allow it to emerge after your daily tratak, or at any other time when your mind is quiet. Setting your intention is akin to choosing a *sankalpa,* a resolve or resolution. In the formal practice of Yoga Nidra as taught by Paramahansa Satyananda Saraswati, the practitioner begins the session by setting such a resolution. While sankalpa "can be used for therapeutic purposes, it should rather be used for a greater purpose, such as achieving self-realization or samadhi." In addition, "the purpose of sankalpa is not to fulfill desires but to create strength in the structure of the mind."[8]

Setting this intention for a magical project is somewhat similar. Yes, you are choosing a modest objective, but it is a good idea to bear in mind Paramahansaji's words on a greater purpose.

In our own practice, we have used the intentions listed below, among others. We hope they give you a sense of what is suitable as you search for your own.

- Treating your partner with even more reverence, kindness, and love.

- Developing more focus on a particular work-related objective: writing, in our case, which is why this book in your hands.

- Maximizing self-confidence or remaining calm in a particularly stressful situation. This can be useful in the context of job interviews, presentations, or any realm in which performance is important.

- Reinforcing positive behaviors, for example, taking an exercise routine to the next level.

The key is to find something positive and reinforce it, rather than focusing on what you'd like to overcome.

EXERCISE 48. **Your Intention**

Once you have settled on your intention, write it in your spiritual journal. The next step is to develop a visual image that expresses your intention. To stay with the exercise routine as an example, you might visualize yourself running at a faster pace, lifting heavier weights, or doing that tricky asana with ease. Describe the visualization in your spiritual journal. It can also be helpful to add a photograph or drawing of something that represents this to you. The more sensory avenues you engage, the more deeply the intention will be embedded in your consciousness.

8 Saraswati, *Yoga Nidra*, 22–25.

Practical Sex Magic: The Method

This practical approach to sex magic works in the context of self-pleasuring, in partnered activity, or in a group sexual ritual. The principles and methods are the same regardless of the number of people involved. The technique outlined here is an enhanced version of the one described in our previous book, which in turn was based on the work of Dr. Jonn Mumford.[9] This version addresses partnered activity more explicitly. If you are practicing with a partner or partners, we encourage you to experiment with the method in both contexts: self-pleasuring and partnered lovemaking. Observe the results and the differences between the two experiences.

Before you begin, familiarize yourself with four core concepts and three simple steps. First, the **four concepts** that are central to this process: (1) arousal, (2) fantasy, (3) suggestibility, and (4) energy.

1. Arousal. It doesn't matter how you get there, but it is crucial to be as intensely aroused as possible. You must identify what truly turns you on, what produces the most intense arousal or results in the strongest orgasm; however, orgasm is not necessary, only a high state of arousal. By now you should have a very good understanding of what arouses you.

2. Fantasy. Use whatever fantasy you find most exciting. There are no taboos here. For partnered activity, fantasy may be unnecessary. Some people find it distracting to fantasize when interacting with another person; for others, fantasy remains a useful tool. There is no right or wrong way to go about this.

3. Suggestibility. Arousal tends to short-circuit intellectual processes and self-consciousness. You enter a highly suggestible mental state somewhat akin to being under hypnosis. At this time, you can implant your intention in such a way that it penetrates into all levels of consciousness, beginning the process of inner transformation.

---

9 *The Essence of Tantric Sexuality*, chapters 6, "Practical Sex Magic," and 7, "Keys to Autoerotic Mysticism," are based on Dr. Jonn Mumford's pioneering work on the subject in the 1970s and 1980s. His approach is both effective and simple. Its theoretical and conceptual aspects are beyond the scope of this book and are not essential for this practice.

4. Energy. Sexual arousal is a highly energized state that affects the mind-body complex on multiple levels; some would say it extends to the energy field beyond the body. The physiological signs of this energized state include increases in blood pressure, respiration, and heart rates; changes in brain wave patterns; and the release of various hormones, including endorphins.

The **three steps** entail: (1) prolonging and heightening arousal, (2) flashing a visual image at the climactic moment, and (3) regulating the breath at climax.

Step 1. Build, prolong, and heighten arousal. The key to virtually all Tantric sexual practices is prolonging arousal, but it is equally important to reach a high level of excitement. Thus, an extended period of mild to moderate arousal may be less effective than a relatively briefer session in which you become highly aroused. This is particularly relevant in the practice of sexual magic, because the mystical experience is less important than the amount of energy you can produce and direct. During step 1, you are not concerned with your magical intention. Focus instead on building arousal through fantasy or any other method, including partnered sexual activity. In addition to building energy, focusing on the arousal will quiet the mind.

Step 2. Visualize. Visualize your intention once you have reached a very high state of arousal (if you do not expect or intend to have an orgasm) or are approaching the "point of no return." Create a vivid image in as much detail as possible and let it flash on and off like a giant neon sign. It can be helpful to add sound, or imagine the sensation of heat, to literally burn the image into your consciousness. If you do have an orgasm, continue to visualize through it and for a few seconds afterwards. (Review dala 8, "Meditation," for pointers on how to visualize.)

Step 3. Regulate your breath as you visualize. Holding the breath lets you direct all your psychic energy into your visualization. Just before you start to visualize, inhale deeply and hold your breath. (Swallowing just after the inhalation makes it easier to retain.) Hold it throughout the visualization process and until the orgasmic sensations subside. To enhance the effect as you finally exhale, imagine that your out-breath is imbuing the image with energy, inflating it. (If holding your breath is uncomfortable, or if you have unregulated high blood pressure, choose a different conscious breathing technique. In any case, use an exhalation to inflate your visualized image.)

Before you begin experimenting with the practice, be completely familiar with the four concepts and the three steps so you won't be preoccupied with remembering them. Your mind should be focused on other things.

EXERCISE 49. **Practical Sex Magic in Practice**

Once you have set your intention and are familiar with the concepts and steps, practice this form of sex magic for at least seven sessions over the course of a week or more, alone or in a partnered setting. The more frequently you do this practice, the more effective it will be.

Keep detailed notes of your experiences in your spiritual journal. Pay attention to whether your intention is manifesting itself, and if so, describe as specifically as possible what changes are taking place.

A Message from Swami Umeshanand

This dala on transformation has been a bit of a departure, drawing more directly on Dr. Jonn Mumford's teachings than the others. Similarly, this message is a departure. It is my personal story, for the most part predating my relationship with Devi Veenanand. She suggested I recount it here because it conveys the transformative power possible in Tantric practice.

As a very young child, I was diagnosed with what was then called minimal brain dysfunction, a term that was later replaced by attention deficit disorder. Although I tested with a very high IQ, I struggled with all the familiar issues that confront gifted people with this syndrome; I did not know of the diagnosis at the time.

Much later, in my mid-thirties, I happened to read about adult ADD, which was a hot topic at the time. After reading Edward M. Hallowell and John J. Ratey's book *Driven to Distraction*, it seemed clear to me that I was still suffering from this syndrome. When I researched my childhood history and found some of my elementary school and medical records, I learned of that early diagnosis. I then had a neuropsychological evaluation including a Continuous Performance Test, the standard way to test attention, at least at that time. My score on the CPT was seven standard deviations from the norm, indicating severe ADD. I started taking Ritalin shortly thereafter, then tried various other similar medications. The general consensus seemed to be that I would need to stay on ADD medication for life. Fortunately, it turned out I would only need it for a couple of years.

The transformation began in my very first session with Satya (Anna Harvey), my first Tantra teacher. She taught me a Neo-Tantric technique popularly known as streaming, and after doing it for about ten minutes I experienced an incredible movement of energy. I told Satya that the sensation was what I imagined a woman's orgasm felt like. I went into an ecstatic state that lasted for days afterwards, and I realized I could stop taking the ADD medication I was on at the time. I have never felt any need for or interest in taking it again.

That change alone was dramatic, but it was only the beginning. Over the next four years I consistently did various forms of meditation. Then, after studying with Dr. Mumford and practicing tratak regularly, I got interested in biofeedback as another tool for working with my consciousness. When I met my biofeedback trainer, I learned that she had worked with people suffering from ADD, both children and adults. Since she was trained in administering the CPT, I asked her to test my attention, more out of curiosity than anything else. To my surprise and delight, all my scores on the test were within normal ranges. The practice of Tantra had measurably transformed my consciousness on a profound level.

I sometimes hesitate to tell this story, because I don't want to create unrealistic hopes or expectations about Tantric practice. Not everyone's story is as dramatic as my own. But, I offer it to you here as a symbol of what might be possible for you. When I made that fateful visit to Satya, I was expecting to learn more about sexuality. I have certainly learned a great deal about sexuality in the course of my Tantric journey, but I had no idea that my entire being would be transformed in the process.

Hari Om.

Nyasa

Consider these questions. Record your thoughts in your spiritual journal.

1. Has your understanding of the word magic changed as a result of your reading and your practice? If so, how?

2. Do you think magical practices work? If so, how and why?

3. List three things that frighten you. How might you be able to transform each of these, and what would it mean to you if you did?

4. Was it difficult for you to choose an intention?

5. Did working in a sexual context make it easier for you to visualize? Were you able to make the image flash?

6. Did you notice any changes in yourself after doing this practice for a week? Do you feel you achieved your objective, either in whole or in part?

DALA 14

Union

If I wish to acquire the burning and lighting Shakti of fire, I must be fire myself; or if I would possess the coolness and Shakti possessed by water, I must be full of water myself; or if I want to acquire the speed and the Shakti of touch possessed by air, I must be full of air myself; or if I wish to have the hardness and the Shakti of smell possessed by earth, I must be full of earth myself; so if I wish to acquire, even in the least degree, the eternal Shakti of Bhagavan (God) or Bhagavati (Goddess), I must be full of Him or Her. I must completely sink my individual existence into the existence of Him or Her whose Shakti is to be communicated to me, otherwise it will never be so communicated. One person becomes full of another to the extent to which he loses himself in the Bhava (nature) of that other person, and the Shakti of the latter is communicated to him to the extent to which he becomes full of such other.

—THE TANTRATATTVA OF SHRIYUKTA SHIVA
CHANDRA VIDYARNAVA BHATTACHARYYA MAHODAYA

In this dala, we will examine the role of love in Tantra, which may not be quite what you expect, and give you an overview of the Panchamakara or 5M ceremony, the quintessential Tantric sex ritual, and the basic principles of Tantric alchemy. As you consider Tantric gender paradigms more deeply, you will create a union of your own masculine and feminine elements through self-pleasuring and/or partnered sex and visualization. The key to erotic empowerment lies in loving yourself. The practices in this dala will give you tools for loving yourself more deeply.

As you work through dala 14, read the reflection on the opposite page every day. Then practice tratak on a candle flame for three to five minutes. Do not try to understand or interpret the text. Instead, let yourself absorb the passage on multiple levels and give your intellect a rest. Record your experiences and observations in your spiritual journal. Do this daily for a minimum of seven days.

The Role of Love in Tantra

Love, in the contemporary Western sense of the word, is not a significant consideration in traditional Hindu Tantra. As you already know, some texts specify that partners in sexual rituals should not be spouses. At the same time, a number of legendary Tibetan Buddhist Tantric siddhas were married or had long-term relationships with their spiritual partners, and some of the legends show that these couples practiced sexual Tantra together.

For example, Miranda Shaw describes the relationship between Dombipa, a king of Assam, and Dombiyogini (from whom *his* name is derived). The king purchased Dombiyogini as a twelve-year-old, paying her parents the dancing girl's weight in gold. The two practiced Tantra together secretly in Dombipa's palace for twelve years. When their relationship was discovered, they were driven from the kingdom, but they stayed together for twelve more years until Dombipa's death. Shaw depicts this as a profoundly interdependent relationship between peers and points out that Dombiyogini spent the rest of her life as a Tantric guru who passed on two important lineages.[1]

Similarly, the Hindu Tantric tradition has a long history of lineages passed down within families, albeit with less emphasis on spiritual partnership than Tantric Buddhism. Thus, we see an established history of Tantric practice encompassing ongoing intimate relationships. (Whether these relationships were imbued with elements of Western romantic love is another question.) We believe that Westerners can find an extraordinary opportunity to approach life Tantrically within an intimate relationship and all its complexities.

Contemporary Western models of love and relationship are profoundly unhealthy. We are taught to believe that we should seek completion outside ourselves, that finding a partner will fill a void within. In fact, finding this partner or "soul mate" is seen as a precondition for becoming complete. Most romantic movies and much popular literature send this message. But from the Tantric perspective, this is rubbish. We are in fact complete, though the experience of living tends to make us lose touch with our own completeness.

Each of us is an expression of the divine. Only when we feel whole within ourselves can we truly worship another and recognize that person's innate divinity. Without this inner sense of integrity, worship is likely to become servility and submission. It may even have a desperate quality, since need is the underlying emotion. There is a vast difference between needing a partner and wanting one. When people are needy, they are dependent and lack freedom. Of course, it is normal to be needy at times and in varying degrees. We humans are social creatures, after all, and we depend on each other for our sanity, indeed for our survival. The problem lies in believing that for each of us, one other person can and should be able to satisfy every need.

Seeking fulfillment through another because one feels incomplete will likely lead to emotional disaster. It imposes an impossible set of expectations on that person, who can only be human and flawed (even as she is

1 Miranda Shaw, *Passionate Enlightenment*, 63–65.

divine). Disappointment will inevitably follow the recognition of the other's defects—defects that will be magnified by the contrast between expectation and reality. This disillusionment and dissatisfaction are often the hidden factors behind relationship failure.

Love does indeed have a place in Tantra, but the Tantric approach to love differs radically from the conventional Western model. As Dr. Swami Gitanada Giri Gurumaharaj once put it: "Love is profound interest." From the Tantric perspective, love can be defined as focused attention on, awareness of, and reverence for the other. It is not infatuation, the starry-eyed, idealized love of popular song. It is not the emotional roller coaster of unrequited love. It is not the complacent and comfortable, if arid, familiarity that many long-term couples share. It is a deep, low-burning fire that requires tending, and you can fan the flames at will.

In this form of love, one devotes great attention and care to one's partner without seeking anything specific in return. Of course, all relationships require some measure of reciprocity, but optimally, the result is synergistic. Partners should enrich and inspire each other, not merely fill in the empty spaces. By constantly reminding yourself that you and your partner are individually complete and divine, and by cultivating interest on an ongoing basis, you can create the conditions for your relationship to flourish and become something utterly extraordinary. This is a process of developing awareness and love, thereby nurturing but not "working on" your relationship.

In Tantric sexuality, the same attitude applies whether you are engaging in ritual activity with someone you barely know or, conversely, are practicing monogamously with a long-term partner. You cannot be seeking to fill a void in yourself, nor can you solely be interested in your own gratification. We are not making a moral judgment and do not object to consensual sexual acts in which people are merely seeking gratification or hoping to feel better; however, in any genuinely Tantric sexual practice, you must be fully present and deeply interested in what is transpiring, not only for your own sake but for your partner's. The participants are collaborating on a shared project—sex as a means to mystical experiences or union with the divine (however they understand it). They must be fully committed to producing this outcome. So for any sexual experience to be truly Tantric, love plays a pivotal role, even if it does not resemble love as it is popularly understood.

Today various forms of alternative relationship styles, including polyamory and other types of open relating, have become more popular and socially acceptable, at least in some circles. While the classical model for Tantric sexual activity is dyadic and heterosexual, we find that Tantric principles are equally valid for those with other types of relationships or orientations. Attitude is the key. Love and reverence need not be restricted to the dyad or to people of "opposite" external genders, although increasing the number of partners creates additional complexities. Whatever your relationship style, sexual orientation, or gender identity, devotion to your partner or partners, and a determination to facilitate those with whom you are interacting are the crucial elements.

In some ways, it is easier to approach a relative stranger with love and reverence than someone you know very well, and this is one reason that some Tantric scriptures recommend a partner other than a spouse. Still, the level of love and trust that can be developed in an ongoing relationship is profound. The mutual decision to treat the relationship as a form of spiritual practice— to approach sexuality with awareness, presence, integrity, and a dedication to recognizing the divine in the other, while facilitating each other's evolution—can create a depth of feeling that is far richer and more complex than conventional romantic love.

Developing Your Inner Tantric Relationship

Your relationship with yourself is essential to your own well-being and to your ability to make the most of your interactions with others. Many of the solo exercises in this book are designed to help you learn to know yourself, primarily as a sexual being, but in other ways as well. Remember the ancient maxim "Know thyself." Pursue this self-knowledge with as much passion, commitment, and creativity as you can muster. This book is a beginning and nothing more.

Once you have developed some measure of self-knowledge, you can begin to treat yourself as your own Tantric partner. In Dakshina Marga Tantra, the practices are solo and do not include sexual ritual. Many of these Dakshina Marga practitioners are married, but their Tantric sadhana is purely internal. They may visualize Shiva and Shakti inside themselves and circulate the energies within their own bodies through *pranayama* (breathing techniques), visualization, mantra, nyasa, and other methods. Kriya Yoga practices (which can also be used in Vama Marga, or Left-Hand Tantra) involve drawing energy up the spine and into the skull and can be quite explicit in terms of sexual imagery. The spine itself becomes the lingam and the skull the yoni. Energy is essentially ejaculated up the spine and into the cranial cavity. You need not be versed in these practices to cultivate a form of inner union, a way of loving yourself.

Loving yourself is generally frowned upon and at best underappreciated in our society, but you cannot truly revere another until you revere yourself. One powerful way to do this is to cultivate a relationship with yourself as if you were somebody else. This may sound strange at first, but it is related to the concept of witness consciousness. It entails standing aside to observe, notice and, above all, appreciate. If love is profound interest, then begin by becoming interested in yourself, not in the conventional egoistic way. This is not self-seeking or arrogance. It is a process of becoming aware and of nurturing.

EXERCISE 50. **Cultivating Interest in Yourself and Becoming Your Own Lover**

List ten things about yourself that you find admirable, interesting, and likable. Write them in your spiritual journal.

Courtship

In the early stages of a relationship, people tend to be very attentive to the interests, needs, and desires of the beloved. They find the new partner fascinating and often view the most mundane characteristics as unique and wonderful. They do thoughtful things—buying flowers or gifts or taking the new beloved out to dinner. For some, this only occurs during courtship, and as the new partner becomes familiar, the attentiveness and appreciation dissipate. We advocate maintaining this attentiveness toward others and cultivating an equivalent attitude toward oneself. We can blame familiarity and routine for our flagging interest in others, but most people have never learned to be attentive to and to court themselves. Even if it seems awkward and unfamiliar at first, developing this kind of appreciation for yourself can transform you.

EXERCISE 51. **Court Yourself Every Day for a Week**

Imagine that you are dating yourself this week. Do something special every day: something small like buying yourself flowers or chocolate, or a bit more ambitious, like treating yourself to a movie or a concert when you really "should" be doing something else. Take some time each day to plan an activity or think of what you will do for yourself. You might approach it by contemplating how you would like to be courted by a lover—and then setting out to do just that. Record your plans and your activities in your spiritual journal. Observe what you experience, both physically and emotionally, over the course of the week and record that too.

Be Kind to Yourself

The Dalai Lama has famously professed that "my religion is kindness." Saints from many religious traditions are renowned for their selfless caring for other creatures. In Tantra, the wrathful goddess Kali transforms into a kindly, benevolent mother when she is worshipped sincerely. And yet, kindness seems to be sorely lacking in the modern world. Our public discourse is often dominated by those most adept at insulting their adversaries. Couples who come to us often seem more concerned with venting emotion than with the possible impact such expression might have. The human potential movement empowered people to speak their truth, but something very important—caring for others—was too often neglected in the process.

Even our educational system is based in significant part on criticism and negativity. The same applies to child rearing, the contemporary emphasis on childhood self-esteem notwithstanding. As adults, we are bombarded by advertising and media imagery that endlessly reinforce our sense of ourselves as inadequate—physically, economically, and emotionally. We are weighed in the balance and found wanting, every day of our lives, and we can't avoid internalizing these messages. As a result, it becomes very difficult to be kind

Figure 23. Kali in her benevolent manifestation. It is
believed that if an aspirant worships Kali sincerely,
the fierce goddess transforms into a tender, loving
mother.

and tender to ourselves, since our inadequacies are so incessantly called to
our attention.

Therefore, become aware of the ways in which you are mentally unkind
to yourself. Begin to cultivate compassion, seeing that while you are human
and flawed, you are also a divine manifestation, worthy of respect, caring,
and kindness—most of all from yourself. This is a lifelong process, but with
a slight change in your thinking and a commitment to treating yourself with
kindness, it can be a transformational force. Being kind to yourself doesn't
mean being complacent, nor does it mean you should refrain from all self-
examination. Continue to recognize and address what you would truly like
to change, but remember that self-flagellation is more often the enemy of
growth than it is its ally.

Your Inner Tantric Sexual Relationship

In dala 12, "Imagination," we considered a Tantric perspective on gender and the idea that we are all both male and female internally. You visualized changing genders and explored what gender means to you. This exploration is the first step in a process of uniting and harmonizing your own inner masculine and feminine aspects, a process of loving yourself internally. In Hindu Tantra, the feminine principle is energy while the masculine is inert consciousness; the feminine is lunar and the masculine is solar; the left side is feminine while the right is masculine. Thus, at the most basic level, certain characteristics are ascribed to masculinity and others to femininity. Gender distinctions are seen as polarities, so that these traits are implicitly opposite. On the surface, this paradigm seems closely related to the widely held Western notion that male and female are opposite sexes, that certain traits are innately male and others are innately female—a narrow, reductionist view of gender difference. We prefer to think of men and women as "neighboring" rather than "opposite" sexes.[2] Indeed, there is a risk that simplistic interpretations of the Tantric model can be even more restrictive and confining than Western stereotypes. We have met a number of people from the lesbian, gay, bisexual, and transgendered communities who have encountered hostility and rejection when exploring contemporary Neo-Tantra. Indeed, a common misconception persists that Tantra is for heterosexual couples only.

---

2 It may come as a surprise to discover that the concept of "opposite" sexes is a modern invention, at least in the West. As Thomas Laqueur, who coined the term "neighboring sexes," documented in his comprehensive and eye-opening *Making Sex: The History of Gender from the Greeks to Freud* (Cambridge, MA: Harvard University Press, 1990), gender was seen as a continuum or hierarchy, and women were deemed to be "lesser men," until the eighteenth century, when the concept of gender polarity became the dominant paradigm. Before the Enlightenment, it was widely believed that people could spontaneously change genders and that, for example, men could lactate under certain circumstances. It was also commonly believed that promiscuity and lust were intrinsically feminine characteristics and that men were predisposed to be chaste, even if they were at times vulnerable to feminine wiles. Laqueur makes a compelling case that our beliefs about the meanings of "male" and "female" are cultural constructs. His book raises profound questions about contemporary "scientific" studies and the current emphasis on sociobiology, since much of this research is founded on a set of unexamined assumptions that are culturally determined. One need not accept Laqueur's argument in its entirety to realize that men and women are more alike than they are different.

While Tantrics identify certain qualities as masculine and others as feminine, these ascriptions should not be taken too literally. Do not confuse the traits of Shiva and Shakti with male and female behavior, or with our culture's own gender distinctions. The Tantric attributions have, however, a certain general, archetypal significance and can offer psychological insights. For example, viewing the feminine principle as active and energizing can remind us that women have far more power in the sexual realm than is commonly recognized. And, while heterosexual men usually think that they initiate courtship, more often than not they are responding to cues from women. Acknowledging feminine power can have an extraordinarily liberating effect, once women understand and embrace that power. Men who develop the ability to be comfortable with empowered women are also liberated.

In Tantra, gender differences are visualized as energetic polarities, not psychic or behavioral ones. These energetic polarities are only tangentially related to one's external genitalia, but understanding them can help you maximize your sexual experience and work effectively with the energies of your own body. This idea of polarity, of binary opposition between male and female, feminine and masculine, can be a gateway to union, to transcending the oppositions and reaching a state in which polarity is no longer meaningful.

Ardhanarishwara (Masculine/Feminine)

Ardhanarishwara is a form of Shiva with particular significance in the Tantric tradition. This manifestation of the deity is male on one side and female on the other, reflecting not only the Tantric concept that we have a feminine energetic channel on the left (*ida*) and a masculine channel on the right (*pingala*), but also the deeper truth that every human is both masculine and feminine and that by bringing these inner elements into harmony and union, we can become fully integrated human beings, to put a Western gloss on the concept of "self-realization."

Tantric iconography is replete with such imagery. The *yantra*, or geometric symbol for the heart chakra, is a hexagram, a six-pointed star, representing the union of male and female. It is no coincidence that this symbol of

Figure 24. Ardhanarishwara, the hermaphroditic form of Shiva, rules the third eye, or ajna chakra, symbolizing the ultimately androgynous nature of the human mind and spirit.

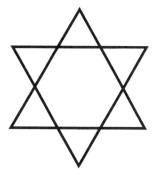

Figure 25. The symbol for the heart chakra, the *anahata yantra* represents the union of male and female elements within us. By bringing these inner aspects into harmony and balance, we can live in and from our hearts.

union resides in the heart. The upward-pointing triangle, the male principle, also implies the upward flow of (Kundalini) energy, which is seen as feminine. The downward-pointing triangle, the feminine, also implies the downward flow of masculine consciousness, which unites with the feminine energy in the heart.[3] A similar concept is perhaps more immediately obvious in the yin-yang symbol of the Taoist tradition. Each half of the circle contains its opposite: the black dot within the white field and vice versa.

To many in the modern West, ambiguously gendered people are disconcerting and threatening. Indeed, they are frequently the targets of violence, as was poignantly illustrated in the film *Boys Don't Cry*. Other cultures take a different view. Many traditional Native American societies recognized various forms of gender-bending as sacred, and people who crossed the line were deemed "two-spirited," not only able to cross gender boundaries, but also particularly gifted at travel between the physical and spiritual realms. There was a concerted effort to suppress these traditions as part of the process of conquest and colonization, but younger generations of gay, lesbian, bisexual, and transgendered Native people are reclaiming their heritage. Similarly, in India, cross-dressers, transgendered people, and eunuchs play a sacred role in certain contexts. They are, however, generally ostracized and scorned in most circumstances, an intolerace that seems to be, in large part, a legacy of British rule.

---

3 For more on this symbolism, the chakra system, and Kundalini energy, see *Essence of Tantric Sexuality*, 9–16 and 109–111.

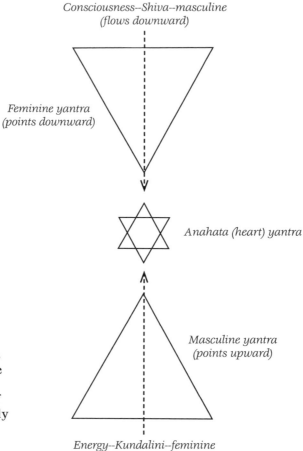

Consciousness--Shiva--masculine
(flows downward)

Feminine yantra
(points downward)

Anahata (heart) yantra

Masculine yantra
(points upward)

Energy--Kundalini--feminine
(flows upward)

Figure 26. In Tantra, feminine energy flows upward; the masculine is drawn down into the body. Thus each of these yantras implicitly contains its opposite.

Figure 27. The yin-yang symbol makes explicit what is implicit in Tantric imagery: each quality contains its opposite.

Even in the West, we find traces of a similar sensibility. Perhaps the most vivid historical example is the superstardom of *castrati,* singers who were castrated as boys before their voices changed. They fascinated the public not only as artists but as objects of sexual desire. This tradition persisted until the late 1800s, and the same undercurrent is echoed in the androgyny of certain rock musicians—Little Richard, Mick Jagger, David Bowie, the New York Dolls, Joan Jett, and Patti Smith, to name a few. From the Tantric perspective, each and every one of us—whether we display any external gender ambiguity or not—has the potential to travel between worlds, as two-spirited Native American people were believed to do. This is an internal alchemical process, a bringing together of our inner male and female elements. In fact, this inner alchemy is one way to think about the "goal" of Tantric sex, if any goal can be said to exist.

Similarly, the Western alchemical tradition, which was at least indirectly influenced by Indian Tantric alchemy, implicitly recognizes this inner process of uniting male and female elements as the key to transforming the "base" into the "pure." Medieval alchemists actually attempted to turn lead into gold and to create the philosopher's stone—a substance that purportedly could bring about this transformation and also had rejuvenating properties. These alchemical processes involved unifying elements that were coded as "male" with those that were coded as "female." Alchemical paradigms have a deeper metaphorical meaning, however literally they may have been understood at times. They represent a search for inner purification, the desire to create something sacred (gold) out of something perceived as profane (lead or "base metal"), or indeed to transcend the distinction between the sacred and the profane altogether.

Tantric Sexual Ritual

The Panchamakara or 5M ceremony involves five forbidden (profane) things, each symbolizing an element.

1. *Mudra* (parched grain): earth

2. *Matsya* (fish): water

3. *Madya* (wine): fire

4. *Mamsa* (meat): air

5. *Maithuna* (union or sexual intercourse, also profane in the minds of many): the fifth element, ether or space.[4]

On a physical level all of these things remain the same. The transformation takes place in the consciousness of the participants. Maithuna is a physical re-enactment of Tantric metaphysics—the view that the universe itself is a concrete manifestation of the ongoing sexual union between Shiva and Shakti. It also enacts a process that is taking place internally, the union of male and female elements that exist in each and every one of us. By bringing awareness to these processes, the very things that make life possible, by removing them from the realm of the reflexive and mechanical, we can transform acts that are perceived as ordinary into acts imbued with meaning and sacredness. The sacredness is there to begin with. The magic lies in recognizing it.

EXERCISE 52. **Connecting Erotically with Your Internal Feminine and Masculine**

In this exercise you will bring together your inner masculine and feminine elements, uniting the heart with the lingam or yoni. Couples and polyamorous configurations should experiment with this practice separately, through self-pleasuring, and together. The basic model is dyadic, so it is perhaps easiest in pairs, but improvise as you wish.

People often talk about the need to connect the heart and the genitals and suggest that men, in particular, experience a disconnect between the two. It is true that people erect barriers between sexuality and emotion, but from the Tantric perspective, the heart (and thus the emotions) and the genitals are linked energetically. Bringing just a little awareness to the emotions that accompany sexual excitement and pleasure makes the connection palpable. Indeed, we may discover that maintaining an artificial barrier be-

---

4 See Mumford, *Ecstasy Through Tantra*, 49–51, for more on the symbolism of this ceremony. Van Lysbeth, *Tantra*, 263–294, includes another valuable analysis. Tantric lineages may differ on which element is identified with which substance.

tween emotion and sexuality requires more psychic energy than embracing their intrinsic relatedness. By becoming aware of the connection between the heart and the genitalia, we can bring a sense of reverence to all of our sexual encounters.

If your external gender is male, imagine that you have a yoni in your heart, and as you self-pleasure, visualize your lingam penetrating that yoni. If your external genitalia are female, imagine that the lingam in your heart is penetrating your yoni. (You may need to use another fantasy to get yourself highly aroused. Try the techniques from dala 13, "Transformation," so that you visualize this sexual union with yourself only as you are approaching orgasm.) Whichever visualization you use, imagine that your lingam is ejaculating golden light into your yoni as you reach orgasm.

If you are a heterosexual couple, use a similar visualization, with the lingam of her heart penetrating the yoni of his, even as his physical lingam penetrates her physical yoni. Same-sex couples should discuss and decide in advance who will enact the masculine and who will enact the feminine. It is also possible for anyone to reverse gender. If you are a single man, for example, you can visualize as if you were a woman. The possibilities are endless and are limited only by your imagination and your capacity to visualize.

Do this practice at least three times over the course of a week, and record the results in your spiritual journal.

A Message from Swami Umeshanand and Devi Veenanand

Our relationship did not develop out of romantic love, as it is commonly understood. When we met, rather than go through the usual form of dating and courtship, we openly discussed an interest in practicing sexual Tantra together. We were both at a point in our lives when the artificial behavior of conventional courtship seemed ridiculous. It quickly became clear to both of us that we were very good together, and love evolved organically. There has been very little drama or unstable emotionality in our relationship; rather, it was comfortable from the start (but not dull!), and our communication was almost always clear and direct. This forthrightness and lack of illusion created a context for us to grow together and avoid the pain and disappointment that often accompany heated infatuation. Instead, today, we have a passionate devotion to each other and a partnership that continues to evolve and surprise us.

We also have maintained a willingness to be open and exploratory in our sexuality, to recognize that there is always more to discover and more to learn. This has entailed a conscious effort to recognize and embrace the inner masculine and feminine elements that dwell within us. Although many of the externals of our relationship fit conventional gender stereotypes, we have arrived at them, for the most part, because they work for us, not because they are what society expects. Approaching as many aspects of our lives as Tantrically as we can has enriched us and made us feel we are freer. We hope the tools we have shared in this book will do the same for you.

Hari Om.

Nyasa

Consider the following questions. Record your thoughts in your spiritual journal.

1. The ritual of the 5Ms may not have the same impact on modern Westerners as it would on traditional Hindus. What substitutes for the traditional five elements might be effective for transforming your consciousness?

2. What aspects of yourself have you learned to appreciate more fully through the exercises in this dala?

3. Have your ideas about love changed as a result of your work on this dala? If so, how?

4. Did your experience of uniting your masculine and feminine aspects (exercise 52) change with practice? Did you experiment with any variations?

5. What qualities do you identify as neither masculine nor feminine?

6. What did you learn about yourself through working with your inner masculine and feminine aspects?

7. "Love is the beginning of silence and the cessation of chaos." How does this definition differ from conventional concepts of love?

Afterword

Congratulations on completing this book, particularly if you did all the exercises, kept your spiritual journal, and completed all the nyasas. Even if you have done only some of the exercises, or have simply read the book, congratulations are in order nonetheless. The rewards of practicing Tantra are great, but that does not mean it is an easy path.

Not long ago, a radio interviewer asked us what it takes to explore Tantric sexuality, and one of us replied, "Guts." While the response was a little flippant, it was not untrue. It has been said that Tantra is the way of the hero, and that is probably even more apt today than it was during the golden age of Indian Tantra.

"Know thyself," an inscription at Delphi admonished the ancient Greeks, and that statement has since been ascribed to Socrates, among many other philosophers. For millennia, self-knowledge, in one form or another, represented perhaps the supreme virtue in many cultures, both Eastern and Western. Indeed, many saw it as the primary goal of human existence. This belief persisted into the modern era. Freud had his shortcomings, but the psychoanalytic approach was perhaps the last echo of the Oracle's advice, at least in the modern West. Today, psychoanalysis has fallen out of favor, supplanted by psychopharmacology and other methods designed to provide quick and easy remedies. Time is money in our society, and as a result, reading a book, never mind thoughtful self-exploration, may seem wasteful and self-indulgent.

If knowing oneself is no longer valued, knowing oneself sexually is virtually forbidden. As we have noted, sex pervades every aspect of our society and permeates our daily lives. We talk about it endlessly and are literally bombarded with sexual imagery. But this sex is formulaic and superficial, a tool for marketing, a form of conditioning. It keeps us in a state of excitement and longing but never delivers on what it promises because it isn't really sex at all. It is a disembodied siren's song, inviting us to seek something we will never find if we listen, for the answer lies within, not without.

At the same time, sex is forbidden, at least in America. We still carry the legacy of not only the Puritan past—which is more ambiguous than the stereotype would lead us to believe—but also all of Western history since Saint Paul. This includes not only religious condemnations of sex but also medical ones. Only in the last hundred years or so has the medical establishment rejected the idea that masturbation is harmful to both physical and mental health. Some people still condemn it for a variety of reasons. It remains a source of guilt and shame for many, and it is still relied on for cheap laughs in lowbrow comedies. The frankness with which we discuss it still retains the power to surprise radio interviewers, more than thirty years after Betty Dodson wrote her groundbreaking book *Liberating Orgasm*.

We have relied heavily on masturbation as a tool for sexual self-discovery, and we are convinced that it can be just that. We hope that your experience with this book has led you to share our perspective. It takes courage to pursue an activity that is so heavily laden with preconceived beliefs, and to make use of it for your own growth. To do so is to go against the weight of history and the force of a society that wants you to remain numb and unaware. The ancient Tantrics refused to be bound by social norms, and the same can be said for modern practitioners who fearlessly explore their own sexuality and thereby their own consciousness. This is not defiance, rebellion, or mere contrariness. At its best, it can be the highest form of resistance, a resistance that has profound implications both for the individual and for society.

There is a growing community of sexual pioneers and explorers. By reading this book, you have become a part of that community. It is up to you whether you choose to go deeper, to push the boundaries a little further. There is no need to do so, but there is always more to learn.

For those interested in a more in-depth exploration of traditional Hindu Tantra, we highly recommend studying online with our guru, Dr. Jonn Mumford. His OM Kara Kriya® courses focus on the non-sexual aspects of Tantra and provide a solid, practical foundation. You may find that both the theoretical and practical aspects of the courses have significant implications in the realm of sexuality. More information about the programs is available at www.jonnmumfordconsult.com. Those interested in studying with us (either online or in person) or simply in receiving our newsletter can visit our website—www.tantrapm.com—for details. You can also find links to other teachers and resources on our website.

We hope that this book has given you a deeper sense of connection with your own sexuality, opened you to new sources of pleasure, provided you with surprising, new experiences, and given you a richer and more nuanced understanding of the Tantric path. At the very least, we hope you discovered one useful practice or one new way of thinking about the world. If any of these things has happened for you, we have accomplished what we set out to do.

Tantra is a way of life for us, and it is not always an easy one. It demands constant practice and attention. In addition, it is rooted in a culture that is alien to modern Westerners. Indeed, it is probably impossible to experience the full depth and breadth of Tantra given our cultural backgrounds. Nevertheless, like many difficult undertakings, living as Tantrically as possible offers huge rewards. Many of the techniques are simple and very powerful, regardless of cultural context, and it is not difficult to start incorporating aspects of Tantric practice into everyday life.

Like so many in the West, our interest in Tantra began with sexuality, and sex remains very important to us. Our first two books have dealt with Tantra's sexual aspects because we believe that developing a deep knowledge of one's sexuality is a key to personal empowerment. This approach is in keeping with the Tantric understanding that sexual energy is perhaps the richest source of personal and spiritual empowerment available to most human beings. We realize that many traditional practitioners might find our approach offensive and think that we have somehow diminished Tantra by focusing too narrowly on what some call its sensational aspects. We also recognize how complex and problematic it can be for Westerners to embrace a foreign spiritual path, one that emanates from a country that suffered under the burden of colonization until relatively recently. Nevertheless, we have done our best to present this material with integrity and with respect for the tradition that inspired us. If this book does nothing but enrich your sex life, we have performed an important service by bringing a little more happiness and pleasure into the world.

Having said that, we hope that you have begun to gain some appreciation for the richness of the Tantric tradition and a genuine understanding of why defining Tantra as "the Yoga of sex" is so misguided. For the Tantric practitioner, every experience is an opportunity to encounter the divine. Sex is a great place to begin, but you can find the opportunities anywhere and everywhere. All it takes is the ability and the willingness to recognize them. Once you have cultivated this ability, you can bring a sense of reverence to everything you do, and today's troubled world desperately needs people who know what it means to be truly reverent.

Hari Om Tat Sat.

Acknowledgements

Our beloved guru, Dr. Jonn Mumford (Swami Anandakapila Saraswati) has been our supporter and guide as we wrote this book. We are profoundly grateful for the guidance and support, the vast quantity of knowledge he has shared with us over the years, and his love and friendship.

Thanks to Tristan Taormino (www.puckerup.com) for her foreword, for her work in the field of sexuality, for helping us gain deeper understanding and new insights, and for introducing us to the community of sexual pioneers at Dark Odyssey. The people we have met at Dark Odyssey, particularly Barbara Carrellas (www.urbantantra.org), Nina Hartley (www.nina.com), Raven Kaldera and Joshua Tenpenny (www.cauldronfarm.com) and FemCar and Phantom, have inspired us, expanded our horizons and given us new insights into how one can be Tantric in twenty-first-century America.

We are also grateful to Dr. Rudy Ballentine for his mentorship and his work with us on the subject of gender in Tantra. He has guided us toward a deeper understanding of the masculine and feminine aspects that reside within us. Helen Boyd (www.myhusbandbetty.com) provided some very helpful, specific comments on the gender issues we have addressed, and we appreciate her insights and suggestions, informed as they were by her work with the transgendered community.

Bhagavan Das (www.bhagavandas.com) and Daniel Odier (www.daniel odier.com) have taught us powerful practices that have become part of our lives and have helped shape our thinking. We are grateful to them both.

Our students, to whom this book is dedicated, have touched our lives and influenced our thinking. The responses of our online students, and the profound impact our course had upon them, inspired us to write this book.

Thanks to Balsam (Sibylle Preuschat) (www.friendlyoils.biz), who was one of those online students, for her careful reading and insightful feedback. Both Paul Skye (Swami Ajnananda Saraswati) (www.skyewriter.com) and Bruce Anderson (Somananda) (www.gaytantra.com) read the manuscript closely and gave us many helpful suggestions. We're grateful to them for their input and their friendship, as we are to Anthony Ambrose and Meryl Harris who gave us both editorial comments and the layperson's perspective. Thanks also to Teresa Ambrose for the photographs.

Dr. Beatrice Beebe's work on infant-mother bonding has influenced our thinking about the practice of eye-gazing. We are deeply indebted to her for a multitude of reasons.

Some of the material in dalas 5, 6, and 11 is based on articles that originally appeared in *Chronogram,* the wonderful upstate New York monthly.

Our great thanks to the following independent bookstores and shops, all of which have been great supporters of our work: Inspired! (Kingston, New York), Aquarius Books (Kansas City, Missouri), The Bodhi Tree (Los Angeles, California), The Dreaming Goddess (Poughkeepsie, New York), Mirabai (Woodstock, New York), Magers and Quinn (Minneapolis, Minnesota), East-West Books (Mountain View, California), The Goddess Gallery (Portland, Oregon), Third Place Books (Lake Forest Park, Washington), Spark of Spirit (College Park, Maryland), Breathe Books (Baltimore, Maryland), Babeland (New York, New York), and Sugar (Baltimore, Maryland).

Finally, we're grateful to those at Llewellyn who made this book possible and helped us get our message out—Carrie Obry, Bill Krause, Alison Aten, Mindy Keskinen, Joanna Willis, and especially Carl Llewellyn Weschcke for his support and belief in us.

Ananda Nidra

Lie down on your back on the floor, your feet apart. If this is uncomfortable for you, place pillows under your knees to relieve any tension in the lower back. The palms of your hands should be pointed upward. You may find it more comfortable to place your hands at your sides with the outer edge of your little fingers on the floor, but do not turn your palms down. Be sure you are warm, and cover yourself with a blanket if necessary. Once you have made yourself as comfortable as you can, close your eyes. (Pause.) Remember that you are about to practice Ananda Nidra, blissful sleep. You will be guided into a deep and pleasurable state of relaxation. Your body will relax totally, but you will remain aware. If you find yourself drifting off, simply bring your attention back to the instructions.

Now take a deep breath. As you inhale, allow a feeling of calm to permeate your body. Now, exhale. With every inhalation, a sense of relaxation washes over you. With every exhalation, you become more deeply relaxed, as you release any anxieties, any thoughts about your day or anything else that might be on your mind.

Relax your body. Feel your body melting into the floor as you keep your awareness on your breath. (Pause.) Breathe naturally and maintain your focus. Breathe naturally. There is no right or wrong way to do this practice. (Pause.) Continue to observe your breathing, and allow yourself to become even more deeply relaxed, sinking into the floor. Sinking, sinking into a deeper and deeper state of relaxation.

(Long pause.)

Now bring your attention to the fact that you are going to practice Ananda Nidra. Silently tell yourself, "I am practicing Ananda Nidra."

Move your awareness from body part to body part, as I name each one.

Begin with the left side: left big toe . . . second toe . . . third toe . . . fourth toe . . . fifth toe . . . sole of the left foot . . . left heel . . . left ankle . . . left calf . . . left knee . . . thigh . . . left hip . . . waist . . . ribs . . . armpit . . . shoulder . . . bicep . . . forearm . . . wrist . . . palm . . . thumb . . . index finger . . . middle finger . . . ring finger . . . little finger.

Now the right side: right big toe . . . second toe . . . third toe . . . fourth toe . . . fifth toe . . . sole of the right foot . . . right heel . . . right ankle . . . right calf . . . right knee . . . thigh . . . right hip . . . waist . . . ribs . . . armpit . . . shoulder . . . bicep . . . forearm . . . wrist . . . palm . . . thumb . . . index finger . . . middle finger . . . ring finger . . . little finger.

Now start with the left hand . . . thumb . . . index finger . . . middle finger . . . ring finger . . . little finger . . . palm . . . wrist . . . left forearm . . . elbow . . . bicep . . . shoulder . . . left armpit . . . ribs . . . waist . . . thigh . . . knee . . . left calf . . . ankle . . . heel . . . sole of the left foot . . . left big toe . . . second toe . . . third toe . . . fourth toe . . . fifth toe.

Now the right side: right thumb . . . index finger . . . middle finger . . . ring finger . . . little finger . . . palm . . . wrist . . . forearm . . . bicep . . . armpit . . . ribs . . . waist . . . right hip . . . thigh . . . knee . . . right calf . . . ankle . . . sole of the right foot . . . right big toe . . . second toe . . . third toe . . . fourth toe . . . fifth toe. (Pause.)

Bring your attention to the back of your body: the left heel . . . calf . . . the back of the left thigh . . . the left buttock . . . the left side of the back . . . the left shoulder . . . the back of the head . . . the right shoulder . . . the right side of the back . . . the right buttock . . . the back of the right thigh . . . the calf . . . the right heel.

Now the back of the body from right to left. The right heel . . . right calf . . . back of the right thigh . . . right buttock . . . the right side of the back . . . right shoulder . . . the back of the head . . . the left shoulder . . . the left side of the back . . . the left buttock . . . the back of the left thigh . . . left calf . . . the left heel.

The back of the body from head to toe: Back of the head . . . left shoulder . . . right shoulder . . . the whole back . . . left buttock . . . right buttock . . .

back of the left thigh . . . back of the right thigh . . . left calf . . . right calf . . . left heel . . . right heel. (Pause.)

Bring your attention to the large body parts: the left leg . . . the right leg . . . the left arm . . . the right arm . . . the back of the torso . . . the front of the torso . . . the head . . . the entire body. Bring your attention to the entire body and visualize it lying on the floor. Repeat the word "body" in your mind as you visualize your body lying on the floor. The body. The body. The body.

(Long pause.)

Next notice the parts of your body where they touch the floor. (Pause.) Notice the contact between the floor and your body. (Pause.) Feel how the floor supports you and allow yourself to sink into it . . . deeper and deeper. You are very relaxed.

(Long pause.)

Experience the feeling of being touched gently on your body. (Pause.) Feel a gentle touch on your toes . . . the soles of your feet . . . the heels . . . ankles . . . calves . . . knees . . . thighs . . . groin . . . torso . . . face.

Now feel a warm embrace that encompasses the entire body . . . all at once . . . as if you were being embraced from head to toe in a tender hug.

(Long pause.)

Now bring your attention to the sense of smell. Bring to your mind the delightful aromas I am describing. Do not linger over any particular scent but move from one to the next as I say them: the smell of a camp fire . . . the scent of roses . . . coffee brewing . . . lavender . . . your lover's body during sex . . . peppermint . . . the air just after a summer rain . . . your favorite meal simmering on the stove . . . burning sage . . . incense . . . a pine forest . . . the ocean air.

(Long pause.)

Bring your attention to the sense of taste: your first french kiss . . . biting into a succulent peach . . . an ice cream cone on a hot summer day . . . a bowl of hearty soup on a winter day . . . your lover's taste . . . chocolate . . . a mango . . . a cold glass of water . . . salt . . . cinnamon . . . watermelon . . . honey.

(Long pause.)

Bring your attention to the sense of sight: snow-capped mountains rising from a plain . . . a sunrise . . . a whale surfacing in the ocean . . . a cloudless sky . . . a clumsy puppy playing with a toy . . . your beloved . . . an erotic scene . . . a beautiful painting . . . a field of flowers . . . a pristine beach . . . a waterfall . . . a cathedral . . . the New York City skyline . . . a starry night . . . the glimpse of an eagle gliding through the sky.

(Long pause.)

Bring your attention to the sense of touch: the sudden thrill of an unexpected caress . . . getting a massage . . . slipping into a warm bath . . . receiving oral sex . . . your lover's warm breath on the back of your neck . . . a pet curling up in your lap . . . satin on your skin . . . leather . . . the moment of penetrating or being penetrated . . . diving into a swimming pool on a hot summer day . . . the warmth of a fire on a cold winter night . . . snowflakes melting on your skin . . . a cool breeze after the air has been hot and still.

(Long pause.)

Now bring your attention to the sense of hearing: the sound of cathedral bells . . . a baby's laughter . . . the moan of a lover in ecstasy . . . a cat's purr . . . wind rustling in the trees . . . the cooing of doves . . . your favorite piece of music . . . waves lapping on the beach . . . the crackling of a fire . . . kind words . . . rain on the roof . . . silence.

(Long pause.)

The body . . . the body . . . the body. Intensify your awareness and become aware of the entire body. (Pause.)

Now emotion: post-coital bliss . . . returning home after a long journey . . . laughing so hard you cry . . . surpassing your abilities . . . knowing you have done a job well . . . seeing a friend after a long absence . . . winning a debate . . . the excitement of meeting someone attractive . . . an evening with friends.

(Long pause.)

Now pleasure. Awaken the sensation of pleasure throughout the body. Concentrate and remember the experience of sexual pleasure in every part of the body. Recall a peak moment of sexual bliss and develop and expand it until you experience ecstatic sensations on all levels; sight . . . sound . . . taste . . . touch . . . smell and emotion. Go deep into that enjoyment of pleasure; relive it. Make it real. Intensify your awareness . . . Intensify the sensation . . . Intensify the pleasure.

(Long pause.)

Become a witness of your own consciousness . . . nothing but your own consciousness. (Pause.) Recognize that you are aware of yourself. (Pause.) Observe yourself, and know that you are aware of the pleasure you have experienced until now. (Pause.)

Go into *chidakash,* the mental screen behind the eyes. (Pause.) In that dark space behind the eyes, you see a small, glowing, golden flame. (Pause.) Take that flame and make it grow, stronger, brighter, golden until your entire body is glowing, bathed in warm, delightful golden light.

(Long pause.)

The body . . . the body . . . the body.

(Long pause.)

Visualize your body lying on the floor. See it as if you were hovering above and looking down on yourself. (Pause.) See your face . . . your arms . . . your legs . . . the front of your body . . . lying on the floor. (Pause.) Visualize your body as if you were seeing your reflection in a mirror. (Pause.) You see your clothes . . . your face . . . your hair, as if looking into a mirror. Your body is prone on the floor and you can see yourself . . . perfectly. (Pause.) See your body as a reflection in a mirror.

(Long pause.)

The body . . . the body . . . the body. Repeat the word "body" in your mind, and see your body lying on the floor. Bring your awareness to your breath and notice it flowing evenly in and out.

(Long pause.)

Keep focusing on your breath, as you realize how deeply relaxed and refreshed you are. (Pause.) Intensify your awareness of relaxation, and of the pleasure you have just experienced. You will carry that pleasure with you as you go back to your everyday activities.

(Long pause.)

Externalize your attention and see yourself lying on the floor. (Pause.) Now visualize the surrounding room. Externalize your attention as completely as you can. Notice any external sounds or physical sensations, contact with the floor, the feeling of your clothing on your skin, or any other sensory experiences. (Pause.) Keep your eyes closed.

You have been practicing Ananda Nidra. Become fully aware of what you have been doing. (Pause.) Lie still until you feel you know this fully.

(Long pause.)

Begin moving your body gently, wiggling your toes and stretching. Take your time. (Pause.) Open your eyes and close them quickly. Open them again and notice the beauty of your surroundings. Sit up slowly. The practice of Ananda Nidra is now complete.

Hari Om Tat Sat.

Reflection Sources

Dala 2: Daniel Odier, *Vijnanabhairava Tantra* in *Yoga Spandakarika: The Sacred Texts at the Origins of Tantra*. Translated from the French by Claire Frock (Rochester, VT: Inner Traditions, 2004), p. 149.

Dala 3: Paramahansa Satyananda Saraswati, *Sure Ways to Self-Realization*, compiled by Swami Gaurishankara Saraswati (Monghyr, Bihar, India: Bihar School of Yoga, 1980), p. 158.

Dala 4: Arthur and Ellen Avalon, *Hymns to the Goddess*, translated from the Sanskrit (London: Luzac, 1913), p. 37.

Dala 5: Abhinavagupta (ca. 960–ca. 1020), *Tantraloka* 12.6–7 in Paul Eduardo Muller-Ortega, *The Triadic Heat of Shiva: Kaula Tantricism of Abhinavagupta in the Non-Dual Shaivism of Kashmir* (Albany: State University of New York Press, 1989), pp. 59–60.

Dala 6: *Gandharva Tantra* 8:12–13 in Arthur Avalon (editor), *Principles of Tantra: The Tantratattva of Shriyukta Shiva Chandra Vidyarnava Bhattacharya Mahodya with an Introduction by Shriyukta Barada Kanta Majumdar* (London: Luzac, 1916) vol. 2, p. 302. (Hereafter *Principles of Tantra*.)

Dala 7: Avalon, *Principles of Tantra*, vol. 2, p. xxi.

Dala 8: Jaideva Singh (trans.), *The Yoga of Delight, Wonder, and Astonishment: A Translation of the Vijnana-bhairava* (Albany: State University of New York Press, 1991), verse 118, p. 105.

Dala 9: Saraswati, *Kundalini Tantra* (Monghyr, Bihar, India: Bihar School of Yoga, 1984), p. 92.

Dala 10: Kamalakar S. Mishra, *Kashmir Saivism: The Central Philosophy of Tantrism* (Delhi: Sri Satguru Publications, 1999), p. 365.

Dala 11: Ajit Mookerjee, *Tantra Asana: A Way to Self-Realization* (Basel: Ravi Kumar, 1971), p. 65.

Dala 12: From the *Gheranda Samhita* in Shyam Ghosh, *The Original Yoga as Expounded in the Sivasamhita, Gherandasamhita and Patanjala Yogasutra,* (New Delhi: Munshiram Manoharlal, 1999), p. 163.

Dala 13: Bhaskar Bhattacharya with Nik Douglas and Penny Slinger, *The Path of the Mystic Lover: Baul Songs of Passion and Ecstasy,* (Rochester, VT: Destiny Books, 1993), Song 31.

Dala 14: Avalon, *Principles of Tantra*, vol. 2, p. 326.

Glossary

Most of the terms listed below are Sanskrit, and Sanskrit words often have multiple meanings. For the most part, the translations found here are most relevant to the content of this book, and additional definitions are provided where appropriate. Most definitions are derived from Sir Monier Monier-Williams's *Sanskrit-English Dictionary.*

Ananda—Commonly translated as bliss, this term can also mean happiness, joy, or sensual pleasure.

Ananda Nidra—Blissful sleep. Our modification of Yoga Nidra (see below). Ananda Nidra focuses exclusively on pleasurable images and sensations.

Anhedonic—Lacking or being incapable of experiencing pleasure. A psychological term probably coined by Freud and dating to the late nineteenth century.

Ardhanarishwara—Hermaphroditic form of the God Shiva. In keeping with Tantric ideas about gender polarities, Ardhanarishwara's left side is female, and the right is male.

Asana—Literally a seat, often a seat for meditation. The word is most familiar to Westerners as the term for postures in Hatha Yoga, since asanas were originally meditative postures.

Ashwini Mudra—Literally "the gesture of the horse," this term refers to the intentional pulsing of the anus. This practice is very important in many

Tantric routines since it is a powerful way to raise energy within the body. It is also reputed to have a wide variety of health benefits.

Bhakti—Like many Sanskrit words, Bhakti has multiple meanings, including separation, but in the context of this book it means devotion, specifically spiritual devotion.

Bhakti Yoga—The Yoga of spiritual devotion. One of its most effective practices is Kirtan or devotional chanting. Chanting for prolonged periods can produce an altered state of consciousness, akin to that produced by prolonged sexual activity.

Bhava—Being or becoming, with the implication of a state of being, a mood, particularly an elevated one. One English slang equivalent is "vibe."

Bhoga—Enjoyment, pleasure, including sexual pleasure, also with the implication of "feeding on."

Bhuta—This word has multiple meanings. Ghost is the relevant one in this context, and Bhuta Sadhana refers to magical rites conducted to gain power over spirits, although Monier-Williams translated it as "leading all creatures toward their end." Bhuta also means element and is sometimes used as a synonym for tattwa.

Brahman—God, the supreme Godhead or universal soul. Despite the fact that Hinduism is described as a polytheistic religion, the concept of Brahman has a certain monotheistic quality. Interestingly enough, the literal meaning of the word is growth or expansion. Not to be confused with Brahma, the creator God of the Hindu trinity.

Brahmin—The highest Hindu caste from which the priesthood is drawn. Subject to stringent taboos, Brahmins are expected to be vegetarian and to abstain from alcohol and certain kinds of contact with members of other castes. Thus, for a Brahmin, the sexual aspects of Tantric ritual have a particular power to shock.

Chakra—Disk or wheel. Chakras are energetic centers in the body that can be used as a roadmap in Tantric practice. Swami Anandakapila defines a chakra as "a whirling vortex of energy at the conjunction point of the mind and the body."

Chakra Puja—The classical Tantric sex ritual. In this context, chakra refers to a circle.

Chela—Student or disciple.

Dakshina Marga—The right-hand path; the form of Tantric practice that involves individual practice and internal ritual.

Dala—Petal.

Darshan—Visual contact with a deity or holy person. In many Hindu rituals, the climactic moment comes when the image of the deity is revealed to the worshippers. This is one form of darshan. Another form involves seeing a spiritual master and perhaps receiving a blessing from that person.

Deva (i)—God/Goddess.

Devata/Devataa—God/Goddess.

Dharma—Path or way; religion. This term can also mean righteousness or virtue.

Diksha—Initiation.

Ekagrata—One-pointedness, the ability to focus intently, a capacity that is developed through various forms of meditative practice.

Guru—Remover of the darkness; a teacher of any kind, but especially a spiritual teacher, an initiator.

Hari Om—A mantra that is also used as a salutation. Hari is a name for Vishnu, the preserver God of the Hindu trinity; the mantra can be used as an invocation, a request to preserve our bodies so that we can attain self-realization.

Heyoka—(Lakota) A contrary, a person who frequently behaves in ways that seem inappropriate at first glance and who turns convention on its head. In the Lakota tradition, heyokas play a particularly sacred role.

Householder—A person who lives an ordinary life but may be pursuing a spiritual path, in contrast to a renunciate, a person who has taken a vow of celibacy and has separated from the world and its social obligations.

Ishtadeva or Ishtadevata—One's personal deity. In Tantra, the practitioner identifies with the Ishtadevata and attempts to embody the qualities of that particular deity.

Jivanmukti—Liberation while living.

Kali—The Hindu Goddess of destruction or transformation, and the central deity in most surviving Tantric traditions. Kali's aspect is fierce, but it is said that she becomes radiant and benign when she is worshipped sincerely.

Karma—The law of cause and effect.

Kashmir Shaivism—The form of Tantra that is generally considered the most sublime and complex. Its most significant scriptures were written between the sixth and twelfth centuries, Abhinavagupta is the most celebrated author of Kashmir Shaivite texts. The tradition has all but disappeared, due in part to the violence in Kashmir over the last thirty years. Swami Lakshmanjoo was among the last great gurus of the tradition, and some of his Western disciples have carried the teachings forward. Daniel Odier also teaches a form of Kashmir Shaivite Tantra.

Kaula—Another word for Vama Marga Tantra; a reference to family or clan that evinces the familial and underground nature of traditional Hindu Tantra.

Kegel Exercises—Exercises of the pubococcygeal (PC) muscles, which comprise the pelvic floor, named for gynecologist Arnold Kegel, who "invented" them in the 1950s. Exercising the PC muscles was well known among Tantric and Yogic practitioners before Kegel made his "discovery."

Kirtan—Devotional call-and-response chanting that can have a powerful consciousness-altering effect. Kirtan is one of the primary forms of spiritual practice in the Bhakti Yoga tradition.

Kriya Yoga—Kriya means action, and Kriya Yoga techniques generally combine subtle head movements, breathing techniques, mantra, and visualization to lead the practitioner into a meditative state. Kriya Yoga was popularized in the West by Paramahansa Yogananda, but there are a number of other lineages. For a discussion of Kriya Yoga and the term Kriya, see chapter 3 of *The Essence of Tantric Sexuality*.

Kundalini—An energy said to reside at the base of the spine. Awakening the Kundalini is one aim of Tantric and Yogic practices. The term literally means coiled, and it also has the implication of a pot. Kundalini can be understood as sexual energy, or as the life-force that resides within all human beings.

Left-Hand Tantra/Path—The form of Tantra that incorporates sexual ritual and other external practices. See Vama Marga.

Lingam—Literally mark or sign, implying the mark or sign of the male deity. Thus, it also means penis. As a symbol, the lingam is associated with Shiva, the destructive or transformational God of the Hindu trinity.

Madya—Wine; the third element in the classical 5M ritual. Drinking wine is taboo for high-caste Hindus.

Maithuna—Sexual union. The fifth of the five Ms in the classical left-hand Tantric ritual. It is sometimes used to refer to the ritual as a whole, which includes four other elements.

Mamsa—Meat; the fourth element in the classical 5M ritual. Eating meat is taboo for high-caste Hindus.

Mantra—Mental tool, from *manas* (mind) and *trayati* (tool), as in Tantra. Mantras are words or sounds that serve to focus the mind or direct energy. Mantras can also function as incantations. They range from the single-syllable *bija,* or "seed mantras," to complex, multisyllabic ones. Mantras can be repeated mentally, under the breath, or as chants. Each method has its own unique impact on the mind of the practitioner and the physical environment. In his younger days, Swami Anandakapila was renowned for his ability to induce trance and imperviousness to pain in others by chanting a mantra, a technique he calls "Mantra Anesthesia."

Matsya—Fish; the second element in the classical 5M ritual. Eating fish is taboo for high-caste Hindus.

Moksha—Liberation, one of the four goals in life, according to the classical Hindu tradition. In this context, the word refers to release from the cycle of death and reincarnation that is a core belief in both Hinduism and Buddhism. One need not believe in reincarnation in the literal sense to accept liberation as something to seek in life. If one recognizes the idea that we die and are reborn from moment to moment, liberation can be seen as a process, something to embrace here and now.

Mudra—A symbolically significant gesture, most often of the hand, that can bring about physiological or psychic changes in the practioner. Mudra also means parched grain, the first M in the 5M ceremony.

Mukti—See Moksha.

Mulabandha—Root lock; a Tantric and Yogic term for contracting and holding the anal muscles, in contrast to Ashwini Mudra, which involves rapid contraction and release of the muscles.

Namaste—I bow to you. This word is widely translated in contemporary New Age circles as "I bow to the divine in you" or "the divine in me bows to the divine in you." The word is a simple greeting in much of India and Nepal, but it does have religious implications, since a variant is also used to salute the gods and goddesses in Hindu ritual.

Neo-Tantra—A term first used by Sir John Woodroffe and others in his circle during their early twentieth-century efforts to revive and reclaim the Tantric tradition. It is more commonly attributed to Bhagwan Shree Rajneesh (Osho) who used it to describe his system, which incorporated ideas and methods from a variety of sources, including other spiritual traditions and human potential movement psychology. The term Neo-Tantra is now used more generally, and sometimes disparagingly, to refer to Western forms of Tantra, particularly those that emphasize sacred sexuality and little or nothing else.

Nirvana—Release from the cycle of death and rebirth; merger of the individual consciousness with all that is, with the result that the individual consciousness is extinguished.

Nyasa—Literally, "writing down." An advanced Tantric practice in which various mantras are implanted in the body by touching the body part, chanting the mantra and naming the body part, usually as a component of a more complex ritual.

Padma—Lotus.

Panchamakara—The ritual of the 5Ms or five "good things" (see above for the definition of each "M"). This is the classical left-hand Tantric ceremony that includes sexual intercourse. Right-hand Tantrikas understand the ritual as symbolic rather than literal and may enact it internally through visualization.

Paramahansa—Literally, great swan. A title given to swamis of very high accomplishment, since the swan, according to legend, could separate milk from water.

Parampara—One after the other, a lineage. The term refers to the way teachings are transmitted from teacher to student in Yoga and Tantra, implying an energetic transmission that is passed from one person to the next over generations.

Polyamory—Loving many. A general term applied to alternate relationship styles that involve more than two people. It can encompass any form of relating other than monogamy (from open marriage to multiple-partner households). Many in the polyamory movement (which emerged in organized form in the 1990s) seek to be all-inclusive and suggest that polyamory is more about examining relationships than it is about a particular form, and from this perspective monogamy and celibacy are equally valid, so long as they are freely chosen.

Prana—Most commonly used to mean the breath. In Tantra, Yoga, and Ayurveda (traditional Indian medicine), one of the five airs of the body, the one with an upward flowing motion. In addition, prana is understood as the energy that surrounds us and pervades the universe at all times. Another way of understanding Kundalini energy (see above) is to recognize it as each individual's highly concentrated dose of inborn prana.

Pranayama—Control of the breath, usually applied to various Tantric and Yogic breathing techniques. Since prana also refers to energy, another way to think about controlling the breath is to understand it as the direction of energy.

Prasad—An offering to the deities that is imbued with their energy and then returned to the worshipper. It is often applied to food, which is offered in Hindu ritual and then consumed by the worshippers, but it can also refer to flowers, sacred ash, and other substances. The fundamental principle is that the substance has been transmuted as a result of the ritual.

Pubococcygeal muscles—The muscles that form the pelvic floor, also known as the "Kegel muscles" or "PC muscles." Learning to work these muscles in various ways is a key part of many Tantric and Yogic practices. More generally, exercising them is very important for uro-genital health, in both men and women.

Puja—Ritual or worship. Puja can refer to any ceremony in the Hindu or Buddhist traditions of India, Nepal, and Tibet. In the West, it is commonly applied to the modern variant of the ancient Tantric Chakra Puja in which participants form two concentric circles, often divided by gender. In this ritual, the inner circle remains stationary, while the outer circle revolves. Participants interact briefly, sometimes bowing, sometimes hugging, sometimes speaking to each other. At its best, this can be a very powerful experience, but many in the contemporary Neo-Tantric movement seem to be unaware of the word's original meaning.

Pujari—Person who conducts a puja. This may or may not be a priest.

Rasa—Nectar or juice; also taste, feeling, or sentiment; frequently a reference to sexual fluids.

Right-Hand Tantra/Path—The form of Tantra that emphasizes internal practices to the exclusion of most, if not all, external enactments, particularly sexual ones. Also known as Dakshina Marga. In contemporary India, almost all Tantric practice is right-handed.

Saddhu—A holy man or renunciate. The word has the same root as sadhaka and sadhana; see below.

Sadhaka—A practitioner or spiritual aspirant.

Sadhana—Spiritual practice. No single form of sadhana is better than another, and there are many different forms.

Sahaja—Natural. It is often suggested that the goal of Tantric sadhana is to achieve a sahaja or natural state; the idea is that, through formalized practice, we can create a framework for becoming more truly ourselves. At a certain point, the forms are discarded and we just live.

Samadhi—The state of mystical union. Treatises on Tantra and Yoga describe several forms of samadhi, but for our purposes the state of samadhi is one in which the mind becomes quiet, time seems to stop, and the world may disappear. Orgasm can produce this subjective experience, which Swami Anandakapila has called a U3 state (Ultimate Universal Unity).

Samsara—Everyday life or the cycle of death and rebirth.

Sandhabasa—Twilight language. A reference to the intentionally obscure style of some Tantric scriptures. Many of these texts were written for initiates only, and the authors took pains to conceal their meaning from outsiders. Not to be confused with the "secret language," a modern term for a sexual technique.

Sankalpa—A divine intention or resolve.

Sanskrit—The ancient language of India. Many Tantric texts were written in Sanskrit, others in regional languages. Sanskrit is still the language of Hindu ritual, although it is no longer living as a conversational tongue.

Secret language—The practice of pulsing the pubococcygeal muscles back and forth during penetrative intercourse.

Shakti—Goddess, particularly the Goddess in the form of energy. It also refers to a goddess in her role as consort to a male deity and hence to a female participant in Tantric sex rituals.

Shamanism—A catchall phrase for indigenous religious traditions in which shamans or medicine men gain spiritual power through various consciousness-altering techniques. The word is Siberian in origin, but it has been applied, perhaps too loosely, to traditions around the world. There are "shamanic traditions" among the peoples of the Indian subcontinent, but the historical relationship between Tantra and shamanism remains in dispute.

Shava Sadhana—Corpse ritual, or corpse practice. One of the more extreme forms of Tantric sadhana, in which the practitioner meditates while seated on a corpse. Cremation and burial grounds are seen as places of danger, power, and impurity, thus Shava Sadhana functions as a way to gain powers while crossing social boundaries and transcending fear.

Shiva—Male deity, one of three Gods of the Hindu trinity, often described as the God of destruction and the lord of the yogis. Shiva is the most important male deity in modern Tantra.

Siddha—An accomplished practitioner or, particularly in the Tibetan Buddhist tradition, a saint.

Siddhis—Powers or accomplishments, some supernatural or magical in nature.

Sri Vidya—A form of Tantra still widely practiced in India today.

Swadharma—One's own path, way, or true nature.

Swami—A Hindu holy man; literally, one's own master, a reference to being released from conventional social obligations. Traditionally swamis were celibate and either resided in monasteries or wandered and taught, depending on alms for their sustenance. Some modern reformers have modified the requirements and have initiated women and married people as swamis. From our perspective, a swami is a person who has dedicated his or her life to the spiritual well-being of others.

Tantric massage—A term that became popular in the 1990s, usually as a euphemism for erotic massage, specifically including stimulation of the genitals. In many instances, the male client is encouraged to refrain from ejaculating. This can be valuable for men who wish to learn to experience full-body orgasms. Tantric massage for women often involves stimulation of the G spot with female ejaculation as a goal. These techniques have nothing to do with traditional Tantra, although a skilled and knowledgeable practitioner can make a "Tantric massage" a very valuable experience for the recipient.

Tantrika—A Tantric practitioner. In some contemporary circles, the term has become associated with practitioners of Tantric massage.

Taoism—A Chinese spiritual tradition that shares some common elements with Tantra, including the recognition of sexuality's sacred dimension. As a general rule, however, Taoist sexual practices focus more on health and longevity than on attaining mystical states. In the Taoist system, there is frequently an emphasis on non-ejaculatory sex for men, based on the belief that the semen contains vital energy that must not be depleted.

Tattva/Tattwa—Element; literally, that which is. In the Hindu system there are five elements or tattwas: earth, water, fire, air, and space.

Theravada Buddhism—The form of Buddhism practiced in much of South Asia. Unlike Tibetan, Chinese, and Zen Buddhism, it is not influenced by the Tantric tradition. Theravada Buddhism tends to have a negative attitude toward sexuality and embodied experience in general.

Tilak—The mark placed in the center of the forehead after a Hindu puja. It is often made out of red kum-kum powder.

Tratak—To gaze without blinking. A technique for developing one-pointed concentration. It can be practiced on a candle flame, a yantra, a statue of a deity, or upon one's beloved.

Vama Marga—The left-hand path. The form of Tantra in which certain sexual rituals are enacted, in contrast to Dakshina Marga Tantra in which they are visualized.

Vira—Hero, the type of personality suited for Vama Marga practice. A person of heroic temperament is energetic and active with a courageous personality, the key element being action.

Yab Yum—(Tibetan) Literally, father-mother. It refers to the classical Tantric lovemaking posture, in which the man sits in the lotus position while his partner straddles him.

Yantra—Tool for conception; a geometric figure that represents something else. Yantras can be quite simple—a triangle, a square, a crescent—or quite complex. The Sri Yantra, which is central to the spiritual practices of the Sri Vidya tradition, is composed of nine major triangles that interconnect to create a total of forty-three triangles, each with spiritual and symbolic significance. (See figure 11.)

Yoga—Literally, yoking or union; an Indian spiritual tradition closely related to Tantra. While most Westerners think of Yoga as a form of exercise characterized by various *asanas* (postures), there are many ways to practice

Yoga, and some do not involve physical postures at all. (See Bhakti Yoga, above, for example.) It can be useful to think of Yoga as a state of mental stillness accompanied by a feeling of union or merger with all that is.

Yoga Nidra—Yogic sleep. A Tantric technique first introduced to the West by Paramahansa Satyananda Saraswati in the 1960s. Yoga Nidra involves the rotation of consciousness through the body and various visualizations. It produces a deep state of relaxation in which the mind often remains quite alert.

Yoni—The female genitalia, including the womb.

Bibliography

Abhinavagupta. *A Trident of Wisdom: Translation of the Paratrisika Vivarana.* Jaideva Singh, trans. Albany: State University of New York Press, 1988.

———. *The Kula Ritual: As Elaborated in Chapter 29 of the Tantraloka.* John R. Dupuche, ed. and trans. Delhi: Motilal Banarsidas, 2003.

The American Heritage Dictionary of the English Language. William Morris, ed. Boston: Houghton Mifflin, 1976.

Anand, Margo. *The Art of Everyday Ecstasy: The Seven Tantric Keys for Bringing Passion, Spirit, and Joy into Every Part of Your Life.* New York: Broadway Books, 1998.

———. *The Art of Sexual Ecstasy: The Path of Sacred Sexuality for Western Lovers.* New York: Jeremy Tarcher/Putnam, 1989.

———. *The New Art of Sexual Ecstasy.* New York: HarperCollins, 2003.

Anderson, Bruce. *Tantra for Gay Men.* Los Angeles: Alyson Books, 2002.

Anonymous. *Nature Worship: An Account of Phallic Faiths and Practices Ancient and Modern; Including the Adoration of the Male and Female Powers in Various Nations and the Sacti Puja of Indian Gnosticism.* Privately printed, 1891.

Beebe, Beatrice and Frank M. Lachmann. *Infant Research and Adult Treatment: Co-Constructing Interactions.* Hillsdale, NJ: The Analytic Press, 2002.

Bharati, Agehananda. *The Tantric Tradition*. London: Rider and Co., 1965.

Bhattacharya, Bhaskar with Nik Douglas and Penny Slinger. *The Path of the Mystic Lover: Baul Songs of Passion and Ecstasy*. Rochester, VT: Destiny Books, 1993.

Bhattacharya, N. N. *Tantrabidhana: A Tantric Lexicon*. New Delhi: Manohar, 2002.

Bonewits, Phillip Emmons Isaac. *Real Magic: An Introductory Treatise on the Principles of Yellow Magic*, rev. ed. York Beach, ME: Samuel Weiser, 1989.

Campbell, Joseph and Bill Moyers. *The Power of Myth*. New York: Doubleday, 1988.

Carrellas, Barbara. *Urban Tantra: Sacred Sex for the Twenty-First Century*. Berkeley, CA: Celestial Arts, 2007.

Comfort, Alex, trans. *The Koka Shastra*. New York: Stein and Day, 1964.

Dodson, Betty. *Self-Love and Orgasm*. New York: privately printed, 1983.

———. *Sex for One: The Joy of Self-Loving*. New York: Harmony Books, 1987.

Douglas, Nik. *Spiritual Sex: Secrets of Tantra from the Ice Age to the New Millennium*. New York: Pocket Books, 1997.

Douillard, John. *Body, Mind and Sport: The Mind-Body Guide to Lifelong Health, Fitness and Your Personal Best*, rev. ed. New York: Three Rivers Press, 2001.

Dubois, Abbé J.A. *Hindu Manners, Customs and Ceremonies*. Henry K. Beauchamp, trans. 3rd ed. Oxford: Clarendon Press, 1906.

Feurstein, Georg. *Tantra: The Path of Ecstasy*. Boston: Shambhala, 1998.

Garrison, Omar. *Tantra: The Yoga of Sex*. New York: Harmony Books, 1964.

Ghosh, Shyam. *The Original Yoga as Expounded in the Sivasamhita, Gherandasamhita and Patanjala Yogasutra*. New Delhi: Manushiram Manoharlal, 1999.

Godbeer, Richard. *Sexual Revolution in Early America*. Baltimore: The Johns Hopkins University Press, 2002.

Gupta, Sanjukta, trans. *Lakshmi Tantra: A Pancaratra Text*. Delhi: Motilal Banarsidas, 2000.

Harper, Katherine Anne and Robert L. Brown, eds. *The Roots of Tantra*. Albany: State University of New York Press, 2002.

Holy Bible: The New King James Version.

Howard, Clifford. *Sex Worship: An Exposition of the Phallic Religion*. Washington DC: privately printed, 1897.

Hughes, John. *Self-Realization in Kashmir Shaivism: The Oral Teachings of Swami Lakshmanjoo*. Albany: State University of New York Press, 1994.

Huxley, Aldous. *Brave New World*. New York: HarperCollins Perennial Classics, 1998.

Inman, Thomas. *Ancient Pagan and Modern Christian Symbolism*, 3rd ed. New York: J. Bouton, 1880.

Johari, Harish. *Tools for Tantra*. Rochester, VT: Destiny Books, 1986.

Kermode, Frank and John Hollander, eds. *The Oxford Anthology of English Literature*. Oxford: Oxford University Press, 1973.

Khanna, Madhu. *Yantra: The Tantric Symbol of Cosmic Unity*. London: Thames and Hudson, 1979, repr. 1997.

Ladas, Alice Kahn, Beverly Whipple and John D. Perry. *The G Spot and Other Discoveries About Human Sexuality*. New York: Dell, 1982.

Lakshman Jee (or Joo), Swami. *Kashmir Shaivism: The Secret Supreme*. Albany: State University of New York Press/The Universal Shaiva Trust, 1988.

———. (under the name Lakshman Joo), commentary. *Vijnana Bhairava: The Practice of Centering Awareness*. Bettina Brauner, trans. New Delhi: Indica Books, 2002.

Laqueur, Thomas. *Making Sex: The History of Gender from the Greeks to Freud*. Cambridge, MA: Harvard University Press, 1990.

———. *Solitary Sex: A Cultural History of Masturbation*. New York: Zone Books, 2004.

McMahon, Darrin M. *Happiness: A History*. New York: Atlantic Monthly Press, 2006.

Michaels, Mark A. (Swami Umeshanand Saraswati) and Patricia Johnson (Devi Veenanand). *The Essence of Tantric Sexuality*. Woodbury, MN: Llewellyn, 2006.

Mishra, Kamalakar. *Kashmir Saivism: The Central Philosophy of Tantrism*. Delhi: Sri Satguru Publications, 1999.

———. *Significance of the Tantric Tradition*. Varanasi, India: Ardhanarisvara Publications, 1971.

Monier-Williams, Sir Monier. *A Sanskrit-English Dictionary: Etymologically and Philologically Arranged with Special Reference to Cognate Indo-European Languages*. Oxford: Oxford University Press, 1899, repr. 1979.

Mookerjee, Ajit. *Tantra Art: Its Philosophy and Physics*. Basel: Ravi Kumar, 1971/2

———. *Tantra Asana: A Way to Self-Realization*. Basel: Ravi Kumar, 1971.

Mookerjee, Ajit, and Madhu Khanna. *The Tantric Way: Art, Science, Ritual*. London: Thames and Hudson, 1977, repr. 1996.

Moor, Edward. *The Hindu Pantheon: A New Edition with Additional Plates, Condensed and Annotated by the Rev. W.O. Simpson*. Madras: J. Higginbotham, 1864.

Moore, Thomas. *The Soul of Sex: Cultivating Life as an Act of Love*. New York: HarperCollins, 1998.

Muir, Charles and Caroline. *Tantra: The Art of Conscious Loving*. San Francisco: Mercury House, 1989.

Muller-Ortega, Paul Eduardo. *The Triadic Heart of Shiva: Kaula Tantricism of Abhinavagupta in the Non-Dual Shaivism of Kashmir*. Albany: State University of New York Press, 1989.

Mumford, Dr. Jonn (Swami Anandakapila Saraswati). *A Chakra & Kundalini Workbook: Psycho-Spiritual Techniques for Health, Rejuvenation, Psychic Powers & Spiritual Realization*. St. Paul, MN: Llewellyn, 1997.

———. *Ecstasy Through Tantra*, 3rd ed. St. Paul, MN: Llewellyn, 1987.

———. *Magical Tattwa Cards: A Complete System for Self-Development*. St. Paul, MN: Lllewellyn, 1987.

Nabokov, Vladimir. *Lolita*. New York: Vintage International, 1989.

Odier, Daniel. *Desire: The Tantric Path to Awakening*. Clare Marie Frock, trans. Rochester, VT: Inner Traditions, 2001.

———. *Tantric Quest: An Encounter with Absolute Love*. Jody Gladding, trans. Rochester, VT: Inner Traditions, 1997.

———. *Yoga Spandakarika: The Sacred Texts at the Origins of Tantra*. Clare Frock, trans. Rochester, VT: Inner Traditions, 2005.

Pandit, M.P. *Gems from the Tantras (Kularnava)*. Madras: Ganesh and Co., 1969.

———. *Lights on the Tantra*. Madras: Ganesh and Co. 1971.

Rai, Ram Kumar, trans. *Damara Tantra*. Varanasi, India: Prachya Prakashan, 1988.

Random House Unabridged Dictionary, Second Edition. Stuart Berg Flexner, ed. New York: Random House, 1993.

Saran, Prem. *Tantra: Hedonism in Indian Culture*. New Delhi: D.K. Print-world, Ltd., 1994.

Saraswati, (Swami or Paramahansa) Satyananda. *Kundalini Tantra*. Monghyr, Bihar, India: Bihar School of Yoga, 1984

———. *Meditations from the Tantras*. Monghyr, Bihar, India: Bihar School of Yoga, 1974.

———. *Sure Ways to Self-Realization*, compiled by Swami Gaurishankara Saraswati. Monghyr, Bihar, India: Bihar School of Yoga, 1980.

———. *Yoga Nidra*, 5th ed. Monghyr, Bihar, India: Bihar School of Yoga, 1984.

Saraswati, Swami Satyasangananda. *Tattwa Shuddhi: The Tantric Practice of Inner Purification*. Monghyr, Bihar: Bihar School of Yoga, 1984.

Sellon, Edward. *Annotations of the Sacred Writings of the Hindus.* London: privately printed, 1902.

SenSharma, Deba Brata. *The Philosophy of Sadhana: With Special Reference to the Trika Philosophy of Kashmir.* Albany: State University of New York Press, 1990.

Shastri, Gaurinath. *Introduction to Tantra.* 2 vols. New Delhi: Cosmo Publications, 2001.

Shaw, Miranda. *Passionate Enlightenment: Women in Tantric Buddhism.* Princeton, NJ: Princeton University Press, 1994.

Silburn, Lilian. *Kundalini: The Energy of the Depths, A Comprehensive Study Based on the Scriptures of Nondualistic Kasmir Saivism.* Jacques Gontier, trans. New York: State University of New York Press, 1988.

Singh, Jaideva, trans. *Pratyabijnahrdyam: Sanskrit Text with English Translation, Notes and Introduction,* 2nd rev. ed. Delhi: Motilal Banarsidas, 1977.

———. *The Yoga of Delight, Wonder and Astonishment: A Translation of the Vijnana-bhairava.* Albany: State University of New York Press, 1991.

Singh, N. K. *Siva Linga.* Delhi: Global Vision Publishing House, 2004.

Svoboda, Robert E. *Aghora: At the Left Hand of God.* Albuquerque, NM: Brotherhood of Life, Inc. 1986.

———. *Aghora II: Kundalini.* Albuquerque, NM: Brotherhood of Life Publishing, 1993.

———. *Aghora III: The Law of Karma.* Albuquerque: Brotherhood of Life Publishing, 1998.

Taylor, Kathleen. *Sir John Woodroffe, Tantra and Bengal: 'An Indian Soul in a European Body?'* Richmond, Surrey, UK: Curzon, 2001.

Thomas, Keith. *Religion and the Decline of Magic.* New York: Charles Scribner's Sons, 1971.

Van Lysbeth, André. *Tantra: The Cult of the Feminine.* York Beach, ME: Samuel Weiser, 1995.

Vecsey, Christopher. *Imagine Ourselves Richly: Mythic Narratives of North American Indians*. New York: HarperCollins, 1991.

Weekley, Ernest. *An Etymological Dictionary of Modern English*. London: John Murray, 1921, repr. New York: Dover, 1967.

Westropp, Hodder M. and C. Staniland Wake. *Ancient Symbol Worship. Influence of the Phallic Idea in the Religions of Antiquity*. New York: J. W. Bouton, 1875.

White, David Gordon. *Kiss of the Yogini: "Tantric Sex" in Its South Indian Contexts*. Chicago: University of Chicago Press, 2003.

Wilkins, J. W. *Hindu Mythology: Vedic and Puranic*. Calcutta: Thacker and Spink and Co., 1882.

Woodroffe, Sir John. *The Great Liberation (Mahanirvana Tantra),* 6th ed. Madras: Ganesh and Co., 1985.

———. *Is India Civilized? Essays on Indian Culture*. Madras: Ganesh and Co., 1922.

———. [Arthur Avalon, pseud.] *Kularnava Tantra*. Readings by M.P. Pandit. Sanskrit text by Taranatha Vidyaratna. Delhi: Motilal Banarsidas, 1965 Repr. 1999.

———. [Arthur Avalon, pseud.] *Principles of Tantra: The Tantratattva of Shriyukta Shiva Chandra Vidyarnava Bhattacharyya Mahodaya*. 2 vols. London: Luzac, 1914.

———. *Sakti and Sakta: Essays and Addresses*, 5th ed. Madras: Ganesh and Co., 1959.

———. [Arthur Avalon, pseud.] *The Serpent Power: Being the Shat-Chakra-Nirupana and Paduka-Panchaka, Two Works on Laya Yoga, Translated from the Sanskrit with Introduction and Commentary*, 3rd ed. Madras: Ganesh and Co., 1931.

———. [Arthur Avalon, pseud.] *Wave of Bliss (Anandalahari)*. London: Luzac and Co., 1917.

Woodroffe, Sir John and Ellen Woodroffe [Arthur and Ellen Avalon, pseuds.]. *Hymns to the Goddess*. London: Luzac, 1913.

Zvelbil, Kamil V., trans. *The Poets of the Powers*. London: Ryder, 1973.

Index

Free Catalog

Get the latest information on our body, mind, and spirit products! To receive a **free** copy of Llewellyn's consumer catalog, *New Worlds of Mind & Spirit,* simply call 1-877-NEW-WRLD or visit our website at www.llewellyn.com and click on *New Worlds.*

LLEWELLYN ORDERING INFORMATION

Order Online:
Visit our website at www.llewellyn.com, select your books, and order them on our secure server.

Order by Phone:
- Call toll-free within the U.S. at 1-877-NEW-WRLD (1-877-639-9753). Call toll-free within Canada at 1-866-NEW-WRLD (1-866-639-9753)
- We accept VISA, MasterCard, and American Express

Order by Mail:
Send the full price of your order (MN residents add 6.5% sales tax) in U.S. funds, plus postage & handling to:

Llewellyn Worldwide
2143 Wooddale Drive, Dept. 978-0-7387-1197-3
Woodbury, MN 55125-2989

Postage & Handling:

Standard (U.S., Mexico, & Canada). If your order is:
$24.99 and under, add $3.00
$25.00 and over, FREE STANDARD SHIPPING

AK, HI, PR: $15.00 for one book plus $1.00 for each additional book.

International Orders (airmail only):
$16.00 for one book plus $3.00 for each additional book

Orders are processed within 2 business days.
Please allow for normal shipping time. Postage and handling rates subject to change.

To Write to the Authors

If you wish to contact the authors or would like more information about this book, please write to the authors in care of Llewellyn Worldwide and we will forward your request. Both the authors and publisher appreciate hearing from you and learning of your enjoyment of this book and how it has helped you. Llewellyn Worldwide cannot guarantee that every letter written to the authors can be answered, but all will be forwarded. Please write to:

Mark A. Michaels & Patricia Johnson
c/o Llewellyn Worldwide
2143 Wooddale Drive, Dept. 978-0-7387-1197-3
Woodbury, MN 55125-2989, U.S.A.
Please enclose a self-addressed stamped envelope for reply,
or $1.00 to cover costs. If outside U.S.A., enclose
international postal reply coupon.

Many of Llewellyn's authors have websites with additional information and resources. For more information, please visit our website at:
www.llewellyn.com